TESTQUBE

Digital SAT®

Published in the United States of America

Table of Content

Table of Content

TEST QUBE

Digital SAT ®

Practice Test #1

I

II

III

IV

V

VI

VII

Section 1, Module 1: Reading & Writing   ⏱ 32:00   📝 Annotate ⋮

The seasoned diplomat Sir Richard Hamilton, a former United Nations ambassador with over three decades of experience in international affairs, was renowned for his adept ability to navigate labyrinthine negotiations with grace and finesse. His ____ demeanor, coupled with an encyclopedic knowledge of international relations and fluency in multiple languages, made him an invaluable asset in high-stakes discussions, especially during pivotal peace talks between warring nations.

1   Mark for Review 🔖

Which choice completes the text with the most logical and precise word or phrase?

- (A) abrasive
- (B) gregarious
- (C) judicious
- (D) capricious

TEST⬛QUBE   Question 1 of 27 >   Back   Next

Section 1, Module 1: Reading & Writing   📝 Annotate ⋮

The young prodigy Alessandro Castellani, a gifted Italian composer barely in his teens, astounded the classical music world with his musical compositions, which exhibited a breathtaking level of sophistication and emotional depth that belied his tender age. His work seemed to ____ the confines of conventional wisdom, seamlessly blending Baroque intricacies with modern symphonic elements, earning him effusive praise and recognition as a groundbreaking artist in prestigious institutions such as the Juilliard School and the Royal Academy of Music.

2   Mark for Review 🔖

Which choice completes the text with the most logical and precise word or phrase?

- (A) transgress
- (B) corroborate
- (C) adhere
- (D) transcend

TEST⬛QUBE   Question 2 of 27 >   Back   Next

Section 1, Module 1: Reading & Writing

Annotate

The following text is adapted from Nathaniel Hawthorne's 1850 novel *The Scarlet Letter*. Hester Prynne, a woman who has been punished for adultery, is out in public.

It may be true, that, to a sensitive observer, there was something exquisitely painful in it. Her attire, which, indeed, she had wrought for the occasion, in prison, and had modelled much after her own fancy, seemed to express the attitude of her spirit, the desperate recklessness of her mood, by its wild and picturesque peculiarity. But the point which drew all eyes, and, as it were, transfigured the wearer,—so that both men and women, who had been familiarly acquainted with Hester Prynne, were now impressed as if they beheld her for the first time,—was that SCARLET LETTER, so fantastically embroidered and illuminated upon her bosom. It had the effect of a spell, taking her out of the ordinary relations with humanity, and enclosing her in a sphere by herself.

3   Mark for Review 🔖

Which choice best describes the function of the underlined sentence in the text as a whole?

(A) It provides a detailed depiction of a character's attire and beauty, enhancing the scene's imagery.

(B) It underscores a marked shift in perception, illustrating the transformative effect of a symbol.

(C) It subtly casts doubt on the claim made in the preceding sentence, prompting further scrutiny.

(D) It effectively expands on the premise introduced in the previous sentence, adding depth to the narrative.

TEST❖QUBE   Question 3 of 27 >   Back   Next

Section 1, Module 1: Reading & Writing

Annotate

A research study by a group of scientists, including biologist Sarah R. Johnson, indicates that the presence of certain bird species can affect the growth rate of nearby plants. The researchers studied the effect of various bird species on the growth of understory plants in different forest ecosystems by monitoring bird visits and plant growth. The team discovered that in some cases, plants grew faster when specific bird species were more frequent visitors.

4   Mark for Review 🔖

Which choice best states the function of the underlined sentence in the overall structure of the text?

(A) To establish a correlation between bird presence and plant growth.

(B) To justify the monitoring of the species observed.

(C) To provide an example of a particular bird species influencing plant growth.

(D) To describe the approach used in the research study to gather data.

TEST❖QUBE   Question 4 of 27 >   Back   Next

Annotate

Text 1

Neuroscientist Dr. Howard Shaw's work focuses primarily on unraveling the mysteries of the cerebral cortex. Central to his research is the hypothesis that the superiority of the cortex in managing these complex tasks is intrinsically linked to its structural complexity. He points out the unusually high density of neurons in the cortex, as well as the intricate, labyrinthine web of connections these neurons form with one another. This level of complexity, according to Shaw, provides the cortex with the processing power necessary for such advanced cognitive tasks, thereby enabling humans to engage in everything from abstract thought to creative endeavors.

Text 2

Dr. Amy Liu, while also a respected figure in the world of neuroscience, takes a slightly different approach in her exploration of the cerebral cortex. Acknowledging the structural complexity of the cortex, her research tends to underscore a distinct yet interrelated aspect of this part of the brain. Her studies focus on the biochemical processes and signaling pathways in the cortex, seeking to understand how these contribute to its function. Liu argues that the secret to the cortex's impressive capabilities may be found not only in its structural intricacies but also in the chemical landscape that exists within its confines. By exploring the nature of neurotransmitters, synaptic functions, and the modulation of neural networks, Liu's work offers a comprehensive and nuanced perspective on the workings of the cerebral cortex.

5 Mark for Review

How might Dr. Liu (Text 2) view the perspective put forth by Dr. Shaw (Text 1)?

(A) She would appreciate its relevance but suggest that it lacks a detailed consideration of the biochemical processes in the cortex.

(B) She would completely agree, given that her work also deals with the complexity of the cerebral cortex, though from a different angle.

(C) She would disregard it as overly simplistic, as it focuses primarily on structural complexity while ignoring biochemical intricacies.

(D) She would argue that Shaw's perspective is outdated, as recent research is more aligned with biochemical than structural explanations for the cortex's function.

Annotate

The Tempest is a circa 1611 play by William Shakespeare. In the play, the character of Prospero demonstrates a change of heart when he decides to give up his magical powers. This decision is evident when he _____.

6 Mark for Review

Which choice most effectively uses a quotation from *The Tempest* to illustrate the claim?

(A) tells Miranda, "O, wonder! How many goodly creatures are there here!"

(B) speaks to Ariel, "Our revels now are ended. These our actors were all spirits, and are melted into air, into thin air."

(C) proclaims to the spirits, "I'll break my staff, bury it certain fathoms in the earth, and deeper than did ever plummet sound, I'll drown my book."

(D) confronts Caliban, "A devil, a born devil, on whose nature can never stick."

Annotate

The following text is adapted from Robert Frost's 1916 poem "Birches."

When I see birches bend to left and right
Across the lines of straighter darker trees,
I like to think some boy's been swinging them.
But swinging doesn't bend them down to stay
As ice-storms do. Often you must have seen them
Loaded with ice a sunny winter morning
After a rain. They click upon themselves
As the breeze rises, and turn many-colored
As the stir cracks and crazes their enamel.

7 Mark for Review

Which choice best describes the overall structure of the text?

(A) The speaker observes the bending of birch trees, then imagines a playful explanation for their curvature.

(B) The speaker describes the destructive forces of nature, then laments the loss of childhood innocence.

(C) The speaker discusses the resilience of birch trees, then contemplates the ephemeral nature of beauty.

(D) The speaker admires the landscape, then ponders the interplay of light and darkness in nature.

TEST QUBE

Back Next

Annotate

The following text is adapted from Ella Wheeler Wilcox's 1883 poem "Solitude."

Laugh, and the world laughs with you;
Weep, and you weep alone;
For the sad old earth must borrow its mirth,
But has trouble enough of its own.
Sing, and the hills will answer;
Sigh, it is lost on the air;
The echoes bound to a joyful sound,
But shrink from voicing care.

8 Mark for Review

Which choice best describes the function of the underlined section in the context of the poem as a whole?

(A) It acknowledges happiness as the core human emotion experienced in nature.

(B) It understates the shared resonance of joy and its ubiquity in nature.

(C) It delineates the world's inclination to engage in collective mirth rather than shared sorrow.

(D) It reinforces the speaker's conviction in the resounding nature of joy and sorrow.

TEST QUBE

Back Next

I
II
III
IV
V
VI
VII

Section 1, Module 1: Reading & Writing

Annotate ⋮

The honeybee dance, often referred to as the waggle dance, is a remarkable form of communication used by foraging honeybees to convey information about the location of food sources to their nestmates. This dance language was first decoded by Austrian ethologist and Nobel laureate Karl von Frisch in the mid-20th century. The dance comprises specific movements and vibrations that provide information about the direction and distance of the food source. An entomologist, Dr. Maria Alvarez, claims that the honeybee dance is a sophisticated form of animal communication, rivaling aspects of human language in its capacity to convey detailed information. She argues that through this dance, honeybees are able to efficiently share geographically relevant information with members of their hive, enabling the colony to mobilize and forage in a coordinated manner.

9 Mark for Review 🔖

Which finding, if true, would most directly support Dr. Maria Alvarez's claim that the honeybee dance is a sophisticated form of animal communication?

(A) Honeybees are social insects that live in large colonies with a complex division of labor, where for agers, workers, and drones all perform specific tasks to maintain the colony's functioning.

(B) The honeybee dance has been decoded by scientists, who discovered that the angle of the dance relative to gravity indicates the direction of the food source, while the duration of the dance indicates the distance.

(C) Honeybees have a remarkable ability to learn and remember the locations of multiple food sources, allowing them to optimize their foraging efforts and maximize the resources available to the colony.

(D) The honeybee dance is not unique to one species of honeybee but has been observed in multiple species across the world, suggesting that it is a highly adaptive and efficient form of communication.

TEST QUBE

Back Next

Section 1, Module 1: Reading & Writing

Annotate ⋮

Decade	Number of Published Novels	Number of Literary Awards	Average Critical Rating
1960s	120	5	7.2
1970s	150	10	9.1
1980s	180	15	8.0
1990s	200	25	7.5
2000s	220	30	7.0
2010s	250	35	9.5

In an article examining the evolution of literature over the second half of the 20th century and early 21st century, literary scholars Dr. Lila Read and Dr. Thomas Write explored the proliferation of published novels, the increasing number of literary awards, and the overall critical reception. Dr. Read posited that the growth in the number of published novels has led to greater recognition within the literary community, as evidenced by the increasing number of literary awards. Dr. Write, however, suggested that while there is an apparent increase in the number of awards, early on, this increase in the number of awards did not necessarily correlate with a rise in the quality of literature, which he measured using average critical ratings.

10 Mark for Review 🔖

Which choice best describes data from the table that weakens Dr. Write's conclusion?

(A) The 1990s saw a substantial increase in the number of published novels and a corresponding rise in the number of literary awards.

(B) The 2010s observed a far greater number of literary awards and higher average critical rating than the 1960s did.

(C) From the 1960s to 1970s, the number of literary awards rose by 5 and the average critical rating increased by 1.9.

(D) Despite the number of novels increasing by 20 from the 1990s to the 2000s, the average critical rating fell by 0.5 points during the same period.

TEST QUBE

Back Next

Section 1, Module 1: Reading & Writing

Annotate

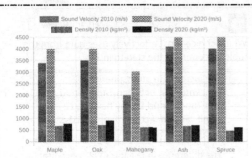

Researchers Dr. Amy Hertz and Dr. Brian Mur conducted a study on the acoustic properties of various wood types, measuring changes in sound velocity and density over ten years. Sound velocity in wood is crucial for musical instrument quality, and it can change due to environmental factors like humidity and temperature. Dr. Hertz and Dr. Mur concluded that while all wood types showed changes in sound velocity over the time analyzed, certain woods displayed more pronounced increases as a result of density changes.

11   Mark for Review 🔖

Which choice best describes data from the bar graph that support the researchers' conclusion?

(A) Mahogany showed the most significant change in sound velocity, indicating its greater sensitivity to environmental changes.

(B) All of the woods observed a change in velocity, but only maple, oak, ash, and spruce observed density changes.

(C) None of the wood types observed a velocity change of less than 100 m/s and maple observed the greatest change in sound velocity when considering woods that underwent density changes.

(D) Maple displayed the least significant velocity change and oak displayed the greatest velocity change when examining woods that underwent density changes.

TEST◆QUBE

Back   Next

Section 1, Module 1: Reading & Writing

Annotate

Population Growth and Urbanization in Five Cities

City	Population Growth Rate (%)	Urbanization Rate (%)	Green Space Area (km²)
C1	1.2	30	100
C2	1.8	45	80
C3	1.9	90	60
C4	3.5	95	40
C5	3.7	97	20

Urban sprawl, characterized by the expansion of human populations away from central urban areas into previously remote and rural areas, often results in a decrease in green space and an increase in urbanization rates.. Researchers have been tracking these changes using metrics such as population growth rate, urbanization rate, and green space area across five cities (C1 to C5).
The data suggests that there might be a correlation between these metrics. A team of researchers led by Dr. Alice Kinsley hypothesizes that even subtle increases in the population growth rate can cause dramatic increases in urbanization rates, contributing to a significant reduction in green space areas. They assert that urban planning policies need to be revised to prioritize the preservation of green spaces and maintain a balance between urban growth and environmental sustainability.

12   Mark for Review 🔖

Which choice best describes data from the table that support Dr. Kinsley's hypothesis?

(A) City C1's green space area is more than double C2's urbanization rate, which suggests an inverse relationship between green space area and urbanization rate.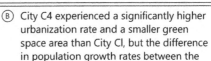

(B) City C4 experienced a significantly higher urbanization rate and a smaller green space area than City CI, but the difference in population growth rates between the two cities is not subtle.

(C) City C3 experienced a much higher urbanization rate and a smaller green space area than City C2, despite the relatively subtle difference in their population growth rates.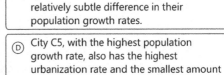

(D) City C5, with the highest population growth rate, also has the highest urbanization rate and the smallest amount of green space.

TEST◆QUBE

Back   Next

Section 1, Module 1: Reading & Writing

Annotate

Earth's Oceanic and Atmospheric Carbon Dioxide Concentrations in Four Time Periods

Time Period	Oceanic CO2 Concentration (ppm)	Atmospheric CO2 Concentration (ppm)
A	1800	280
B	1900	300
C	1950	310
D	2000	370

Researchers studying carbon dioxide (CO2) concentrations in the Earth's atmosphere and oceans are also interested in the impacts of CO2 on marine life and ecosystems. An increase in CO2 levels can lead to ocean acidification, which negatively affects marine organisms such as coral reefs, mollusks, and some species of plankton. Additionally, higher CO2 concentrations in the atmosphere can contribute to climate change, causing disruptions to weather patterns and impacting both terrestrial and aquatic ecosystems. In their recent study, Dr. Jane Smith and her team aimed to examine the correlation between the rise in atmospheric CO2 levels and the health of marine ecosystems. From examining their results, as expected, the researchers posited that _____

13   Mark for Review

Which choice most effectively uses data from the table to complete the statement?

(A) The increase in atmospheric CO2 concentration between Time Period A and Time Period D may have had a significant impact on marine ecosystems due to ocean acidification.

(B) The difference in oceanic CO2 concentration between Time Period A and Time Period B might not have been significant enough to affect marine organisms.

(C) The relatively stable oceanic CO2 concentration between Time Period B and Time Period C could indicate a period of reduced impact on marine ecosystems.

(D) The substantial increase in atmospheric CO2 concentration between Time Period B and Time Period C could have led to a more rapid decline in the health of marine ecosystems.

Section 1, Module 1: Reading & Writing

Annotate

Despite constituting a modest fraction of the audience at public speeches, skilled rhetoricians tend to exert a disproportionate influence over crowd reactions. A likely rationale for this skewed influence might be that seasoned orators understand the nuances of persuasive communication, and their grasp of these subtleties could _____

14   Mark for Review

Which choice most logically completes the text?

(A) encourage the crowd to develop their rhetorical skills to match the orators.

(B) amplify the orators' ability to sway public sentiment during speeches.

(C) prompt the uninitiated in the crowd to disregard the speech entirely.

(D) increase the demand for public speeches that employ sophisticated rhetorical techniques.

Section 1, Module 1: Reading & Writing

Annotate

The artist Frida Kahlo, known for her self-portraits and exploration of ___ has inspired generations of artists with her unique style and powerful themes. Her work continues to captivate audiences worldwide.

15   Mark for Review

Which choice completes the text so that it conforms to the conventions of Standard English?

(A) identity,

(B) identity

(C) identity–

(D) identities

TEST❖QUBE

Back   Next

Section 1, Module 1: Reading & Writing

Annotate

According to astronomers, the Milky Way is a barred spiral galaxy, and ____ contains over 100 billion stars. This celestial marvel is also home to our Solar System, with its diverse and unique planetary bodies. Its structure is defined by vast dusty spiral arms that encompass a dense, elongated central bar, the origin of its classification as a barred spiral galaxy.

16   Mark for Review

Which choice completes the text so that it conforms to the conventions of Standard English?

(A) itself

(B) it

(C) they

(D) one

TEST❖QUBE

Back   Next

I   II   III   IV   V   VI   VII

Section 1, Module 1: Reading & Writing

Annotate

____ famous for his dystopian novels 1984 and Animal Farm—was also a prolific essayist and journalist. His insights into power and totalitarianism remain relevant today.

17   Mark for Review 🔖

Which choice completes the text so that it conforms to the conventions of Standard English?

- (A) The author, George Orwell,
- (B) The author George Orwell –
- (C) The author, George Orwell –
- (D) The author George Orwell,

Section 1, Module 1: Reading & Writing

Annotate

The redwood trees of California are known for their incredible height, with some reaching over 300 feet tall. These magnificent trees, which can live for more than 2,000 years, ____ a unique ecosystem and are considered a natural wonder.

18   Mark for Review 🔖

Which choice completes the text so that it conforms to the conventions of Standard English?

- (A) supports
- (B) support
- (C) has supported
- (D) have supported

Annotate

Jane Goodall, a renowned primatologist and anthropologist, has spent decades studying the behavior of wild chimpanzees in their natural habitat in Gombe Stream National Park, Tanzania. Through her research, Goodall discovered that chimpanzees exhibit complex social behaviors, use tools, and _____ thereby challenging the conventional understanding of what distinguishes humans from other primates.

19　　　　　　　　　　Mark for Review 🔖

Which choice completes the text so that it conforms to the conventions of Standard English?

(A) communicate　　　　　Ⓐ

(B) communicate;　　　　　Ⓑ

(C) communicate,　　　　　Ⓒ

(D) communicate:　　　　　Ⓓ

TEST QUBE　　　Question 19 of 27 >　　　Back　Next

II

III

Annotate

Microbes, such as bacteria and fungi, are essential to various processes that sustain life on Earth. For example, nitrogen-fixing bacteria like Rhizobium convert atmospheric nitrogen into a form that plants can use, facilitating _____ growth. Additionally, the human microbiome, composed of trillions of microbes residing within and on our bodies, plays a crucial role in maintaining our health.

20　　　　　　　　　　Mark for Review 🔖

Which choice completes the text so that it conforms to the conventions of Standard English?

(A) their　　　　　Ⓐ

(B) your　　　　　Ⓑ

(C) its　　　　　Ⓒ

(D) they　　　　　Ⓓ

TEST QUBE　　　Question 20 of 27 >　　　Back　Next

IV

V

VI

VII

Annotate

II

After losing her left arm in a horrific shark attack at the age of 13, Bethany Hamilton was told she might never surf again. Defying all odds, Hamilton didn't just return to the water, she _____ the 2004 NSSA National Championships in California, she won first place in the Explorer Women's division and secured her position as a top-ranked female surfer, inspiring millions with her story of courage and determination.

III

21   Mark for Review 🔖

Which choice completes the text so that it conforms to the conventions of Standard English?

(A) blew her competition out of the water — figuratively — during   Ⓐ

(B) blew her competition out of the water — figuratively during   Ⓑ

(C) blew her competition out of the water — figuratively, during   Ⓒ

(D) blew her competition out of the water — figuratively. During   Ⓓ

IV

TEST●QUBE

Back Next

Annotate

V

Pioneering physicist Albert Einstein developed the theory of relativity, which fundamentally changed our understanding of space, time, and gravitation. His famous equation, $E=mc^2$, revealed the equivalence of mass and energy. _____ Einstein's work laid the foundation for various modern technologies, such as nuclear power and GPS.

22   Mark for Review 🔖

Which choice completes the text with the most logical transition?

(A) Nonetheless,   Ⓐ

(B) In summary,   Ⓑ

(C) Accordingly,   Ⓒ

(D) Despite this,   Ⓓ

VI

VII

TEST●QUBE

Back Next

Section 1, Module 1: Reading & Writing

Annotate

The Roman Empire, at its height, spanned three continents and included diverse cultures and languages. It maintained order and stability through a complex system of government and law. _____ the empire eventually succumbed to a combination of internal strife and external pressures.

23   Mark for Review

Which choice completes the text with the most logical transition?

(A) Therefore,

(B) Nevertheless,

(C) Furthermore,

(D) In contrast,

Section 1, Module 1: Reading & Writing

Annotate

The jazz age, a period during the 1920s, witnessed the flourishing of African American music, literature, and art. Jazz musicians like Louis Armstrong and Duke Ellington garnered widespread acclaim. _____ writers of the Harlem Renaissance, such as Langston Hughes and Zora Neale Hurston, challenged racial inequality through their creative works.

24   Mark for Review

Which choice completes the text with the most logical transition?

(A) Conversely,

(B) Simultaneously,

(C) As a consequence,

(D) On the contrary,

Annotate

The advent of social media has transformed the way people communicate, providing a platform for instant sharing of information and ideas. However, its impact on mental health and privacy has raised concerns. _____ studies have shown that excessive use of social media can lead to increased anxiety and decreased self-esteem.

25   Mark for Review 🔖

Which choice completes the text with the most logical transition?

(A) For instance,   Ⓐ

(B) On the other hand,   Ⓑ

(C) In addition,   Ⓒ

(D) Instead,   Ⓓ

Annotate

While researching a topic, a student has taken the following notes

- The Roman Empire was one of the most powerful and influential civilizations in history.
- At its height, the empire included much of Europe, North Africa, and the Middle East.
- Rome's political system was characterized by a complex mix of monarchy, oligarchy, and democracy.
- The Pax Romana was a period of relative peace and stability throughout the empire.
- The Roman Empire eventually declined due to a combination of political, economic, and military factors.

26   Mark for Review 🔖

The student wants to emphasize the geographical extent of the Roman Empire. Which choice most effectively uses relevant information from the notes to accomplish this goal?

(A) The Roman Empire's political system consisted of a mix of monarchy, oligarchy, and democracy, contributing to its vast influence across Europe and beyond.

(B) The Roman Empire, one of history's most powerful civilizations, spanned much of Europe, North Africa, and the Middle East at its peak.

(C) During the Pax Romana, the Roman Empire experienced a period of peace and stability that extended across its vast territories.

(D) The decline of the Roman Empire was due to various factors, despite its impressive geographical extent covering multiple continents.

Section 1, Module 1: Reading & Writing

 Annotate ⋮

While researching a topic, a student has taken the following notes:

- "1984" is a dystopian novel by George Orwell, published in 1949.
- The story is set in a totalitarian state called Oceania, ruled by the Party and its leader, Big Brother.
- The protagonist, Winston Smith, works at the Ministry of Truth, where he alters historical records to fit the Party's narrative.
- The novel explores themes of surveillance, propaganda, and the power of language to control thought.
- "1984" serves as a warning against the dangers of totalitarianism and the erosion of individual freedom.

27   Mark for Review 🔖

The student wants to explain the role of the protagonist in "1984." Which choice most effectively uses relevant information from the notes to accomplish this goal?

Ⓐ "1984" is a dystopian novel by George Orwell that explores the impact of surveillance, propaganda, and the power of language on society and individual freedom. Ⓐ

Ⓑ Winston Smith, works at the Ministry of Truth in Oceania, where he alters historical records to fit the Party's narrative, reflecting the themes of propaganda and control in "1984." Ⓑ

Ⓒ George Orwell's "1984" is set in the totalitarian state of Oceania, where Winston Smith struggles against oppression, exploring the themes of surveillance and propaganda. Ⓒ

Ⓓ As a warning against the dangers of totalitarianism, "1984" by George Orwell examines the erosion of individual freedom in a society characterized by surveillance and manipulation. Ⓓ

Back Next

Move on to the
Next Section 》

⏱ 32:00   Annotate ⋮

1   Mark for Review 🔖

Which choice completes the text with the most logical and precise word or phrase?

In the quaint coastal town of Whitby, England, a dense fog enveloped the city, making it nearly impossible for pedestrians and motorists alike to navigate the cobblestone streets. With the famous Whitby Abbey barely visible in the background, people struggled to ____ their way through the limited visibility, proceeding with extreme caution as the foghorn from the harbor sounded intermittently.

(A) circumvent

(B) conjure

(C) discern

(D) meander

TEST⬛QUBE   Question 1 of 27 >   Back Next

Annotate ⋮

2   Mark for Review 🔖

Which choice completes the text with the most logical and precise word or phrase?

Detroit, once the pulsating heart of the American automotive industry, has, over the years, fallen into a state of decay with its once-gleaming architecture, including the iconic Packard Automotive Plant, now showing signs of age and neglect. This ____ state of disrepair stands as a stark reminder of the city's former glory and industrious past.

(A) nascent

(B) immutable

(C) desolate

(D) auspicious

TEST⬛QUBE   Question 2 of 27 >   Back Next

Section 1, Module 2: Reading & Writing

Annotate ⋮

Brazilian artist, Vik Muniz, known for his ingenious use of unconventional materials, has a new exhibit that challenges conventional notions of beauty. By presenting a diverse array of subjects, ranging from portraits made of scrap metal to images composed of chocolate syrup, Muniz _____ the idea that beauty is subjective and multifaceted.

3   Mark for Review 🔖

Which choice completes the text with the most logical and precise word or phrase?

(A) repels

(B) censures

(C) ratifies

(D) champions

Section 1, Module 2: Reading & Writing

Annotate ⋮

Samantha Power, a renowned diplomat and former United States Ambassador to the United Nations, exhibited exceptional skill in navigating tense international discussions. Her ability to _____ compromise from seemingly intractable positions, particularly during negotiations on Syrian conflict resolution, earned her widespread respect and admiration.

4   Mark for Review 🔖

Which choice completes the text with the most logical and precise word or phrase?

(A) extort

(B) admonish

(C) broach

(D) elicit

Dr. Karl von Frisch, an Austrian ethologist, made groundbreaking discoveries concerning honeybees' remarkable ability to communicate through intricate dance patterns, famously known as the "waggle dance." This method of communication allows honeybees to _____ the location of food sources to other members of the hive, ensuring their collective survival and efficiency in foraging.

5   Mark for Review 🔖

Which choice completes the text with the most logical and precise word or phrase?

(A) obfuscate

(B) misappropriate

(C) divulge

(D) misconstrue

TEST QUBE   Question 5 of 27 >   Back   Next

The discovery of the ancient city of Machu Picchu by explorer Hiram Bingham in 1911 captivated historians and archaeologists, as it provided a _____ insight into the lives of the Inca civilization. Nestled among the Andes mountains, the site's well-preserved structures and artifacts, including the Intihuatana stone and Temple of the Sun, continue to offer valuable information about this once-dominant culture.

6   Mark for Review 🔖

Which choice completes the text with the most logical and precise word or phrase?

(A) fleeting

(B) cursory

(C) evocative

(D) palpable

TEST QUBE   Question 6 of 27 >   Back   Next

Section 1, Module 2: Reading & Writing

Annotate ⋮

In the United States Congress, the contentious debates between the Republican and Democratic parties often lead to legislative stalemates, hindering the passage of crucial policies such as healthcare reform and immigration. Each party's _____ insistence on its own ideals, exemplified by figures like Senator Mitch McConnell and Senator Bernie Sanders, only serves to exacerbate the polarization and gridlock.

7   Mark for Review 🔖

Which choice completes the text with the most logical and precise word or phrase?

- Ⓐ congenial — Ⓐ
- Ⓑ dogmatic — Ⓑ
- Ⓒ pliable — Ⓒ
- Ⓓ ambivalent — Ⓓ

TEST⬤QUBE

Back   Next

Section 1, Module 2: Reading & Writing

Annotate ⋮

Off the coast of Florida, marine biologists from the Harbor Branch Oceanographic Institute have observed that dolphins employ a variety of hunting strategies, including a remarkable technique known as "mud-ring feeding." This fascinating technique involves dolphins _____ their tails on the water's surface, creating a mud ring that serves as a barrier to trap fish, demonstrating their intelligence and adaptability in foraging for food.

8   Mark for Review 🔖

Which choice completes the text with the most logical and precise word or phrase?

- Ⓐ languishing — Ⓐ
- Ⓑ suppressing — Ⓑ
- Ⓒ thrashing — Ⓒ
- Ⓓ dismantling — Ⓓ

TEST⬤QUBE

Back   Next

Section 1, Module 2: Reading & Writing

Annotate ⋮

The following text is from Leo Tolstoy's 1877 novel *Anna Karenina*. The Oblonskys are a family in Imperial Russian society.

Everything was in confusion in the Oblonskys' house. The wife had discovered that the husband was carrying on an intrigue with a French girl, who had been a governess in their family, and she had announced to her husband that she could not go on living in the same house with him. This position of affairs had now lasted three days, and not only the husband and wife themselves, but all the members of their family and household, were painfully conscious of it. Every person in the house felt that there was no sense in their living together, and that the stray people brought together by chance in any inn had more in common with one another than they, the members of the family and household of the Oblonskys.

9

Mark for Review 🔖

According to the text, what is true about the Oblonskys?

(A) The Oblonskys are a close-knit family with strong bonds, despite internal struggles.

(B) The Oblonskys' household is in turmoil due to the husband's indiscretion.

(C) The Oblonskys endure a sense of disconnection caused by the stray people.

(D) The Oblonskys encounter friction with the stray people due to the French governess.

TEST⬜QUBE

Back   Next

Section 1, Module 2: Reading & Writing

Annotate ⋮

In 1928, Scottish biologist Alexander Fleming discovered penicillin, the first antibiotic, revolutionizing medicine and leading to the treatment of countless bacterial infections. However, the widespread use of antibiotics has also contributed to the emergence of antibiotic-resistant bacteria, posing a significant threat to public health. A medical researcher claims that the development of new antibiotics is critical to combat antibiotic resistance.

10

Mark for Review 🔖

Which finding, if true, would most directly support the researcher's claim?

(A) The discovery of penicillin was a serendipitous event, as Fleming noticed that a mold called Penicillium notatum produced a substance that killed a wide range of bacteria.

(B) Antibiotic resistance can develop through various mechanisms, such as mutations in bacterial genes or the acquisition of resistance genes from other bacteria through horizontal gene transfer.

(C) The development of new antibiotics with novel mechanisms of action can target resistant bacteria and help to preserve the effectiveness of existing antibiotics by reducing the selective pressure for resistance.

(D) Antibiotic stewardship programs, which promote the appropriate use of antibiotics, are important for minimizing the emergence and spread of antibiotic-resistant bacteria.

TEST⬜QUBE

Back   Next

Section 1, Module 2: Reading & Writing

Annotate   ⋮

"If—" is a 1910 poem by Rudyard Kipling. In the poem, Kipling urges the readers, whom he addresses directly, to remain resilient in the face of adversity, writing, ____

11   Mark for Review 🔖

Which quotation from "If—" most effectively illustrates the claim?

(A) If you can dream—and not make dreams your master; / If you can think—and not make thoughts your aim; / If you can meet with Triumph and Disaster   Ⓐ

(B) If neither foes nor loving friends can hurt you, / If all men count with you, but none too much: / If you can fill the unforgiving minute   Ⓑ

(C) If you can force your heart and nerve and sinew / To serve your turn long after they are gone, / And so hold on when there is nothing in you   Ⓒ

(D) If you can talk with crowds and keep your virtue, / Or walk with Kings—nor lose the common touch, / Yours is the Earth and everything that's in it,   Ⓓ

TEST⬛QUBE   Question 11 of 27 >   Back   Next

Section 1, Module 2: Reading & Writing

Annotate   ⋮

The Underground Railroad was a clandestine network of people, African American as well as white, offering shelter and aid to escaped enslaved people from the South. Harriet Tubman, a famous abolitionist known for her work in the Underground Railroad, contributed to the escape of numerous slaves to freedom. Tubman's accomplishments include personally guiding around 70 slaves to freedom, providing instructions for 50 to 60 others to escape independently, and creating a network of contacts to assist her missions. A historian asserts that Tubman's actions had a substantial impact on the success of the Underground Railroad.

12   Mark for Review 🔖

Which finding, if true, would most directly support the historian's claim?

(A) During her missions, Tubman used her knowledge of the terrain and safe houses, and her network of contacts to meticulously plan trips, ensuring the safe passage of slaves to freedom.   Ⓐ

(B) Tubman was a key figure in the women's suffrage movement, advocating for equal rights for women and people of color in the late 19th and early 20th centuries.   Ⓑ

(C) During the Civil War, Tubman served as a nurse, cook, and laundress, supporting the Union Army in various capacities.   Ⓒ

(D) Tubman settled in Auburn, New York, where she established a home for the elderly and provided care for her own aging parents.   Ⓓ

TEST⬛QUBE   Question 12 of 27 >   Back   Next

Section 1, Module 2: Reading & Writing

Annotate

The following text is adapted from Friedrich Nietzsche's 1886 philosophical work, *Beyond Good and Evil*. The book is an extended critique of the philosophical tradition, with a particular focus on philosophers of the Enlightenment.

SUPPOSING that Truth is a woman—what then? Is there not ground for suspecting that all philosophers, in so far as they have been dogmatists, have failed to understand women—that the terrible seriousness and clumsy importunity with which they have usually paid their addresses to Truth, have been unskilled and unseemly methods for winning a woman? Certainly she has never allowed herself to be won; and at present every kind of dogma stands with sad and discouraged mien—IF, indeed, it stands at all! For there are scoffers who maintain that it has fallen, that all dogma lies on the ground—nay more, that it is at its last gasp.

13   Mark for Review 🔖

Which choice best states the main purpose of the text?

- (A) To critique the seriousness and persistence with which philosophers approach Truth

- (B) To assert that dogmatic philosophers have misunderstood Truth, metaphorically depicted as a woman

- (C) To portray the current state of philosophical dogma as downtrodden and potentially obsolete

- (D) To suggest that Truth, like a woman, resists simplistic and heavy-handed attempts at understanding

TEST🧊QUBE   Back   Next

Section 1, Module 2: Reading & Writing

Annotate

In predictive modeling, data scientists employ machine learning algorithms to anticipate future outcomes based on historical data. Dr. Lena Petrovich, a data science researcher, argues that while predictive models are naturally inclined to perform best on data similar to their training set, robust models should also account for potential outliers. Thus, incorporating data from extreme cases, even if they deviate from the majority of observations, might _____

14   Mark for Review 🔖

Which choice most logically completes the text?

- (A) align the predictive models with the theoretical distributions postulated in statistical textbooks.

- (B) prevent data scientists from developing predictive models without considering outlier data.

- (C) simplify the modeling process for novice data scientists unfamiliar with machine learning algorithms.

- (D) enhance the model's capacity to generalize and make accurate predictions in diverse scenarios.

TEST🧊QUBE   Back   Next

The philosophical doctrine of hedonism, associated predominantly with the Greek philosopher Epicurus, posits that the pursuit of pleasure is the highest good. Nevertheless, several of Epicurus's writings emphasize the avoidance of pain, rather than the pursuit of pleasure. If both the generally accepted interpretation of hedonism and the focus of Epicurus's writings are correct, it could be posited that ____

15   Mark for Review

Which choice most logically completes the text?

A) Epicurus held an atypical interpretation of hedonism, in which the avoidance of pain was equated to the pursuit of pleasure.

B) Epicurus was an anomaly among Greek philosophers, often contradicting the philosophical doctrines he himself endorsed.

C) Hedonism was an esoteric philosophy, understood and interpreted differently among various Greek philosophers.

D) The writings of Epicurus were misattributed, and in reality, he didn't propagate hedonism at all.

II

III

During an extensive study of tectonic activities, geologists replaced the mineral olivine, commonly found in Earth's mantle, with a synthetic analogue in their laboratory model. The viscosity of the mantle was then measured under conditions mimicking those at a depth of 410 kilometers (where the transition zone in Earth's mantle begins) at 1000 and 1300 degrees Celsius respectively. The experiment showed no significant difference in mantle viscosity at 1000 degrees Celsius between the olivine model and the synthetic one. However, at 1300 degrees Celsius, the model with olivine exhibited markedly reduced viscosity compared to its synthetic counterpart, implying that ____

16   Mark for Review

Which choice most logically completes the text?

A) the transition zone in Earth's mantle predominantly contains olivine.

B) the viscosity of Earth's mantle increases beyond the transition zone.

C) the synthetic analogue of olivine exhibits properties identical to those of natural olivine at 1000 degrees Celsius.

D) olivine is crucial for the reduction of mantle viscosity at high temperatures.

IV

V

VI

VII

Section 1, Module 2: Reading & Writing

Annotate ⋮

Leonardo da Vinci, a true Renaissance man, excelled in various ___ painting, sculpture, architecture, and science. His innovative ideas and inventions were far ahead of his time.

17   Mark for Review 🔖

Which choice completes the text so that it conforms to the conventions of Standard English?

- (A) fields, including
- (B) fields,
- (C) fields including:
- (D) fields including

Section 1, Module 2: Reading & Writing

Annotate ⋮

In ancient Rome, Julius Caesar initiated significant reforms during his time as a political leader. Among his accomplishments ____ the creation of the Julian calendar, which served as a precursor to the modern Gregorian calendar.

18   Mark for Review 🔖

Which choice completes the text so that it conforms to the conventions of Standard English?

- (A) was
- (B) were
- (C) is
- (D) are

Annotate

Harriet Tubman, a courageous abolitionist and conductor on the Underground Railroad, risked her life numerous times to help enslaved people escape to ___ efforts saved countless lives and left a lasting impact on American history.

19   Mark for Review

Which choice completes the text so that it conforms to the conventions of Standard English?

(A) freedom, her   (A)

(B) freedom; her   (B)

(C) freedom – her   (C)

(D) freedom her   (D)

II

III

IV

Annotate

The mathematician Ada Lovelace—often considered the world's first computer ___ collaborated with inventor Charles Babbage on the Analytical Engine. This early computing device laid the groundwork for modern computers.

20   Mark for Review

Which choice completes the text so that it conforms to the conventions of Standard English?

(A) programmer—   (A)

(B) programming—   (B)

(C) programmer,   (C)

(D) programmer;   (D)

V

VI

VII

Annotate

The Great Barrier Reef, located off the coast of Australia, is the world's largest coral reef system. Spanning over 1,400 miles, the reef ___ a diverse range of marine life and plays a vital role in maintaining the health of our oceans.

21   Mark for Review 🔖

Which choice completes the text so that it conforms to the conventions of Standard English?

- (A) is home to
- (B) has been home to
- (C) are home to
- (D) have been home to

TEST QUBE

Back   Next

Annotate

Marie Curie, a pioneering physicist and chemist, was the first person to win Nobel Prizes in two different scientific ___ . Her discoveries in radioactivity revolutionized the field of science.

22   Mark for Review 🔖

Which choice completes the text so that it conforms to the conventions of Standard English?

- (A) fields: physics and chemistry
- (B) fields; physics and chemistry
- (C) fields, such as physics and chemistry
- (D) fields physics and chemistry

TEST QUBE

Back   Next

Section 1, Module 2: Reading & Writing

Annotate

The Industrial Revolution brought significant advancements in manufacturing, transportation, and communication. It led to urbanization and improved living standards for many people. _____ the revolution also had negative consequences, such as environmental degradation and labor exploitation.

23   Mark for Review

Which choice completes the text with the most logical transition?

- (A) Moreover,
- (B) In conclusion,
- (C) As a result,
- (D) However,

TEST QUBE

Back   Next

Section 1, Module 2: Reading & Writing

Annotate

The human brain is an intricate organ responsible for processing sensory information, regulating vital functions, and enabling complex thought. It consists of billions of neurons that communicate through electrical and chemical signals. _____ the study of the brain, known as neuroscience, continues to uncover new insights into its structure and function.

24   Mark for Review

Which choice completes the text with the most logical transition?

- (A) Despite this,
- (B) As such,
- (C) Conversely,
- (D) In comparison,

TEST QUBE

Back   Next

I

II

III

IV

V

VI

VII

Section 1, Module 2: Reading & Writing

Annotate ⋮

The Sistine Chapel, located in Vatican City, is renowned for its remarkable frescoes painted by the celebrated artist Michelangelo. The ceiling, completed in 1512, depicts scenes from the Book of Genesis. _____ The Last Judgment, a powerful portrayal of the Second Coming of Christ, adorns the chapel's altar wall.

25   Mark for Review 🔖

Which choice completes the text with the most logical transition?

- (A) Subsequently,
- (B) In addition,
- (C) Contrarily,
- (D) As a result,

Section 1, Module 2: Reading & Writing

Annotate ⋮

While researching a topic, a student has taken the following notes:

- Plate tectonics is the theory that the Earth's lithosphere is divided into several large and small plates that move over the asthenosphere.
- The movement of these plates is driven by the convection currents in the Earth's mantle.
- Plate boundaries can be categorized into three types: divergent, convergent, and transform.
- The movement of tectonic plates causes various geological events, such as earthquakes, volcanic eruptions, and the formation of mountains.

26   Mark for Review 🔖

The student wants to discuss the consequences of plate tectonics. Which choice most effectively uses relevant information from the notes to accomplish this goal?

- (A) Plate tectonics is a theory that explains the movement of the Earth's lithosphere, with large and small plates shifting over the asthenosphere due to convection currents in the mantle
- (B) The movement of tectonic plates causes various geological events, such as earthquakes, volcanic eruptions, and the formation of mountains, as a result of interactions at divergent, convergent, and transform boundaries.
- (C) Plate boundaries in the theory of plate tectonics can be classified into three types: divergent, convergent, and transform, which are responsible for the movement of the Earth's lithosphere.
- (D) Convection currents in the Earth's mantle drive the movement of tectonic plates, leading to the formation of geological features and the occurrence of natural disasters like earthquakes and volcanic eruptions.

Section 1, Module 2: Reading & Writing

Annotate

While researching a topic, a student has taken the following notes:

- The Dyatlov Pass incident occurred in the northern Ural Mountains in 1959.
- Nine experienced hikers died under mysterious circumstances.
- Investigations found that the hikers tore their tent from the inside and fled without proper clothing or shoes.
- Injuries found on the bodies could not be explained by human actions.

27   Mark for Review 🔖

The student wants to convey the peculiar circumstances and the mystery surrounding the Dyatlov Pass incident. Which choice most effectively uses relevant information from the notes to accomplish this goal?

(A) In the Dyatlov Pass incident, nine hikers died under mysterious circumstances in the northern Ural Mountains.

(B) The Dyatlov Pass incident is puzzling because the hikers, found dead, had inexplicable injuries and had fled their tent without proper clothing or shoes.

(C) The Dyatlov Pass incident, which occurred in 1959, involved the mysterious death of nine experienced hikers.

(D) Investigations of the Dyatlov Pass incident found that the hikers tore their tent from the inside, an action that remains unexplained.

TEST QUBE

End of Test 1 Reading/Writing Section

Back   Next

Upcoming Math Section: Reference Formula Sheet

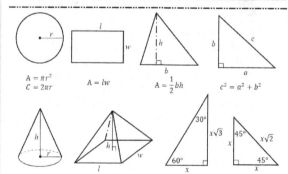

$A = \pi r^2$
$C = 2\pi r$

$A = lw$

$A = \frac{1}{2}bh$

$c^2 = a^2 + b^2$

$V = \frac{1}{3}\pi r^2 h$

$V = \frac{1}{3}lwh$

Special Right Triangles

$V = lwh$

$V = \pi r^2 h$

$V = \frac{3}{4}\pi r^3$

The number of degrees of arc in a circle is 360.
The number of radians of arc in a circle is 2π.
The sum of the measures in degrees of the angles of a triangle is 180.

Directions for Student-Produced Response

- **TEST QUBE** recommends students to use decimals for most answers but suggests using fractions only in cases where the answers involve repeating decimals (e.g., 0.333 = 1/3)
- For cases with more than one answer, enter **just one of the answers.**
- You can enter up to 5 characters for your answer. (For negative answers, the **negative sign** does not count as one character)
- For **fractions** that don't fit the answer box, enter the decimal equivalent (Unless advised to do otherwise)
- For **decimals** that exceed the answer box, round to the fourth digit. (Unless advised to do otherwise)
- For mixed number (such as $4\frac{1}{4}$), enter it as an improper fraction ($17/4$) or its decimal equivalent (4.25)
- For all answers, you may omit the symbols and units such as $, %, cm^3, m^2, etc.

Acceptable vs Non-Acceptable Answers

Answer	Acceptable ways to receive credit	Ways you WON'T receive credit
4.25	4.25 , 17/4	41/4 , 4 1/4
4/6	2/3 .6666 , .6667 0.666 , 0.667	0.66 , .66 0.67 , .67
-1/6	-1/6 -0.166 , -0.167 -.1666 , -.1667	-0.16 , -.16 -0.17 , -.167

Move on to the Next Section ≫

1   Mark for Review 🔖

If $6y = 12$, what is the value of y?

(A)   12   Ⓐ

(B)   6   Ⓑ

(C)   3   Ⓒ

(D) ●   2   Ⓓ

TEST⬛QUBE   Question 1 of 22 >

2   Mark for Review 🔖

Each side of a fair 2-sided coin is denoted heads and tails. If Jake flips the coin twice, what is the probability of having only heads as the result?

(A) $\frac{1}{2}$ Ⓐ

(B) $\frac{1}{3}$ Ⓑ

(C) ● $\frac{1}{4}$ Ⓒ

(D) $\frac{1}{8}$ Ⓓ

$$\frac{1}{2} \cdot \frac{1}{2}$$

TEST⬛QUBE   Question 2 of 22 >

3   Mark for Review 🔖

What is 16% of 25?

(A) ●   4   Ⓐ

(B)   14   Ⓑ

(C)   16   Ⓒ

(D)   400   Ⓓ

TEST⬛QUBE   Question 3 of 22 >

4   Mark for Review 🔖

$$F(x) = 120,000 + 4600x$$

Function $F(x)$ models a nuclear power plant's total monthly operation cost, in dollars, where x represents the number of workers working at the nuclear power plant. If 27 workers work at the nuclear power plant this month, how much is the total operation cost, in dollars, of the nuclear power plant for this month?

(A)   124,200   Ⓐ

(B)   124,600   Ⓑ

(C)   200,600   Ⓒ

(D) ●   244,200   Ⓓ

TEST⬛QUBE   Question 4 of 22 >   Back   Next

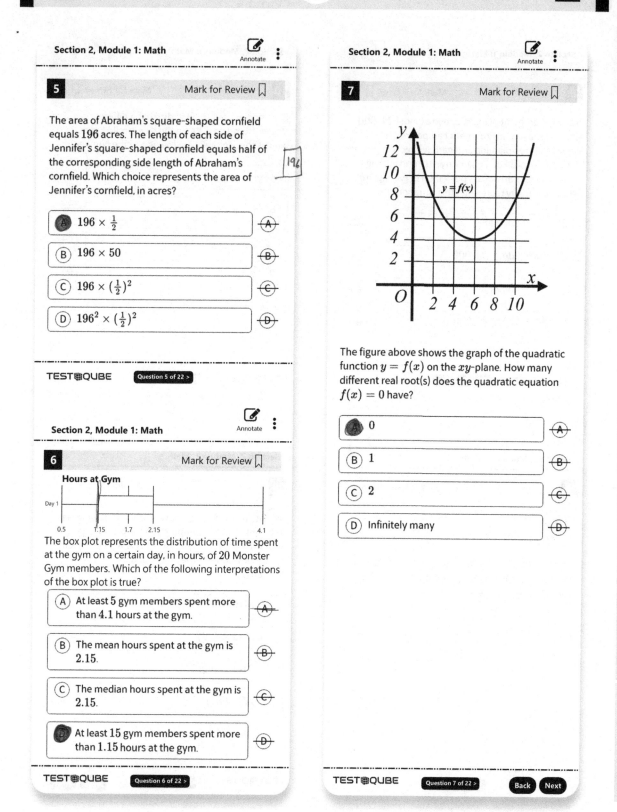

5   Mark for Review 🏷

The area of Abraham's square-shaped cornfield equals 196 acres. The length of each side of Jennifer's square-shaped cornfield equals half of the corresponding side length of Abraham's cornfield. Which choice represents the area of Jennifer's cornfield, in acres?

196

Ⓐ $196 \times \frac{1}{2}$

Ⓑ 196×50

Ⓒ $196 \times (\frac{1}{2})^2$

Ⓓ $196^2 \times (\frac{1}{2})^2$

TEST◉QUBE   Question 5 of 22 >

6   Mark for Review 🏷

Hours at Gym

Day 1

0.5   1.15   1.7   2.15   4.1

The box plot represents the distribution of time spent at the gym on a certain day, in hours, of 20 Monster Gym members. Which of the following interpretations of the box plot is true?

Ⓐ At least 5 gym members spent more than 4.1 hours at the gym.

Ⓑ The mean hours spent at the gym is 2.15.

Ⓒ The median hours spent at the gym is 2.15.

Ⓓ At least 15 gym members spent more than 1.15 hours at the gym.

TEST◉QUBE   Question 6 of 22 >

7   Mark for Review 🏷

$y = f(x)$

The figure above shows the graph of the quadratic function $y = f(x)$ on the xy-plane. How many different real root(s) does the quadratic equation $f(x) = 0$ have?

Ⓐ 0

Ⓑ 1

Ⓒ 2

Ⓓ Infinitely many

TEST◉QUBE   Question 7 of 22 >   Back   Next

8   Mark for Review 🔖

A city government plans to spend at most $24,000$ dollars for a city environment campaign, which consists of tree planting and garbage recycling. Tree planting costs 55 dollars per tree (t), and garbage recycling costs 90 dollars per gallon of garbage (g). Which inequality represents this situation?

(A) $55t \leq 24,000$

(B) $55t + 90g \leq 24,000$

(C) $90t + 55g \leq 24,000$

(D) $55t + 90t \leq 24,000$

TEST🧊QUBE   Question 8 of 22 >

9   Mark for Review 🔖

$$x + 2y = 11$$
$$4xy = 20$$

(x,y) is the solution for the system of equations above. Find one value of y that satisfies the system of equations.

5

TEST🧊QUBE   Question 9 of 22 >

10   Mark for Review 🔖

Each side of a fair 6-sided dice has a different integer from 1 to 6. When the dice is rolled once, what is the probability of rolling a prime number?

(A) $\frac{1}{6}$

(B) $\frac{1}{4}$

(C) $\frac{1}{3}$

(D) $\frac{1}{2}$

2, 3, 5

TEST🧊QUBE   Question 10 of 22 >

11   Mark for Review 🔖

Mountain A erodes every year, causing a decrease in height by 0.1% compared to the previous year. If the current height of mountain A is M feet, which choice best models the height of mountain A, in feet, after x years?

(A) $M(0.1)^x$

(B) $M(1 - 0.9)^x$

(C) $M(1 - 0.001)^x$

(D) $M(0.001)^x$

TEST🧊QUBE   Question 11 of 22 >   Back   Next

Section 2, Module 1: Math Annotate ⋮

12 Mark for Review 🔖

Student	Credits
A	11
B	14
C	13
D	18
E	12
F	10
G	13

Seven students $A, B, C, D, E, F,$ and G take credit courses at Wharton High School. The total credits each student takes this semester are shown in the table above. What is the median value of the seven students' credits at Wharton High School?

13

10, 11, 12, 13, 13, 14, 18

Section 2, Module 1: Math Annotate ⋮

13 Mark for Review 🔖

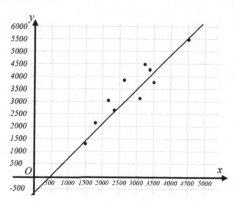

The scatterplot above shows the statistics of major cities in data set P, where the x-values represent the land area (in square kilometers) and the y-values represent the population (in thousands). Which choice most appropriately models the line of best fit for data set P?

(A) $y = -1.41x + 560$

(B) $y = -1.41x - 560$

(C) $y = 1.41x + 560$

(D) $y = 1.41x - 560$

Section 2, Module 1: Math　Annotate ⋮

14　　　Mark for Review 🔖

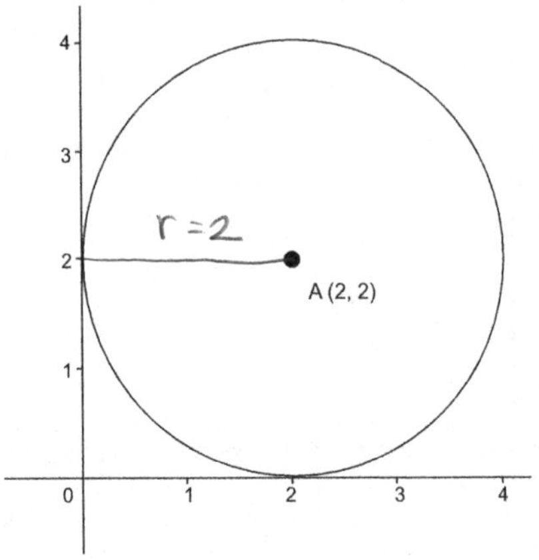

r = 2

A (2, 2)

What is the area of a circle whose center is $A(2, 2)$ and is tangent to both x-axis and y-axis?

- (A) π
- (B) 2π
- ● (C) 4π
- (D) 8π

$A = \pi r^2$

Section 2, Module 1: Math　Annotate ⋮

15　　　Mark for Review 🔖

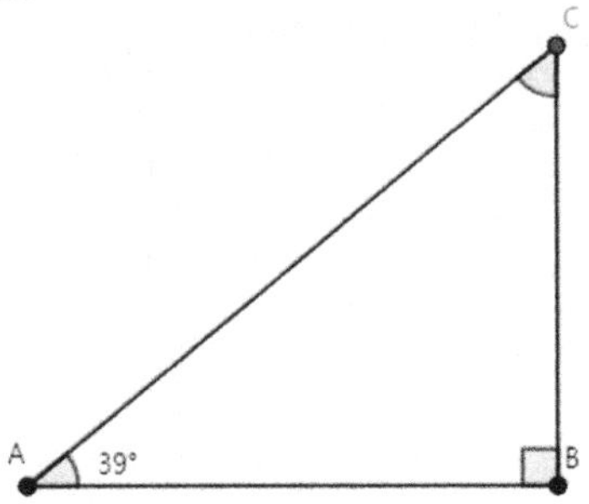

C

A 39°　B

Among the internal angles in right triangle ABC, angle B has the largest value. If angle A equals $39°$, what is the value, in degrees, of angle C?

51

Section 2, Module 1: Math　Annotate ⋮

16　　　Mark for Review 🔖

Which expression is equivalent to $\overparen{x(xy)}^3 \times \frac{x}{y}$ where x and y are different positive real numbers?

- ● (A) $x^5 y^2$
- (B) $x^4 y^3$
- (C) $x^3 y^{-2}$
- (D) $(xy)^3$

$x\left(x^3 y^3\right)$

$x^4 xy^3$

$x^5 y^3 \times \frac{x}{y}$ ×

17 Mark for Review ⬚

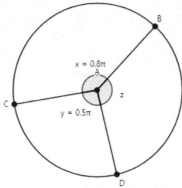

x = 0.8π

y = 0.5π

Points B, C, and D are on a circle with center A. Angle BAC (angle x) equals 0.8π and angle CAD (angle y) equals 0.5π, each in radians. What is the measure of the smaller angle BAD, in radians? (The picture is not drawn to scale.)

 (A) 2π

 (B) 1.5π

 (C) 0.7π

(D) 0.5π

$0.8\pi + 0.5\pi = 360$
$= 2\pi$

18 Mark for Review ⬚

What is the correct set of solutions for equation $x^2 - 12x + 27 = 0$?

 $x = 3$ or $x = 9$ — (A)

(B) $x = -3$ or $x = 9$ — (B)

(C) $x = 3$ or $x = -9$ — (C)

(D) $x = -3$ or $x = -9$ — (D)

I
II
III
IV
V
VI
VII

19 Mark for Review 🔖

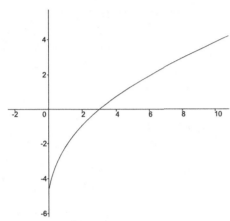

A part of the graph of $f(x) = 2\sqrt{2x} - 5$ on the xy-plane is shown above. Each point of the graph of $f(x)$ is translated by 6 to the positive x-direction, forming a new graph identical to the graph of $g(x)$. Which equation defines $g(x)$?

(A) $g(x) = 2\sqrt{12x} - 5$ ~~A~~

(B) $g(x) = 2\sqrt{x - 6} - 5$ ~~B~~

(C) $g(x) = 2\sqrt{2(x - 6)} - 5$ ~~C~~

(D) $g(x) = 2\sqrt{2x} - 11$ ~~D~~

20 Mark for Review 🔖

$f(x) = \frac{1}{x - 11}$
What is the value of x, if $f(x) = \frac{1}{35}$?

46

21 Mark for Review 🔖

In a city, 60% of the population owns a car, and 40% of those car owners also own a motorcycle. If the city has a population of 50,000, how many people own both a car and a motorcycle?

22   Mark for Review 🔖

Table

Suit	Numerals	Faces
Spades	1, 2, 3, 4, 5, 6, 7, 8, 9, and 10	Jack, Queen, and King
Hearts	1, 2, 3, 4, 5, 6, 7, 8, 9, and 10	Jack, Queen, and King
Clubs	1, 2, 3, 4, 5, 6, 7, 8, 9, and 10	Jack, Queen, and King
Diamonds	1, 2, 3, 4, 5, 6, 7, 8, 9, and 10	Jack, Queen, and King

Example

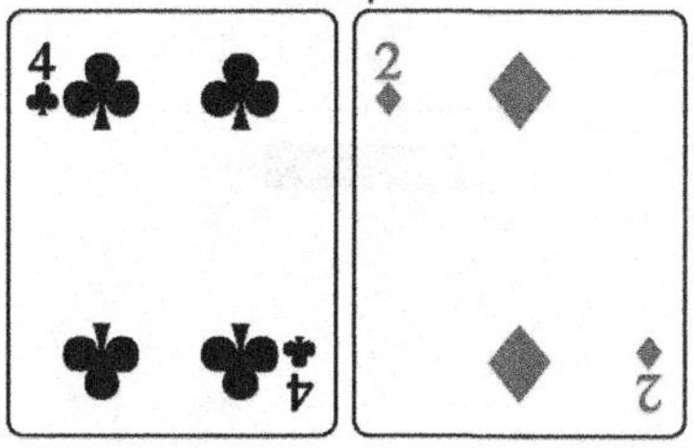

A standard card deck contains 52 unique cards. On each card, either a numeral or a face is denoted as shown in the table. (Aces are considered as 1.) Julia randomly picked two different numeral cards from a deck and placed one on the left and one on the right. What is the chance of the numeral denoted on the card Julia placed on the left is exactly two times bigger than the one on the right?

(A) $\frac{80}{40 \times 39}$

(B) $\frac{16}{40 \times 39}$

(C) $\frac{80}{52 \times 52}$

(D) $\frac{16}{52 \times 52}$

Move on to the Next Section

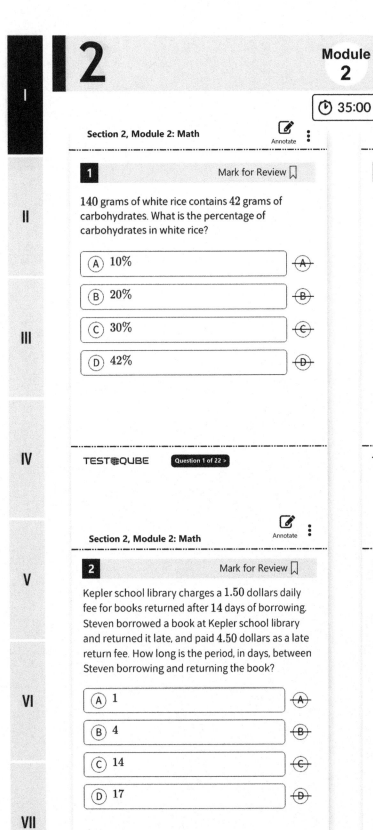

1   Mark for Review 🔖

140 grams of white rice contains 42 grams of carbohydrates. What is the percentage of carbohydrates in white rice?

Ⓐ 10%   Ⓐ

Ⓑ 20%   Ⓑ

Ⓒ 30%   Ⓒ

Ⓓ 42%   Ⓓ

TEST🔳QUBE   Question 1 of 22 >

2   Mark for Review 🔖

Kepler school library charges a 1.50 dollars daily fee for books returned after 14 days of borrowing. Steven borrowed a book at Kepler school library and returned it late, and paid 4.50 dollars as a late return fee. How long is the period, in days, between Steven borrowing and returning the book?

Ⓐ 1   Ⓐ

Ⓑ 4   Ⓑ

Ⓒ 14   Ⓒ

Ⓓ 17   Ⓓ

TEST🔳QUBE   Question 2 of 22 >

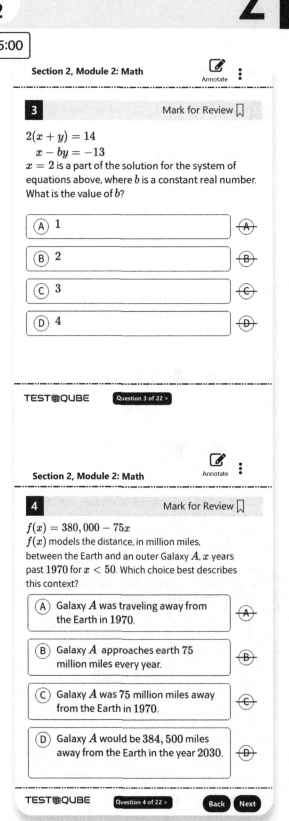

3   Mark for Review 🔖

$$2(x + y) = 14$$
$$x - by = -13$$

$x = 2$ is a part of the solution for the system of equations above, where b is a constant real number. What is the value of b?

Ⓐ 1   Ⓐ

Ⓑ 2   Ⓑ

Ⓒ 3   Ⓒ

Ⓓ 4   Ⓓ

TEST🔳QUBE   Question 3 of 22 >

4   Mark for Review 🔖

$f(x) = 380,000 - 75x$

$f(x)$ models the distance, in million miles, between the Earth and an outer Galaxy A, x years past 1970 for $x < 50$. Which choice best describes this context?

Ⓐ Galaxy A was traveling away from the Earth in 1970.   Ⓐ

Ⓑ Galaxy A approaches earth 75 million miles every year.   Ⓑ

Ⓒ Galaxy A was 75 million miles away from the Earth in 1970.   Ⓒ

Ⓓ Galaxy A would be 384,500 miles away from the Earth in the year 2030.   Ⓓ

TEST🔳QUBE   Question 4 of 22 >   Back   Next

5 Mark for Review 🔖

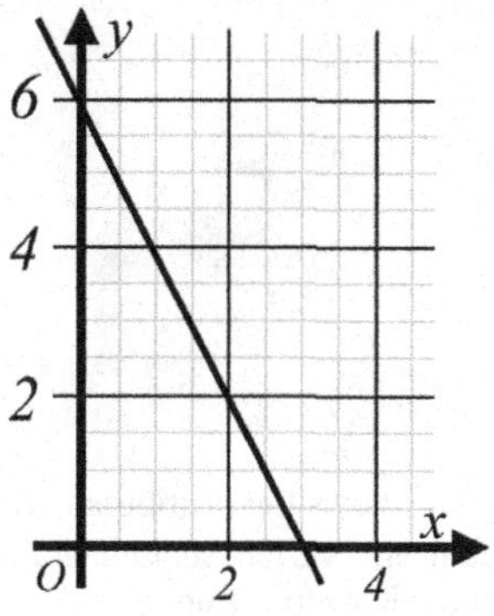

What is the y-intercept of the graph shown?

(A) 6 —(A)—

(B) 4 —(B)—

(C) 3 —(C)—

(D) 0 —(D)—

6 Mark for Review 🔖

Vigo's school band consists of guitar players and flute players, where a band member plays exactly one kind of instrument between the two. If there are twice as many guitar players as there are flute players, and there are 18 members in Vigo's band, how many guitar players are present in Vigo's band?

(A) 12 —(A)—

(B) 8 —(B)—

(C) 6 —(C)—

(D) 4 —(D)—

7 Mark for Review 🔖

Factory F has a 2% chance of producing defective products. Out of $5,000$ items produced from factory F, which of the following values is closest to the expected quantity of defective products?

(A) 2 —(A)—

(B) 10 —(B)—

(C) 100 —(C)—

(D) 1,000 —(D)—

8   Mark for Review 🔖

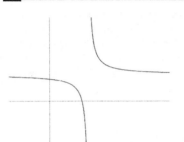

An overview of the graph of $y = \frac{1}{x-3} + 2$ is shown. What is the x-intercept of the graph?

9   Mark for Review 🔖

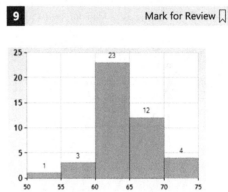

The histogram shows the distribution of the ages of all 43 students in a certain senior literature course. Which of the following is true?

(A) The median age of the students is greater than or equal to 60, and less than 65.

(B) A student at the age of 57 is above the 90th percentile of age.

(C) 60 students are 23 years old.

(D) 12 students are older than or at the age of 70.

10   Mark for Review 🔖

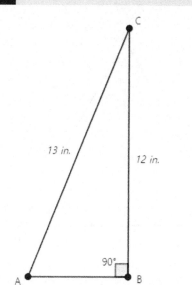

In a right triangle ABC where angle $B = 90°$, the hypotenuse A is 13 inches long, and the opposite B is 12 inches long. What is $\cos(A)$?

(A) $\frac{1}{13}$

(B) $\frac{5}{13}$

(C) $\frac{13}{5}$

(D) $\frac{13}{12}$

11   Mark for Review 🔖

Approve Relocation	44
Against Relocation	56

This winter, City A is planning a vote for or against the relocation of the city hall. Kristin visited 100 restaurants near the city hall to interview restaurant owners and collected the data above. Based on the data, she concluded that among 200,000 voters in City A, approximately 88,000 will vote for the relocation. Which of the following is the best strategy Kristin can apply to improve the accuracy of her research?

(A) Interviewing 10 restaurant owners instead of 100.

(B) Revising the conclusion such that 112,000 voters will vote for the relocation.

(C) Calling random voters in City A on the phone to conduct the interview rather than visiting the restaurants.

(D) Interviewing additional 100 restaurant owners in another city to enlarge the sample size.

I   II   III   IV   V   VI   VII

12 Mark for Review 🔖

$f(x) = \frac{1}{3}\sqrt{x}$
What is the x-value when $f(x) = 3$?

TEST◻QUBE Question 12 of 22 >

Section 2, Module 2: Math

13 Mark for Review 🔖

$f(x) = 2,260(1.05)^{\frac{x}{6}}$

$f(x)$ models the population of certain fungi per square centimeter of an experimental medium x hours after the initial observation. Which of the following functions best models the population of the fungi per square centimeter of the medium y days after the initial observation?

(A) $24 \times 2,260(1.05)^{\frac{y}{6}}$

(B) $2,260(1.05)^{4y}$

(C) $2,260(1.05)^{\frac{y}{6}}$

(D) $2,260(1.05 \times 24)^{\frac{y}{6}}$

TEST◻QUBE Question 13 of 22 >

Section 2, Module 2: Math

14 Mark for Review 🔖

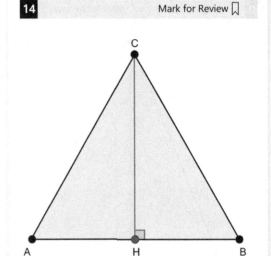

Straight line CH bisects the area of an equilateral triangle ABC. What is the value of angle ACH in radians?

(A) $\frac{\pi}{6}$

(B) $\frac{\pi}{4}$

(C) $\frac{\pi}{3}$

(D) $\frac{\pi}{2}$

Section 2, Module 2: Math   Annotate ⋮

15   Mark for Review ☐

$x^2 + 16x + k = 0$

The given equation has two distinct real solutions for x, where k is a constant. Which of the following values can k be to satisfy the condition above?

- (A) 0
- (B) 64
- (C) 128
- (D) 1,024

TEST⬛QUBE   Question 15 of 22 >

Section 2, Module 2: Math   Annotate ⋮

16   Mark for Review ☐

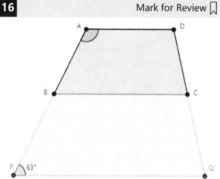

Trapezoids $ABCD$ and $BPQC$ are similar, where sides CD and DA of $ABCD$ correspond to QC and CB of $BPQC$, respectively. If angle P measures $63°$, what is the value, in degrees, of angle A?

TEST⬛QUBE   Question 16 of 22 >

Section 2, Module 2: Math   Annotate ⋮

17   Mark for Review ☐

$x = \dfrac{1}{3}(y + 1)$

$xz = 27$

$c = x + y + z$

$x = 3$ is a part of the solution to the given system of equations where c is a constant real number. What is the value of c?

TEST⬛QUBE   Question 17 of 22 >   Back Next

18 Mark for Review 🔖

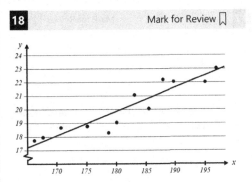

A group of geologists analyzed fossils from the Jurassic Era excavated in a certain region to measure the average atmospheric temperature at the time when the fossil was formed. The x values of the scatterplot represent the ages of the fossil records (in million years ago), and the y values represent the calculated average atmospheric temperature of the region based on each record (in degrees Celsius). The slope of the line of best fit is 0.19. Which of the following interpretations for the number 0.19 is most appropriate in this context?

(A) The average atmospheric temperature increased approximately 0.19 degrees Celsius per million years during the Jurassic Era.

(B) The average atmospheric temperature in the Jurassic Era was 0.19 degrees Celsius.

(C) The average atmospheric temperature in the Jurassic Era was 0.19 degrees Celsius higher than now.

(D) The average atmospheric temperature increased 0.19 degrees Celcius every year during the Jurassic Era.

19 Mark for Review 🔖

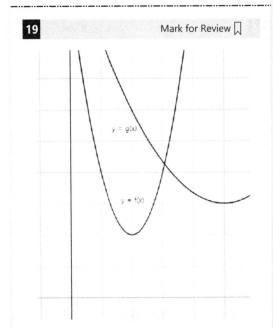

$f(x) = 2(x - 2)^2 + 2$
$g(x) = \frac{1}{3}(x - 5)^2 + 3.$
The distance between the vertex of $y = f(x)$ and the vertex of $y = g(x)$ plotted on xy-plane is $\sqrt{d}$. What is the value of d?

Annotate ⋮

20   Mark for Review 🔖

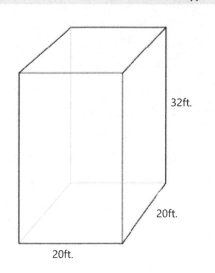

32ft.

20ft.

20ft.

The base of a 32-foot-deep cuboid diving pool is a square with 20 feet of each side. The pool is full of water with which the density equals 62.4 pounds per cubic foot. Which of the following is closest to the total mass of the water in pounds?

(A) $800,000$ pounds — A

(B) $40,000$ pounds — B

(C) $13,000$ pounds — C

(D) 200 pounds — D

 Annotate ⋮

21   Mark for Review 🔖

Dot Plot A: Data Set X

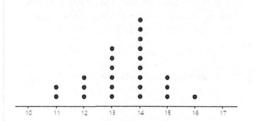

Dot Plot B: Data Set Y

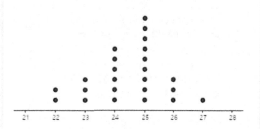

Dot plots A and B represent the distribution of 25 integer values each from data sets X and Y, respectively. Each value in data set Y is greater than the corresponding value in data set X by 11. Which of the following descriptions about the relationship between data sets X and Y is true?

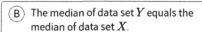
(A) The mean value of data set X equals 15, and the mean value of Y equals 26. — A

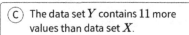
(B) The median of data set Y equals the median of data set X. — B

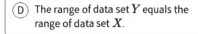
(C) The data set Y contains 11 more values than data set X. — C

(D) The range of data set Y equals the range of data set X. — D

Section 2, Module 2: Math

22   Mark for Review 🔖

$f(x) = 39.1(0.98)^{\frac{x}{12}}$ models the air pressure of a car tire, in psi, after x hours of filling the tire with air. What does the number 0.98 mean in this context?

(A) An average rate of decrease in the tire pressure per 12 hours in percent.

(B) The ratio of the tire pressure at a certain time to the tire pressure 12 hours after the certain time.

(C) An average decrease in the tire pressure per 12 hours in psi/hour.

(D) The ratio of the tire pressure 12 hours after a certain time to the tire pressure at the certain time.

TEST█QUBE

Digital SAT ®

Practice Test #2

Section 1, Module 1: Reading & Writing

⏱ 32:00

✎ Annotate ⋮

Detective James Caldwell's keen observational skills and attention to detail, honed through years of experience and training with Scotland Yard, enabled him to pick up on clues that others might overlook. His ability to _____ patterns and connections, akin to the legendary fictional detective Sherlock Holmes, was instrumental in solving complex cases, including the infamous Whitmore Heist and the enigmatic case of the Vanishing Violinist.

1 Mark for Review 🔖

Which choice completes the text with the most logical and precise word or phrase?

Ⓐ distort ～Ⓐ～

Ⓑ obfuscate ～Ⓑ～

Ⓒ distinguish ～Ⓒ～

Ⓓ trivialize ～Ⓓ～

TEST⬛QUBE

Question 1 of 27 >

Back Next

Section 1, Module 1: Reading & Writing

✎ Annotate ⋮

Jiu-jitsu, a martial art that originated in Japan, has gained popularity worldwide for its emphasis on technique, leverage, and ground fighting. Advocates of jiu-jitsu often ____ its effectiveness as a practical form of self-defense for individuals of any size or strength.

2 Mark for Review 🔖

Which choice completes the text with the most logical and precise word or phrase?

Ⓐ disparage ～Ⓐ～

Ⓑ undermine ～Ⓑ～

Ⓒ extol ～Ⓒ～

Ⓓ neglect ～Ⓓ～

TEST⬛QUBE

Question 2 of 27 >

Back Next

Section 1, Module 1: Reading & Writing

Annotate

The following text is adapted from Anton Chekov's 1904 play "Cherry Orchard."

EPIKHODOV: There's a frost this morning--three degrees, and the cherry-trees are all in flower. I can't approve of our climate. [Sighs] I can't. Our climate is <u>indisposed</u> to favour us even this once. And, Ermolai Alexeyevitch, allow me to say to you, in addition, that I bought myself some boots two days ago, and I beg to assure you that they squeak in a perfectly unbearable manner. What shall I put on them?

LOPAKHIN: Go away. You bore me.

EPIKHODOV: Some misfortune happens to me every day. But I don't complain; I'm used to it, and I can smile. [DUNYASHA comes in and brings LOPAKHIN some kvass] I shall go. [Knocks over a chair] There... [Triumphantly] There, you see, if I may use the word, what circumstances I am in, so to speak. It is even simply marvellous. [Exit.]

3   Mark for Review 🔖

An used in the text, what does the word "indisposed" most nearly mean?

- (A) infirm
- (B) reluctant
- (C) anxious
- (D) inclined

TEST⬛QUBE   Question 3 of 27 >   Back   Next

Section 1, Module 1: Reading & Writing

Annotate

The discovery of Teflon, a nonstick polymer accidentally invented by chemist Roy Plunkett in 1938, led to a wide range of innovative applications, from nonstick cookware to aerospace engineering. This _____ material has been praised for its unique properties, including its resistance to heat and chemical reactions.

4   Mark for Review 🔖

Which choice completes the text with the most logical and precise word or phrase?

- (A) mundane
- (B) versatile
- (C) adept
- (D) enchanting

TEST⬛QUBE   Question 4 of 27 >   Back   Next

I

II

III

IV

V

VI

VII

Section 1, Module 1: Reading & Writing

Annotate ⋮

The following text is adapted from Robert Frost's 1923 poem "Stopping by Woods on a Snowy Evening." The poem describes a serene, snowy scene.

Whose woods these are I think I know.
His house is in the village though;
He will not see me stopping here
To watch his woods fill up with snow.
My little horse must think it queer
To stop without a farmhouse near
Between the woods and frozen lake
The darkest evening of the year.

5 Mark for Review 🔖

Which choice best states the main purpose of the text?

A) To convey a sense of solitude and quiet contemplation, as the speaker observes the snow falling in the woods.

B) To evoke a feeling of warmth and cheerful camaraderie, as the speaker shares a moment with his horse.

C) To express a strong desire for adventure and exploration, with the woods and frozen lake providing a backdrop for discovery.

D) To create an overwhelming sense of fear and unease, as the speaker stops in the woods on the darkest evening of the year.

TEST QUBE

Back Next

Section 1, Module 1: Reading & Writing

Annotate ⋮

The following text is adapted from Adam Smith's 1776 work "An Inquiry into the Nature and Causes of the Wealth of Nations."

In every other art and manufacture, the effects of the division of labour are similar to what they are in this very trifling one, though, in many of them, the labour can neither be so much subdivided, nor reduced to so great a simplicity of operation. The division of labour, however, so far as it can be introduced, occasions, in every art, a proportionable increase of the productive powers of labour. The separation of different trades and employments from one another, seems to have taken place in consequence of this advantage. This separation, too, is generally carried furthest in those countries which enjoy the highest degree of industry and improvement; what is the work of one man, in a rude state of society, being generally that of several in an improved one. In every improved society, the farmer is generally nothing but a farmer; the manufacturer, nothing but a manufacturer.

6 Mark for Review 🔖

Which choice best describes the function of the underlined sentence in the text as a whole?

A) It elaborates on the premise of division of labor, illustrating its variance between societies with disparate levels of advancement.

B) It provides a historical account of how different trades and employments evolved and separated overtime.

C) It depicts the limiting factors that impede the full implementation of the division of labor in certain societies.

D) It emphasizes the role of the individual as solely a farmer or a manufacturer in societies that have undergone industrial improvement.

TEST QUBE

Back Next

Section 1, Module 1: Reading & Writing

Annotate

The following text is adapted from John Masefield's 1902 poem "Sea Fever."

I must go down to the seas again, to the lonely sea and the sky,
And all I ask is a tall ship and a star to steer her by;
And the wheel's kick and the wind's song and the white sail's shaking,
And a grey mist on the sea's face, and a grey dawn breaking.

I must go down to the seas again, for the call of the running tide
Is a wild call and a clear call that may not be denied;
And all I ask is a windy day with the white clouds flying,
And the flung spray and the blown spume, and the sea-gulls crying.

7   Mark for Review 🔖

Which choice best describes the function of the underlined portion in the text as a whole?

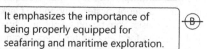

(A) It highlights the solitude and loneliness that the sea represents.   Ⓐ

(B) It emphasizes the importance of being properly equipped for seafaring and maritime exploration.   Ⓑ

(C) It contrasts the serenity and peace of the sea with the turmoil of the speaker's life.   Ⓒ

(D) It conveys the speaker's deep longing for the sea and the simplicity of his desires.   Ⓓ

TEST◼QUBE   Question 7 of 27 >   Back   Next

Section 1, Module 1: Reading & Writing

Annotate

Marie Tharp, a trailblazing American geologist and oceanographic cartographer, revolutionized the field of oceanography in the mid-20th century. Her groundbreaking research, conducted alongside Bruce Heezen in the 1950s and 1960s, culminated in the creation of the first detailed maps of the ocean floor. These maps revealed the presence of a continuous underwater mountain range, known as the mid-ocean ridge, which had previously eluded discovery. Some geologists of that era asserted that the features of the ocean floor were largely static and unchanging. Tharp's work, however, hinted at a dynamic ocean floor and provided critical support for the then-emerging theory of plate tectonics, which posits that the Earth's lithosphere is divided into plates that move over the asthenosphere.

8   Mark for Review 🔖

Which finding, if true, would most directly support the geologists' claim?

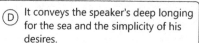

(A) Observations of the ocean floor made several decades after Tharp's maps showed virtually no changes in the position or structure of the midocean ridges, suggesting that they might be static.   Ⓐ

(B) Technological advancements enabled the capture of high- resolution images of the ocean floor, revealing that the features identified by Tharp remained unchanged in form and location over an extended period.   Ⓑ

(C) Sediment samples taken from the mid-ocean ridges showed a consistent composition over time, indicating that there has been little to no geological activity in those areas for thousands of years.   Ⓒ

(D) Comparisons of Tharp's original maps with contemporary mapping data revealed striking similarities, with no evidence of shifts or changes in the underwater mountain ranges or other features of the ocean floor.   Ⓓ

TEST◼QUBE   Question 8 of 27 >   Back   Next

Section 1, Module 1: Reading & Writing

Annotate

The following text is adapted from Kate Chopin's 1893 short story "Désirée's Baby." Désirée, a young mother, begins to sense something amiss in her environment.

When the baby was about three months old, Désirée awoke one day to the conviction that there was something in the air menacing her peace. It was at first too subtle to grasp. It had only been a disquieting suggestion; an air of mystery among the blacks; unexpected visits from far-off neighbors who could hardly account for their coming. Then a strange, an awful change in her husband's manner, which she dared not ask him to explain. When he spoke to her, it was with averted eyes, from which the old love-light seemed to have gone out.

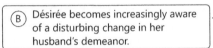

9 Mark for Review 🔖

Which choice best states the main idea of the text?

(A) Désirée is concerned about her husband's health as he seems to be distancing himself.

(B) Désirée becomes increasingly aware of a disturbing change in her husband's demeanor.

(C) Désirée is desperately trying to confront her husband about his infidelity.

(D) Désirée regrets not communicating openly with her husband about family matters.

TEST⬢QUBE

Back Next

Section 1, Module 1: Reading & Writing

Annotate

The following text is adapted from Samuel Taylor Coleridge's 1798 poem "The Rime of the Ancient Mariner." The poem narrates the tale of a mariner who faces supernatural events during a sea voyage.

The ship drove fast, loud roared the blast,
And southward aye we fled.
And now there came both mist and snow,
And it grew wondrous cold:
And ice, mast-high, came floating by,
As green as emerald.
And through the drifts the snowy clifts
Did send a dismal sheen.

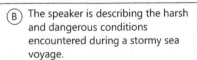

10 Mark for Review 🔖

Which choice best states the main idea of the text?

(A) The speaker is recalling a peaceful and idyllic journey at sea.

(B) The speaker is describing the harsh and dangerous conditions encountered during a stormy sea voyage.

(C) The speaker is lamenting the beauty of the icy landscape they left behind.

(D) The speaker is celebrating the safe arrival at their destination after a perilous journey.

TEST⬢QUBE

Back Next

Section 1, Module 1: Reading & Writing

Annotate

"Ode to the West Wind" is an 1818 poem by Percy Bysshe Shelley. In the poem, Shelley seeks a transformative connection with the natural force of the wind, writing, _____

11 Mark for Review

Which quotation from "Ode to the West Wind" most effectively illustrates the claim?

A) "O wild West Wind, thou breath of Autumn's being / Thou, from whose unseen presence the leaves dead / Are driven, like ghosts from an enchanter fleeing."

B) "Make me thy lyre, even as the forest is: / What if my leaves are falling like its own! / The tumult of thy mighty harmonies."

C) "Drive my dead thoughts over the universe/ Like wither'd leaves to quicken a new birth!"

D) "A heavy weight of hours has chain'd and bow'd/ One too like thee: tameless, and swift, and proud."

Section 1, Module 1: Reading & Writing

Annotate

Volcano	Eruption Intensity	Sulfur Emissions (tons)	Ash Emissions (tons)
V1	2	5,000	10,000
V2	4	10,000	15,000
V3	6	15,000	100,000
V4	8	20,000	500,000
V5	10	25,000	3,000,000

The table presents data on eruption intensity, sulfur emissions, and ash emissions for five volcanoes. Researchers claim that of high-intensity eruptions have a more negative impact on the environment by emitting harmful sulfur and ash. They posit that while sulfur emissions tend to reflect a linear increase, ash emissions exponentially increase with eruption intensity increases.

12 Mark for Review

Which choice best describes data from the table that support the researchers' claim?

A) Volcano V1 has a lower eruption intensity and lower sulfur and ash emissions than Volcano V4.

B) Volcano V2, in comparison to Volcano V1, experienced considerable increases in ash emissions while more minor increases in sulfur emissions.

C) Volcano V5, in comparison to Volcano V2, experienced considerable increases in ash emissions while more minor increases in sulfur emissions.

D) Volcano V5 has the highest eruption intensity and the highest sulfur and ash emissions.

Section 1, Module 1: Reading & Writing

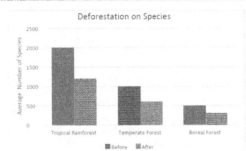
Deforestation on Species

Ecologists are investigating the impact of deforestation on the biodiversity of three different ecosystems: tropical rainforests, temperate forests, and boreal forests. They have collected data on the average number of species found in these ecosystems before and after deforestation events. Ecologists claim depending on the kinds of species existing within a certain ecosystem, the extent to which deforestation impacts species varies, for certain species have immunity to the effects of the less-oxygen filled environment created by deforestation.

13   Mark for Review 🔖

Which choice best describes data from the table that support the ecologists' claim?

- (A) Biodiversity remained constant in all three ecosystems after deforestation events.

- (B) Biodiversity decreased in all three ecosystems after deforestation events, with the greatest decrease in tropical rainforest, demonstrating tropical rainforest's limited susceptibility to deforestation.

- (C) Biodiversity decreased in all three ecosystems after deforestation events, with the least pronounced decrease in temperate forests, demonstrating temperate forest's must have species who can survive in less oxygenated environments.

- (D) Biodiversity decreased in all three ecosystems after deforestation events, with the least pronounced decrease in borreal forests, demonstrating borreal forest's limited susceptibility to deforestation.

Section 1, Module 1: Reading & Writing

The Middle East has a long and complex history marked by geopolitical conflicts, cultural diversity, and natural resource abundance. The Sykes-Picot Agreement, signed in 1916 by the United Kingdom and France, is considered a pivotal moment in the region's history, as it divided the region into spheres of influence, leading to the modern borders of many Middle Eastern countries. Critics argue that the Sykes-Picot Agreement disregarded ethnic and religious groups, contributing to tensions and conflicts that persist today. If historical analyses demonstrate that the territories defined by the Sykes-Picot Agreement experienced a higher prevalence of conflict than areas with borders determined by natural or pre-existing cultural boundaries, this would suggest that ____

14   Mark for Review 🔖

Which choice most logically completes the text?

- (A) the Sykes-Picot Agreement may have played a role in exacerbating ethnic and religious tensions in the Middle East.

- (B) the Sykes-Picot Agreement was a successful diplomatic endeavor that fostered regional stability to an extent.

- (C) natural and pre-existing cultural boundaries are not significant factors in determining the likelihood of conflict.

- (D) the historical context in which the Sykes-Picot Agreement was signed had no lasting impact on the Middle East.

Section 1, Module 1: Reading & Writing   Annotate ⋮

Skara Brae is an archaeological site on the Orkney Islands in present-day Scotland and was a remarkably well-preserved Neolithic settlement dating from around 3180 BCE to about 2500 BCE. Archaeologist Fiona McLeod recently traveled to Skara Brae to study its ancient dwellings and ____ into a midden mound and initially revealed by a severe storm, these stone-built houses, interconnected by covered passageways, seem to offer an intimate window into the daily lives and social structures of the Neolithic people, painting a vivid tapestry of human ingenuity and adaptability in an era shrouded by the mists of time.

15   Mark for Review 🔖

Which choice completes the text so that it conforms to the conventions of Standard English?

(A) artifacts built   Ⓐ

(B) artifacts, built   Ⓑ

(C) artifacts and built   Ⓒ

(D) artifacts. Built   Ⓓ

TEST⬛QUBE   Back   Next

Section 1, Module 1: Reading & Writing   Annotate ⋮

The ancient city of Rome, once the center of a vast empire, is home to many remarkable architectural wonders, such as the Colosseum, the Roman Forum, and the ____ flock to the city to explore its rich history and culture.

16   Mark for Review 🔖

Which choice completes the text so that it conforms to the conventions of Standard English?

(A) Pantheon – tourists

(B) Pantheon. Tourists

(C) Pantheon, tourists

(D) Pantheon

TEST⬛QUBE   Back   Next

I   II   III   IV   V   VI   VII

Section 1, Module 1: Reading & Writing

Annotate

⋮

The theory of plate tectonics, which explains the movement of Earth's lithosphere, has deepened our understanding of geological processes, such as earthquakes, volcanic activity, _____ the formation of mountain ranges.

17   Mark for Review 🔖

Which choice completes the text so that it conforms to the conventions of Standard English?

(A) even

(B) and even,

(C) and even

(D) and, even

Section 1, Module 1: Reading & Writing

Annotate

⋮

Inventor and aviation pioneer Igor Sikorsky made remarkable strides in the field of aeronautics, forever changing the landscape of air transportation. Celebrated as one of the most influential contributions to aviation history, _____ was the first aircraft of its kind to enter full-scale production. This revolutionary helicopter opened up new possibilities for air travel, rescue operations, and military applications, leaving a lasting legacy on the industry.

18   Mark for Review 🔖

Which choice completes the text so that it conforms to the conventions of Standard English?

(A) Sikorsky developed the Vought-Sikorsky VS-300 in 1939; it

(B) in 1939 Sikorsky developed the Vought - Sikorsky VS-300, which

(C) Sikorsky's 1939 Vought-Sikorsky VS-300

(D) the Vought-Sikorsky VS-300 was developed by Sikorsky in 1939 and

Section 1, Module 1: Reading & Writing

Annotate ⋮

The ancient Maya civilization, which flourished in present-day Mexico and Central America, developed an advanced system of writing, mathematics, and astronomy, leaving behind a rich legacy that _____ modern scholars and archaeologists.

19   Mark for Review 🔖

Which choice completes the text so that it conforms to the conventions of Standard English?

(A) continually fascinate,   ⊝Ⓐ

(B) continues to fascinate   ⊝Ⓑ

(C) fascinates —   ⊝Ⓒ

(D) fascinating   ⊝Ⓓ

TEST⬛QUBE   Question 19 of 27 >   Back Next

Section 1, Module 1: Reading & Writing

Annotate ⋮

The 19th-century author Jane Austen's novels, which often explore the complexities of social class and gender roles in her time, continue to be appreciated by readers today; many of her works have been adapted into films and television series. Her keen observations and wit make her stories ____.

20   Mark for Review 🔖

Which choice completes the text so that it conforms to the conventions of Standard English?

(A) relatable, even, two centuries later   ⊝Ⓐ

(B) relatable; even two centuries later.   ⊝Ⓑ

(C) relatable even two centuries later.   ⊝Ⓒ

(D) relatable even, two centuries later.   ⊝Ⓓ

TEST⬛QUBE   Question 20 of 27 >   Back Next

Section 1, Module 1: Reading & Writing

Annotate

The concept of natural selection, introduced by Charles Darwin and Alfred Russel Wallace, revolutionized our understanding of biological evolution. According to this theory, organisms with advantageous traits are more likely to survive and reproduce. _____, over generations, these favorable traits become more common within a population.

21   Mark for Review

Which choice completes the text with the most logical transition?

- (A) Therefore,
- (B) On the contrary,
- (C) In contrast,
- (D) Meanwhile,

TEST QUBE   Question 21 of 27 >   Back   Next

Section 1, Module 1: Reading & Writing

Annotate

While researching a topic, a student has taken the following notes:

- "Animal Farm" is an allegorical novella by George Orwell, published in 1945.
- The story is set on a farm where the animals revolt against their human owner, Mr. Jones, and establish a new society.
- The novel serves as a satirical critique of the Russian Revolution and the rise of Stalinism.
- The characters in "Animal Farm" represent various historical figures and factions involved in the Russian Revolution and its aftermath.
- The story explores themes of power, corruption, and the dangers of totalitarianism.

22   Mark for Review

The student wants to explain the allegorical nature of "Animal Farm." Which choice most effectively uses relevant information from the notes to accomplish this goal?

- (A) "Animal Farm" is a satirical novella by George Orwell that tells the story of a group of animals who revolt against their human owner and establish a new society on the farm.
- (B) The characters in "Animal Farm" represent various historical figures and factions involved in the Russian Revolution, serving as a critique of Stalinism and the dangers of totalitarianism.
- (C) Set on a farm where animals overthrow their human owner, "Animal Farm" explores themes of power, corruption, and the perils of unchecked authority through its allegorical representation of the Russian Revolution.
- (D) As an allegorical novella, "Animal Farm" uses the story of a farm animal rebellion to satirize the Russian Revolution and critique the rise of Stalinism, highlighting the destructive effects of animal exploitation.

TEST QUBE   Question 22 of 27 >   Back   Next

Section 1, Module 1: Reading & Writing

Annotate ⋮

While researching a topic, a student has taken the following notes:

- Photosynthesis is the process by which plants, algae, and some bacteria convert light energy into chemical energy.
- During photosynthesis, carbon dioxide and water are used to produce glucose and oxygen.
- Photosynthesis occurs in the chloroplasts of plant cells, which contain chlorophyll.
- Chlorophyll is a pigment that absorbs light energy and plays a crucial role in photosynthesis.

23   Mark for Review 🔖

The student wants to describe the role of chlorophyll in photosynthesis. Which choice most effectively uses relevant information from the notes to accomplish this goal?

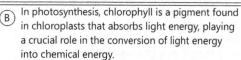
(A) Photosynthesis is a process that occurs in the chloroplasts of plant cells, where light energy is used to produce glucose and oxygen from carbon dioxide and water.

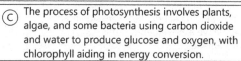
(B) In photosynthesis, chlorophyll is a pigment found in chloroplasts that absorbs light energy, playing a crucial role in the conversion of light energy into chemical energy.

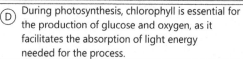
(C) The process of photosynthesis involves plants, algae, and some bacteria using carbon dioxide and water to produce glucose and oxygen, with chlorophyll aiding in energy conversion.

(D) During photosynthesis, chlorophyll is essential for the production of glucose and oxygen, as it facilitates the absorption of light energy needed for the process.

Ⓐ
Ⓑ
Ⓒ
Ⓓ

TEST🔲QUBE

Back   Next

Section 1, Module 1: Reading & Writing

Annotate ⋮

While researching a topic, a student has taken the following notes:

- The mantis shrimp is a marine crustacean known for its powerful punch.
- It uses its specialized appendages to strike prey at incredibly high speeds.
- The mantis shrimp's punch can generate cavitation bubbles, which produce a secondary shockwave.
- Its eyes have a highly complex structure and can detect multiple types of light.
- Mantis shrimp can be divided into two main groups: "smashers" and "spearers."

24   Mark for Review 🔖

The student wants to emphasize the mantis shrimp's unique visual abilities. Which choice most effectively uses relevant information from the notes to accomplish this goal?

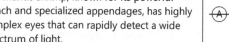
(A) The mantis shrimp, known for its powerful punch and specialized appendages, has highly complex eyes that can rapidly detect a wide spectrum of light.

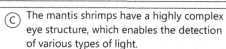
(B) Mantis shrimp are marine crustaceans that use their powerful punch to generate cavitation bubbles, which produce a secondary shockwave.

(C) The mantis shrimps have a highly complex eye structure, which enables the detection of various types of light.

(D) Mantis shrimp are divided into two main groups, "smashers" and "spearers," and are known for their powerful punch and ability to strike prey at high speeds.

Ⓐ
Ⓑ
Ⓒ
Ⓓ

TEST🔲QUBE

Back   Next

Section 1, Module 1: Reading & Writing

 Annotate :

While researching a topic, a student has taken the following notes:

- The civil rights movement in the United States aimed to end racial segregation and discrimination against African Americans.
- The movement took place primarily between the 1950s and the 1960s.
- Key figures in the movement included Martin Luther King Jr., Rosa Parks, and Malcolm X.
- Nonviolent protest and civil disobedience were central strategies used by activists.
- The Civil Rights Act of 1964 and the Voting Rights Act of 1965 were significant legislative achievements of the movement.

25   Mark for Review 🔖

The student wants to emphasize the strategies used by civil rights activists. Which choice most effectively uses relevant information from the notes to accomplish this goal?

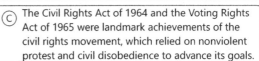

(A) The civil rights movement sought to end racial segregation and discrimination, with key figures like Martin Luther King Jr. and Rosa Parks utilizing nonviolent protest and civil disobedience as central strategies.   Ⓐ

(B) Martin Luther King Jr., Rosa Parks, and Malcolm X were influential leaders in the civil rights movement, which aimed to end racial discrimination and segregation in the United States.   Ⓑ

(C) The Civil Rights Act of 1964 and the Voting Rights Act of 1965 were landmark achievements of the civil rights movement, which relied on nonviolent protest and civil disobedience to advance its goals.   Ⓒ

(D) Taking place primarily in the 1950s and 1960s, the civil rights movement was marked by the use of nonviolent protest and civil disobedience to challenge racial segregation and discrimination.   Ⓓ

TEST🌐QUBE   Question 25 of 27 >   Back   Next

Section 1, Module 1: Reading & Writing

 Annotate :

While researching a topic, a student has taken the following notes:

- The Stanford prison experiment was a social psychology study conducted in 1971.
- Philip Zimbardo led the study, which aimed to investigate the psychological effects of perceived power and authority.
- Participants were randomly assigned the roles of prisoners and guards in a simulated prison environment.
- The experiment was terminated early due to the extreme behaviors exhibited by the participants.
- The study raised ethical concerns and highlighted the power of situational factors in human behavior.

26   Mark for Review 🔖

The student wants to emphasize the main findings of the Stanford prison experiment. Which choice most effectively uses relevant information from the notes to accomplish this goal?

(A) The Stanford prison experiment led by Philip Zimbardo, demonstrated the powerful influence of situational factors on human behavior, as participants exhibited extreme behaviors in their assigned roles.   Ⓐ

(B) Conducted in 1971, the Stanford prison experiment aimed to investigate the psychological effects of power and authority, with participants randomly assigned roles as prisoners or guards in a simulated environment.   Ⓑ

(C) The Stanford prison experiment was terminated early due to ethical concerns and the extreme behaviors of participants, shedding light on the potential dangers of unchecked power dynamics in social settings.   Ⓒ

(D) Philip Zimbardo's controversial Stanford prison experiment revealed the impact of perceived power and authority on human behavior, sparking debates on ethical considerations in psychological research.   Ⓓ

TEST🌐QUBE   Question 26 of 27 >   Back   Next

Section 1, Module 1: Reading & Writing Annotate ⋮

While researching a topic, a student has taken the following notes:

- The Hanseatic League was a commercial and defensive confederation of merchant guilds and market towns in Northwestern and Central Europe.
- It was formed in the late 12th century and lasted until the 17th century.
- The league protected economic interests and diplomatic privileges in the cities and countries and along the trade routes the merchants visited.
- The Hanseatic cities had their own legal system and furnished their own protection and mutual aid.

27   Mark for Review 🔖

The student wants to discuss the main functions of the Hanseatic League. Which choice most effectively uses relevant information from the notes to accomplish this goal?

- (A) The Hanseatic League was a group of merchant guilds and market towns that existed from the late 12th to the 17th century.

- (B) The Hanseatic League was a commercial and defensive confederation that protected economic interests, diplomatic privileges, and provided mutual aid among the members.

- (C) The Hanseatic League was a confederation that had its own legal system and provided protection for its members.

- (D) The Hanseatic League lasted until the 17th century, providing a unique legal system and mutual aid among its members. 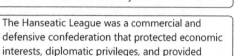

I   II   III   IV   V   VI   VII

Move on to the Next Section »

Section 1, Module 1: Reading & Writing

⏱ 32:00

✎ Annotate ⋮

Dr. Marissa Baskett, a revered marine biologist from the University of California, Davis, dedicated her illustrious career to the extensive study of coral reefs, specifically honing in on the pernicious impacts of climate change on these resplendent yet fragile underwater ecosystems. Her research, featured in premier journals such as "Nature," has had a _____ effect on the concerted global conservation efforts to protect the biodiversity housed within these delicate aquatic habitats.

1   Mark for Review 🔖

Which choice completes the text with the most logical and precise word or phrase?

Ⓐ undermining   (A̶)

Ⓑ galvanizing   (B̶)

Ⓒ refuting   (C̶)

Ⓓ obfuscating   (D̶)

TEST⬛QUBE   Question 25 of 27 >   Back   Next

Section 1, Module 1: Reading & Writing

✎ Annotate ⋮

Film director Christopher Nolan frequently _____ non-linear storytelling in his movies: this technique is evident in his film Memento, which tells the story of a man with short-term memory loss using a disjointed, reverse-order timeline.

2   Mark for Review 🔖

Which choice completes the text with the most logical and precise word or phrase?

Ⓐ shuns   (A̶)

Ⓑ employs   (B̶)

Ⓒ debunk   (C̶)

Ⓓ derides   (D̶)

TEST⬛QUBE   Question 26 of 27 >   Back   Next

Section 1, Module 2: Reading & Writing

Annotate ⋮

Led by the indomitable Dr. Robert Ballard, best known for his discovery of the Titanic shipwreck, the team of intrepid scientists from the Ocean Exploration Trust faced arduous weather conditions, technical glitches, and the treacherous depths of the ocean during their expedition aboard the research vessel E/V Nautilus. Despite the multitude of adversities, they remained unwaveringly ____ in their dogged pursuit of valuable data. Their determination culminated in several groundbreaking discoveries that enriched our understanding of marine geology and biology.

3   Mark for Review 🔖

Which choice completes the text with the most logical and precise word or phrase?

- (A) dauntless   Ⓐ
- (B) apprehensive   Ⓑ
- (C) listless   Ⓒ
- (D) vacillating   Ⓓ

TEST⬡QUBE   Back   Next

Section 1, Module 2: Reading & Writing

Annotate ⋮

Dr. Danielle Fong, a relatively lesser-known but immensely significant figure in the scientific community, and co-founder of LightSail Energy, has been passionately working towards revolutionizing energy storage solutions. With her forward-thinking vision, she aims to facilitate a future where sustainable energy solutions are not just a dream but a widespread reality. This____ idea, marked by its inventiveness, galvanized a cohort of researchers and enthusiasts to join the burgeoning movement for a cleaner, more sustainable world, and has kindled interest among stakeholders to recognize the potential of renewable energy storage.

4   Mark for Review 🔖

Which choice completes the text with the most logical and precise word or phrase?

- (A) divisive  Ⓐ
- (B) antiquated Ⓑ
- (C) quitoxic  Ⓒ
- (D) audacious  Ⓓ

TEST⬡QUBE   Back   Next

Section 1, Module 2: Reading & Writing

Text 1

Many political scientists accept the conventional wisdom that democracies are inherently stable and less likely to experience political upheaval compared to autocratic regimes. Democratic institutions, such as free elections and an independent judiciary, are believed to facilitate peaceful transitions of power and provide avenues for dissent. Critics, however, argue that democracies can still be susceptible to internal strife and polarization, which may threaten their stability.

Text 2

Recent research into the stability of democracies worldwide suggests that while democratic systems may generally be more stable than autocracies, they are not immune to internal challenges. The study found that factors such as economic inequality, political polarization, and eroding trust in institutions can undermine the stability of democracies. The researchers recommend addressing these issues to ensure the long-term resilience of democratic systems.

5 Mark for Review 🔖

Based on the texts, how would the researchers mentioned in Text 2 most likely respond to the "conventional wisdom" discussed in Text 1?

- (A) By dismissing the idea that democracies are inherently stable and instead arguing that their stability is contingent upon various factors.

- (B) By agreeing that democracies are generally more stable than autocracies but recognizing the need to address internal challenges to maintain stability.

- (C) By asserting that the stability of a political system is unrelated to its democratic or autocratic nature and depends solely on external factors.

- (D) By suggesting that the perceived stability of democracies is an illusion and that they are no less susceptible to upheaval than autocratic regimes.

Section 1, Module 2: Reading & Writing

The following text is an excerpt from James Joyce's 1914 story *The Sisters*. In the story, the narrator describes the protagonist's complex emotions towards death.

There was no hope for him this time: it was the third stroke. Night after night I had passed the house (it was vacation time) and studied the lighted square of window: and night after night I had found it lighted in the same way, faintly and evenly. If he was dead, I thought, I would see the reflection of candles on the darkened blind for I knew that two candles must be set at the head of a corpse. He had often said to me: "I am not long for this world," and I had thought his words idle. Now I knew they were true.

6 Mark for Review 🔖

Which choice best states the main purpose of the text?

- (A) To express the protagonist's denial and eventual acceptance of a friend's impending death.

- (B) To illustrate the protagonist's nightly ritual of passing by the dying man's house.

- (C) To underscore the protagonist's fascination with the symbolism of candles in death rituals.

- (D) To highlight the morbid conversations between the protagonist and the dying man.

Section 1, Module 2: Reading & Writing   Annotate ⋮

During the Industrial Revolution, which began in the late 18th century, significant technological advancements transformed the manufacturing and production industries. Factories emerged as a result of these advancements, replacing small-scale, home-based industries. One such invention, the spinning jenny, was developed by English inventor James Hargreaves in 1764. This machine revolutionized the textile industry by allowing workers to spin multiple threads simultaneously, increasing productivity and lowering costs. As a result, the textile industry shifted from a predominantly domestic enterprise to a factory-based system, leading to urbanization and the growth of cities.

7   Mark for Review 🔖

According to the text, what was the primary impact of the spinning jenny on the textile industry?

- (A) The spinning jenny made textile production more labor-intensive
- (B) It facilitated the transition from home-based industries to factory-based systems
- (C) The spinning jenny led to a decline in textile production
- (D) It caused textile prices to skyrocket due to increased demand

Section 1, Module 2: Reading & Writing   Annotate ⋮

The following text is from Nathaniel Hawthorne's 1852 novel *The Blithedale Romance*. Zenobia is a character who is noted for her commanding presence.

Zenobia was truly a magnificent woman. The homely simplicity of her dress could not conceal, nor scarcely diminish, the queenliness of her presence. The image of her form and face should have been multiplied all over the earth. It was wronging the rest of mankind to retain her as the spectacle of only a few. The stage would have been her proper sphere. She should have made it a point of duty, moreover, to sit endlessly to painters and sculptors, and preferably to the latter; because the cold decorum of the marble would consist with the utmost scantiness of drapery, so that the eye might chastely be gladdened with her material perfection in its entireness.

8   Mark for Review 🔖

According to the text, what is true about Zenobia?

- (A) Zenobia often tries to conceal her beauty with her simple dress, but fails to do so.
- (B) Zenobia can be overly conscious about her appearance.
- (C) Zenobia believes that only a few deserving people should behold her beauty.
- (D) Zenobia is remarkably stunning and would be suited to be a model or actress.

Section 1, Module 2: Reading & Writing

Annotate

"Invictus" is an 1875 poem by William Ernest Henley. In the poem, Henley emphasizes the indomitable spirit of an individual in the face of adversity and expresses gratitude, writing, _____.

9   Mark for Review 🔖

Which quotation from "Invictus" most effectively illustrates the claim?

(A) "Out of the night that covers me, / Black as the pit from pole to pole, / I thank whatever gods may be / For my unconquerable soul."

(B) "In the fell clutch of circumstance / I have not winced nor cried aloud. / Under the bludgeonings of chance / My head is bloody, but unbowed."

(C) "Beyond this place of wrath and tears / Looms but the Horror of the shade, / And yet the menace of the years / Finds and shall find me unafraid."

(D) "It matters not how strait the gate, / How charged with punishments the scroll, / I am the master of my fate, / I am the captain of my soul."

TEST🎲QUBE   Question 9 of 27 >   Back   Next

Section 1, Module 2: Reading & Writing

Annotate

Energy Consumption and Renewable Energy Share in Five Countries

City	Gini Coefficient	Crime Rate (per 1,000 residents)
City 1	0.35	25
City 2	0.40	35
City 3	0.45	39
City 4	0.50	42
City 5	0.55	43

The table presents data on income inequality, measured by the Gini coefficient, and crime rates in five cities. The Gini coefficient ranges from 0 (perfect equality) to 1 (perfect inequality), while the crime rate represents the number of crimes per 1,000 residents. Researchers claim that cities with higher income inequality tend to have higher crime rates, but that the increase in this crime rate diminishes as the gini coefficient increases, a classic diminishing returns phenomenon.

10   Mark for Review 🔖

Which choice best describes data from the table that support the researchers' claim?

(A) City 1 has the lowest Gini coefficient and the lowest crime rate.

(B) City 2 has a lower Gini coefficient and a lower crime rate than City 3.

(C) City 5's crime rate only marginally increased compared to City 4.

(D) City 2's crime rate only marginally increased compared to City 1.

TEST🎲QUBE   Question 10 of 27 >   Back   Next

Annotate ⋮

Madagascar, an island nation with a plethora of unique flora, is home to the critically endangered plant species, Madagascan periwinkle (Catharanthus roseus). This enigmatic plant is renowned for its medicinal properties, as it produces alkaloids that are utilized in the treatment of various cancers. Some botanists have posited that this plant is endemic to very specific environmental conditions, citing evidence of its limited distribution across the island and its proclivity for growing in well-drained soils with ample sunlight. They argue that these stringent requirements have contributed to the plant's vulnerability and precarious conservation status. However, the Madagascan periwinkle has also demonstrated adaptability, as it has been successfully cultivated in various countries for its medicinal applications.

11   Mark for Review 🔖

Which finding, if true, would most directly weaken the botanists' claim regarding the Madagascan periwinkle's specific environmental requirements?

- (A) Evidence emerges that the Madagascan periwinkle can thrive in a variety of environmental conditions, both in the wild and in cultivation, without compromising its medicinal properties.   Ⓐ
- (B) A new population of Madagascan periwinkle is discovered in a microhabitat with slightly different environmental conditions than those of previously known populations.   Ⓑ
- (C) The Madagascan periwinkle exhibits a proclivity for propagating through both sexual and asexual reproduction.   Ⓒ
- (D) The method for determining the environmental requirements of the Madagascan periwinkle is discovered to be less effective when used to analyze other endemic plant species in Madagascar.   Ⓓ

TEST❖QUBE   Question 11 of 27 >   Back   Next

Annotate ⋮

The RNA world hypothesis posits that RNA molecules, capable of both storing genetic information and catalyzing chemical reactions, played a central role in the early stages of life on Earth. A biochemist claims that RNA molecules could have acted as a precursor to both DNA and proteins in the development of life.

12   Mark for Review 🔖

Which finding, if true, would most directly support the biochemist's claim?

- (A) RNA is composed of nucleotides, the building blocks of genetic material, and can form complex three-dimensional structures.
- (B) The discovery of ribozymes, RNA molecules with catalytic activity, supports the idea that RNA can perform functions typically associated with proteins.
- (C) Both DNA and RNA use a similar language of four nucleotide bases to store genetic information, although RNA uses uracil instead of thymine.
- (D) The central dogma of molecular biology describes the flow of genetic information from DNA to RNA to protein.

TEST❖QUBE   Question 12 of 27 >   Back   Next

Section 1, Module 2: Reading & Writing

The hukou system is a household registration policy in China that was initially implemented in the late 1950s as a means of controlling the population's movement between rural and urban areas. The system has been criticized for creating a socioeconomic divide by limiting access to social services, such as healthcare and education, for those with a rural hukou. In recent years, the Chinese government has introduced reforms aimed at reducing the disparities caused by the hukou system. If these reforms were successful in addressing the negative consequences of the hukou system, they would likely ____

13 Mark for Review

Which choice most logically completes the text?

(A) exacerbate the rural-urban divide by further restricting access to public services.

(B) remedy the inequalities faced by rural hukou holders in accessing social benefits.

(C) perpetuate the existing system without making any significant changes.

(D) nullify the original intent of the hukou system and increase internal migration.

TEST QUBE Question 13 of 27 > Back Next

Section 1, Module 2: Reading & Writing

The intricate cave systems of the Yucatan Peninsula in Mexico are home to a unique and diverse array of aquatic life, including various species of blind cavefish. These fish have adapted to their dark environment by losing their eyes and developing enhanced sensory systems, such as the lateral line system, which enables them to detect changes in water pressure and navigate their surroundings. Additionally, these fish exhibit traits like reduced pigmentation, slower metabolic rates, and the ability to tolerate low oxygen levels. Some researchers speculate that these adaptations may have arisen through a process known as regressive evolution, in which the loss or reduction of certain traits becomes advantageous in specific environments. With this in mind, the blind cavefish's unique adaptations ____

14 Mark for Review

Which choice most logically completes the text?

(A) indicate that the cave environment is not as harsh as previously thought.

(B) suggest that the loss of eyesight in these species was detrimental to their survival.

(C) provide evidence of how organisms can adapt to extreme environmental conditions.

(D) imply that these fish are likely to regain their eyesight if introduced to well-lit environments.

TEST QUBE Question 14 of 27 > Back Next

Section 1, Module 2: Reading & Writing

Annotate

The crested ibis (Nipponia nippon), once widespread across East Asia, is now primarily found in the Shaanxi province of China. By the late 20th century, habitat destruction and overhunting had driven the species to the brink of extinction. However, concerted conservation efforts, such as captive breeding programs and habitat restoration, have helped revive the crested ibis population in recent years. The successful recovery of the crested ibis in China demonstrates that _____

15   Mark for Review

Which choice most logically completes the text?

(A) the role of human intervention in species decline is often overstated.

(B) conservation efforts are invariably futile in the face of environmental degradation.

(C) concerted and targeted actions can mitigate and potentially reverse the effects of human-induced threats.

(D) species like the crested ibis are impervious to environmental changes on their habitats.

TEST QUBE

Back   Next

Section 1, Module 2: Reading & Writing

Annotate

The biologist Charles _____ theory of evolution by natural selection transformed our understanding of the natural world—spent decades refining his ideas before publishing On the Origin of Species. His work laid the foundation for modern evolutionary biology.

16   Mark for Review

Which choice completes the text so that it conforms to the conventions of Standard English?

(A) Darwin,

(B) Darwin–whose

(C) Darwin; whose

(D) Darwin, who's

TEST QUBE

Back   Next

I
II
III
IV
V
VI
VII

Section 1, Module 2: Reading & Writing

Annotate ⋮

The development of ___ against infectious diseases by stimulating the immune system, has saved countless lives, eradicated smallpox, and dramatically reduced the incidence of other diseases, such as polio and measles.

17   Mark for Review 🔖

Which choice completes the text so that it conforms to the conventions of Standard English?

(A) vaccines, which protect

(B) vaccines - protecting

(C) vaccines protect

(D) vaccines: which protect

TEST◼QUBE

Back Next

Section 1, Module 2: Reading & Writing

Annotate ⋮

The effectiveness of acupuncture in pain relief has been a subject of debate among medical professionals for years. However, after conducting extensive clinical trials and meta-analyses, _____ that acupuncture can indeed provide significant relief for certain types of pain.

18   Mark for Review 🔖

Which choice completes the text so that it conforms to the conventions of Standard English?

(A) researcher Andrew Vicker's study concludes

(B) researcher Andrew Vickers has found

(C) the study of researcher Andrew Vickers suggests

(D) finding, researcher Andrew Vickers concludes

TEST◼QUBE

Back Next

Section 1, Module 2: Reading & Writing

Annotate ⋮

Living under constant fear and manipulation, the citizens struggled to discern truth from propaganda; according to the renowned author George Orwell in his book *1984*, the government's _____ is Peace. Freedom is Slavery. Ignorance is Strength."

19 Mark for Review 🔖

Which choice completes the text so that it conforms to the conventions of Standard English?

- (A) slogan was: "War
- (B) slogan was "War
- (C) slogan was, "War
- (D) slogan was; "War

TEST⬛QUBE

Back Next

Section 1, Module 2: Reading & Writing

Annotate ⋮

In evaluating the novels of British author Virginia Woolf, _____ have overlooked her subtle references to Greek mythology that enrich the depth of her stories.

20 Mark for Review 🔖

Which choice completes the text so that it conforms to the conventions of Standard English?

- (A) numerous scholars have concentrated on Woolf's innovative narrative techniques but
- (B) Woolf's innovative narrative techniques have been the focus of numerous scholars, who
- (C) there are numerous scholars who have concentrated on Woolf's innovative narrative techniques, but they
- (D) the focus of numerous scholars has been on Woolf's innovative narrative techniques; they

TEST⬛QUBE

Back Next

Section 1, Module 2: Reading & Writing

Annotate ⋮

To protect themselves from predators, some species of cuttlefish _____ an impressive ability to change their color and texture. This natural camouflage allows them to blend seamlessly with their surroundings, making it difficult for predators to detect them.

21   Mark for Review 🔖

Which choice completes the text so that it conforms to the conventions of Standard English?

(A) posses   (A)

(B) to possess   (B)

(C) having possessed   (C)

(D) possessing   (D)

TEST⬛QUBE   Back   Next

Section 1, Module 2: Reading & Writing

Annotate ⋮

After winning the lottery and using the money to help his community, he referred to it as "the best day of his _____ little did he know what was to come.

22   Mark for Review 🔖

Which choice completes the text so that it confirms to the conventions of Standard English?

(A) life"-

(B) life";

(C) life,"

(D) life"

TEST⬛QUBE   Back   Next

Annotate

William Shakespeare, often regarded as the greatest playwright in the English language, authored numerous plays and sonnets. His works explore a wide range of themes, from love and betrayal to ambition and power. _____ his plays have been translated into every major living language and continue to be performed worldwide.

23 Mark for Review

Which choice completes the text with the most logical transition?

- (A) For example,
- (B) However,
- (C) Accordingly,
- (D) In fact,

Back Next

Annotate

The Eurasian lynx, a solitary and enigmatic wildcat native to the dense, sprawling forests of Europe, is endowed with impressive agility and stealth, attributes it harnesses to master the art of ambush predation. When silently prowling through the underbrush in search of prey, this adept hunter utilizes its acute senses of hearing and sight to pinpoint the location of unsuspecting quarry, typically consisting of small to medium-sized mammals. _____ when the mating season arrives, shattering the wintry stillness, these ordinarily reticent predators undergo a marked transformation as they employ an assortment of calls, ranging from growls to yowls, in an effort to communicate with potential mates across the forest.

24 Mark for Review

Which choice completes the text with the most logical transition?

- (A) Analogously,
- (B) For example,
- (C) However,
- (D) Morever,

Back Next

I

II

III

IV

V

VI

VII

Annotate

The invention of the telephone by Alexander Graham Bell in 1876 revolutionized communication, allowing people to converse across great distances. Over time, the technology has evolved from wired devices to wireless cellular phones. _____ the advent of smartphones has further transformed the way we communicate and access information.

25   Mark for Review

Which choice completes the text with the most logical transition?

(A) Therefore,

(B) In comparison,

(C) Moreover,

(D) Conversely,

TEST**QUBE**   Back   Next

Annotate

While researching a topic, a student has taken the following notes:

- Maslow's hierarchy of needs is a motivational theory in psychology.
- The hierarchy is often represented as a pyramid with five levels.
- The levels are, from the bottom to the top: physiological needs, safety needs, love and belonging needs, esteem needs, and self-actualization needs.
- According to Maslow, individuals must fulfill lower-level needs before focusing on higher-level needs.

26   Mark for Review

The student wants to explain the structure of Maslow's hierarchy of needs. Which choice most effectively uses relevant information from the notes to accomplish this goal?

(A) Maslow's hierarchy of needs is structured as a five-level pyramid, with physiological needs at the base, followed by safety, love and belonging, esteem, and self- actualization needs at the top.

(B) As a motivational theory in psychology, Maslow's hierarchy of needs emphasizes the importance of fulfilling basic needs before pursuing higher-level psychological and self-actualization needs.

(C) Maslow's hierarchy of needs represents the different levels of human motivation, with the bottom levels focused on basic survival and the top levels aimed at personal growth and fulfillment.

(D) According to Maslow, the hierarchy of needs progresses from physiological needs to self-actualization needs, with each level building upon the fulfillment of the previous level's needs.

TEST**QUBE**   Back   Next

Section 1, Module 2: Reading & Writing

Annotate

While researching a topic, a student has taken the following notes:

- The "Stolen Generations" refers to Aboriginal children who were forcibly removed from their families by Australian government policies between 1910 and 1970.
- The policies were justified by a belief in the assimilation of these children into white society.
- It is estimated that between one in ten and one in three indigenous Australian children were taken from their families during this period.
- The impacts of these policies include a loss of cultural identity and psychological effects.

27   Mark for Review 🔖

The student wants to emphasize the impact of these policies on Aboriginal communities. Which choice most effectively uses relevant information from the notes to accomplish this goal?

(A) The Australian government's policies forcibly removed Aboriginal children from their families, causing a loss of cultural identity and psychological effects.

(B) The "Stolen Generations" policies aimed at assimilating Aboriginal children into white society, resulting in the loss of cultural identity for many.

(C) Between 1910 and 1970, Australian government policies resulted in between one in ten and one in three indigenous children being taken from their families.

(D) The Australian government justified the "Stolen Generations" policies with a belief in the assimilation of these children into white society.

TEST⬛QUBE

End of Test 2 Reading/Writing Section

Back   Next

Upcoming Math Section: Reference Formula Sheet

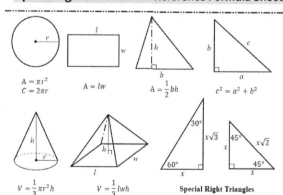

$A = \pi r^2$
$C = 2\pi r$

$A = lw$

$A = \frac{1}{2}bh$

$c^2 = a^2 + b^2$

$V = \frac{1}{3}\pi r^2 h$ $V = \frac{1}{3}lwh$ **Special Right Triangles**

$V = lwh$ $V = \pi r^2 h$ $V = \frac{3}{4}\pi r^3$

The number of degrees of arc in a circle is 360.
The number of radians of arc in a circle is 2π.
The sum of the measures in degrees of the angles of a triangle is 180.

Directions for Student-Produced Response

- **TEST QUBE** recommends students to use decimals for most answers but suggests using fractions only in cases where the answers involve repeating decimals (e.g., 0.333 = 1/3)
- For cases with more than one answer, enter **just one of the answers.**
- You can enter up to 5 characters for your answer. (For negative answers, the **negative sign** does not count as one character)
- For **fractions** that don't fit the answer box, enter the decimal equivalent (Unless advised to do otherwise)
- For **decimals** that exceed the answer box, round to the fourth digit. (Unless advised to do otherwise)
- For mixed number (such as $4\frac{1}{4}$), enter it as an improper fraction (17/4) or its decimal equivalent (4.25)
- For all answers, you may omit the symbols and units such as \$,%, cm^3, m^2, etc.

Acceptable vs Non-Acceptable Answers

Answer	Acceptable ways to receive credit	Ways you **WON'T** receive credit
4.25	4.25 , 17/4	41/4 , 4 1/4
4/6	2/3 .6666 , .6667 0.666 , 0.667	0.66 , .66 0.67 , .67
-1/6	-1/6 -0.166, -0.167 -.1666, -.1667	-0.16 , -.16 -0.17, -.167

Move on to the Next Section ≫

35:00

1   Mark for Review 🔖

If $4x + y = 10$, what is the value of $16x + 4y$?

- (A) 10
- (B) 20
- (C) 40
- (D) 80

TEST🌐QUBE   Question 1 of 22 >

Section 2, Module 1: Math   📝 Annotate   ⋮

2   Mark for Review 🔖

Shakil intends to buy a $98 calculator and p pencils that cost $2 each. He has a maximum of $110 budget for his purchase. Which of the following inequalities best represents this situation?

- (A) $98 + 2p \leq 110$
- (B) $2 + 98p \leq 110$
- (C) $2p \leq 98$
- (D) $110 + 2p \leq 98$

TEST🌐QUBE   Question 2 of 22 >

Section 2, Module 1: Math   📝 Annotate   ⋮

3   Mark for Review 🔖

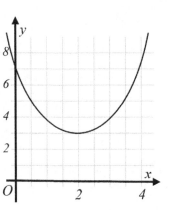

The graph of $y = f(x)$ is shown. What is the y-intercept of the graph?

- (A) 2
- (B) 7
- (C) 12
- (D) 17

TEST🌐QUBE   Question 3 of 22 >   Back Next

76

4   Mark for Review 🔖

$PQ = 15$
$QR = 12$
$RP = 9$
The side lengths of a right triangle PQR is given. What is the value of angle R, in degrees?

TEST◈QUBE   Question 4 of 22 >

5   Mark for Review 🔖

Function g is defined by $g(x) = \frac{1}{2}(x-3)^2 + 1$. The graph of $h(x)$ is generated by shifting the graph of $g(x)$ on the xy-plane by 3 units to the negative x direction. Which equation correctly defines $h(x)$?

(A) $h(x) = \frac{1}{2}(x^2 + 3)$ Ⓐ

(B) $h(x) = \frac{1}{2}x^2 + 3$ Ⓑ

(C) $h(x) = \frac{1}{2}x^2 + 1$ Ⓒ

(D) $h(x) = \frac{1}{2-3}(x^2 - 3)$ Ⓓ

TEST◈QUBE   Question 5 of 22 >

6   Mark for Review 🔖

The equation $y = x - 8$ defines the relation between x and y. What is the x value when $y = 1$?

(A) 7

(B) 9

(C) -1

(D) -9 Ⓓ

TEST◈QUBE   Question 6 of 22 >   Back   Next

7 Mark for Review

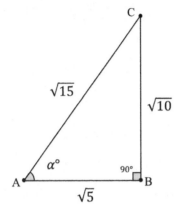

Note: Figure Not Drawn to Scale

A right triangle ABC is shown, where α represents the value of angle A. What is the value of $\cos \alpha$?

(A) $\sqrt{5}$

(B) $\frac{\sqrt{5}}{\sqrt{15}}$

(C) $\sqrt{15}$

(D) $\frac{\sqrt{15}}{\sqrt{5}}$

8 Mark for Review

The standard English set of alphabets consists of 26 unique letters, of which exactly 5 (a, e, i, o, u) are vowels. What is the probability of randomly choosing a standard English letter that is not a vowel?

(A) $\frac{6}{26}$

(B) $\frac{11}{26}$

(C) $\frac{16}{26}$

(D) $\frac{21}{26}$

TEST QUBE   Question 8 of 22 >

9 Mark for Review

Quadratic equation $x^2 - x + c = 0$ has two distinct real solutions when a constant real number c is less than k. What is the maximum value of k?

(A) 16

(B) 4

(C) $\frac{1}{2}$

(D) $\frac{1}{4}$

10   Mark for Review 🔖

Aniya found out that of 25 students in her class, there were twice as many students who had cats, c, as there were those who had dogs, d. There were no students who had both cats and dogs. s students, however, did not have cats or dogs. Which set of expressions best describes this context?

A)
$$\begin{cases} s = 25 - d \\ s + d = c \end{cases}$$

B)
$$\begin{cases} s + d - c = 25 \\ d + 25 = c \end{cases}$$

C)
$$\begin{cases} c = 2d \\ s = 25 - (c + d) \end{cases}$$

D)
$$\begin{cases} c = 2d \\ s = 25 + (c + d) \end{cases}$$

11   Mark for Review 🔖

$A(x)$ is defined as $A(x) = |x| - 4$. At how many different points do the graph of $A(x)$ and the x-axis intersect?

A) 2

B) 1

C) 0

D) Infinitely many

12   Mark for Review 🔖

$$L(x) = 130{,}000\,(1.1)^x$$

$L(x)$ represents the total number of tree leaves in a certain area of forest on every July 15th, x years after 2020. How many more tree leaves does the area contain on July 15th, 2021, when compared to July 15th, 2020?

A) $1{,}300$

B) $13{,}000$

C) $15{,}730$

D) $26{,}000$

I II III IV V VI VII

13   Mark for Review 🔖

In an isosceles triangle DEF, both the values of angle E and angle F are **30** degrees. What is the value of angle D in radians?

- (A) $\frac{\pi}{2}$
- (B) $\frac{\pi}{3}$
- (C) $\frac{2\pi}{3}$
- (D) π

TEST◉QUBE   Question 13 of 22 >

14   Mark for Review 🔖

$P(1, 17), Q(3, 29)$
What is the slope of a linear function whose graph passes both points P and Q?

[   ]

TEST◉QUBE   Question 14 of 22 >

15   Mark for Review 🔖

$f(x)$ is defined as $f(x) = x(x - 2)(x - 11)^2$. How many different x-intercepts does the graph of $f(x)$ have?

- (A) 3
- (B) 4
- (C) 5
- (D) 6

TEST◉QUBE   Question 15 of 22 >   Back   Next

2

Module 1

2

I

II

III

IV

V

VI

VII

Section 2, Module 1: Math Annotate

16 Mark for Review

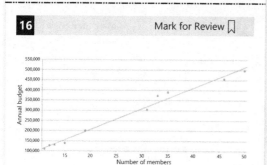

Cathay conducted research on the number of member and the annual budgets of 10 senior daycare centers in her city. The scatterplot shows the relationship between the annual budget and the number of numbers enrolled in each daycare center. Which of the choices best describes the meaning of the slope of the linear model, 10,200, in this context?

 (A) An additional member in a daycare center takes $10,200$ dollars more annual budget on average.

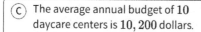 (B) Cathay researched $10,200$ daycare centers.

(C) The average annual budget of 10 daycare centers is $10,200$ dollars.

(D) The minimum of the annual budget of 10 daycare centers is $10,200$ dollars.

Section 2, Module 1: Math Annotate

17 Mark for Review

What is an equivalent form of $3x^3y^{12} + 6x^3$?

(A) $3x(x^{12} + 2)$

(B) $3x^3(y^{12} + 2)$

(C) $3x^3(y^6 + 2)$

(D) $3x(y^{12} + 2)$

Section 2, Module 1: Math Annotate

18 Mark for Review

A state imposes a 6% sales tax for each purchase in the state. How much in total should a person pay, in dollars including sales tax, when he/she purchases 3 desks, each costing 200 dollars, before the purchase tax in the state?

(A) 606

(B) 616

(C) 626

(D) 636

Section 2, Module 1: Math

Annotate

19 Mark for Review

A car of a certain model loses its fuel mileage as the car engine gets old. $F(y) = 20(0.95)^y$ models the fuel mileage of the car, in miles per gallon, y years after purchase. Which of the choices is closest to the maximum distance, in miles, a car can travel with 50 gallons of fuel at the moment of 2 years after purchase?

(A) 25

(B) 350

(C) 900

(D) $2,750$

TESTQUBE Question 19 of 22 >

Section 2, Module 1: Math

Annotate

20 Mark for Review

Data set	A	B
Values	105, 107, 109, 115, 116	101, 103, 105, 110, 111, 112, x

Data sets A and B contain 5 and 7 values, respectively, as shown above. The median of the values in data set A and B are the same. What is the value of x?

TESTQUBE Question 20 of 22 >

Section 2, Module 1: Math

Annotate

21 Mark for Review

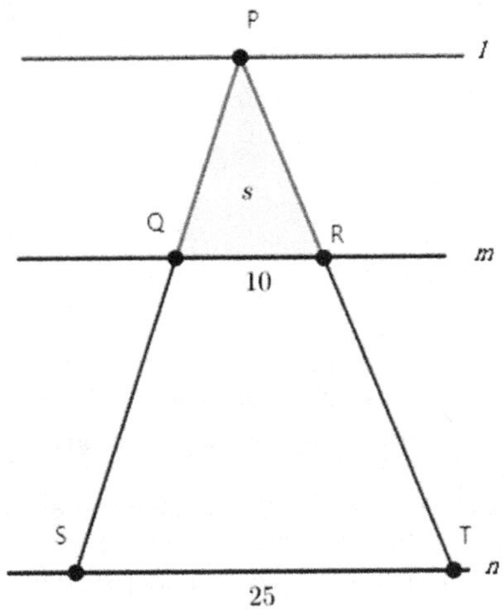

In the diagram above, lines l, m, and n are parallel to each other. The length of QR equals 10 units, and the length of ST equals 25 units. The area of triangle PQR is s. Which of the following expression equals the area of triangle PST?

(A) $4s$

(B) $\frac{25}{4}s$

(C) $9s$

(D) $\frac{49}{7}s$

TESTQUBE Question 21 of 22 > Back Next

Annotate

22   Mark for Review 🔖

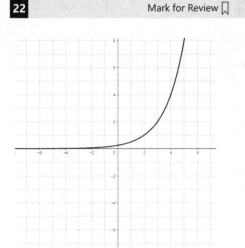

The graph of $g(x) = 2^{x-2}$ is shown. Which of the following interprets the relationship between $g(t)$ and $g(t+3)$, when t is a constant?

(A) $g(t) + 6 = g(t+3)$

(B) $g(t)^3 = g(t+3)$

(C) $g(3t) = g(t+3)$

(D) $2^3 g(t) = g(t+3)$

I

II

III

IV

V

VI

VII

Move on to the
Next Section »

⏱ 35:00

1 Mark for Review 🔖

What is 18% of 400?

[   ]

2 Mark for Review 🔖

Ben is planning to print 110 pages of documents at a print shop. c pages should be printed in color, and the rest should be printed in gray-scale. The print shop charges 1.5 dollars for printing a colored page, and 0.5 dollars for printing a gray-scale page. Which expression best describes the total price of Ben's printing in dollars?

(A) $1.5c + 0.5(110 - c)$ —A—

(B) $1.5c - 0.5(110 + c)$ —B—

(C) $0.5c + 1.5(110 - c)$ —C—

(D) $0.5c + 1.5(110 + c)$ —D—

3 Mark for Review 🔖

$x - 2y = 11$
$\quad\ 2y = 15$
The solution for the given system of equations is (x, y). What is xy?

(A) 15 —A—

(B) 97.5 —B—

(C) 150 —C—

(D) 195 —D—

4   Mark for Review 🔖

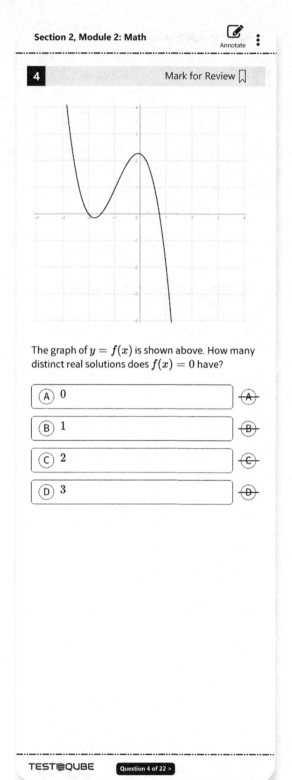

The graph of $y = f(x)$ is shown above. How many distinct real solutions does $f(x) = 0$ have?

(A) 0   (A)

(B) 1   (B)

(C) 2   (C)

(D) 3   (D)

5   Mark for Review 🔖

Oliver spent 29.6 dollars when he purchased 8 bottles of orange and prune juice at a grocery store. The price of orange juice and prune juice are 3.40 and 4.00 dollars per bottle, respectively. What is the number of bottles of orange juice Oliver bought?

(A) 3   (A)

(B) 4   (B)

(C) 5   (C)

(D) 6   (D)

6   Mark for Review 🔖

Which is an equivalent form of $15x(xy)^3$?

(A) $15x^4y^3$ (A)

(B) $15x^2y$ (B)

(C) $15xy^3$ (C)

(D) $15y(xy)^3$ (D)

Section 2, Module 2: Math

 Annotate

7 Mark for Review

The daily revenue of a movie theater is directly proportional to t, the number of tickets sold. If the theater's revenue on a certain day was $7.95t$ dollars, which of the choices best suggests the meaning of the number 7.95 in this context?

(A) The number of tickets sold on that day

(B) The annual average revenue of the movie theater

(C) The number of movies showing at the theater

(D) The price per ticket

Section 2, Module 2: Math

 Annotate

8 Mark for Review

A square-bottomed monument is surrounded by a square-shaped plaza with a three times longer side length. The area of the plaza excluding the bottom of the monument is 720 square feet. What is the area of the bottom of the monument in square feet?

(A) 40

(B) 90

(C) 240

(D) 270

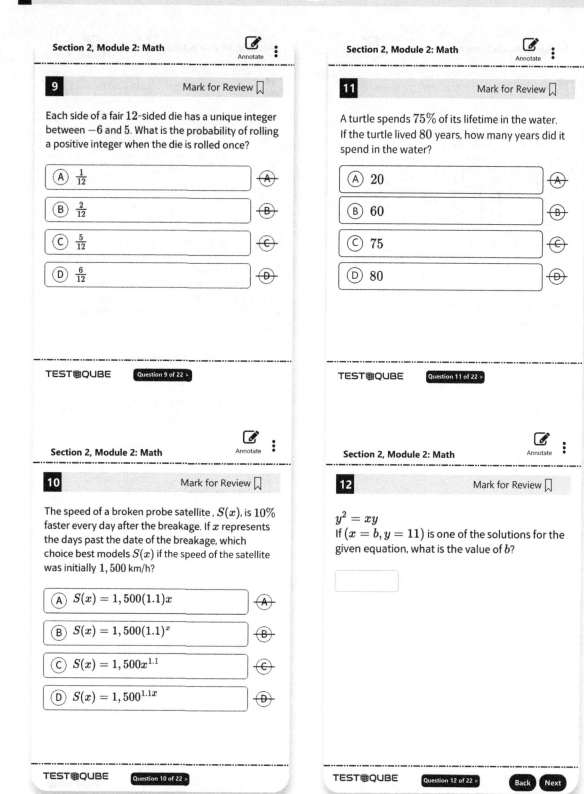

9   Mark for Review

Each side of a fair 12-sided die has a unique integer between -6 and 5. What is the probability of rolling a positive integer when the die is rolled once?

- (A) $\frac{1}{12}$
- (B) $\frac{2}{12}$
- (C) $\frac{5}{12}$
- (D) $\frac{6}{12}$

TEST🔳QUBE   Question 9 of 22 >

10   Mark for Review

The speed of a broken probe satellite , $S(x)$, is 10% faster every day after the breakage. If x represents the days past the date of the breakage, which choice best models $S(x)$ if the speed of the satellite was initially $1,500$ km/h?

- (A) $S(x) = 1,500(1.1)x$
- (B) $S(x) = 1,500(1.1)^x$
- (C) $S(x) = 1,500x^{1.1}$
- (D) $S(x) = 1,500^{1.1x}$

TEST🔳QUBE   Question 10 of 22 >

11   Mark for Review

A turtle spends 75% of its lifetime in the water. If the turtle lived 80 years, how many years did it spend in the water?

- (A) 20
- (B) 60
- (C) 75
- (D) 80

TEST🔳QUBE   Question 11 of 22 >

12   Mark for Review

$y^2 = xy$
If $(x = b, y = 11)$ is one of the solutions for the given equation, what is the value of b?

TEST🔳QUBE   Question 12 of 22 >   Back   Next

I

II

III

IV

V

VI

VII

13   Mark for Review

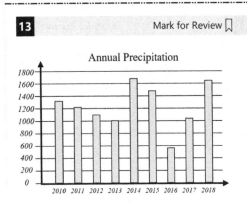

The chart shows the recorded annual precipitation of a certain city, in millimeters per year. From 2010 to 2018, in which year did the city experience the least amount of precipitation?

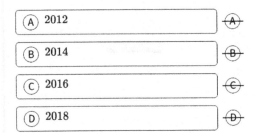

(A) 2012

(B) 2014

(C) 2016

(D) 2018

14   Mark for Review

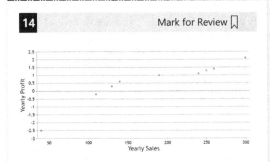

The scatterplot is generated by analyzing a company's total sales, in thousand products, and the net profit, in million dollars, for each fiscal year over a nine-year period. A linear function $y = f(x)$ models the data where x and y represent the sales and profit, respectively. Which of the following descriptions of $f(x)$ is true?

(A) Both the slope and the y-intercept are positive.

(B) The slope is positive and the y-intercept is negative.

(C) The slope is negative and the y-intercept is positive.

(D) Both the slope and the y-intercept are negative.

Section 2, Module 2: Math   Annotate ⋮

15   Mark for Review 🔖

Last winter, Alexia visited a ski resort x times to take ski lessons. At every visit, she paid l dollars to take a lesson. In addition, she paid m dollars registration fee on her first visit. What is the average payment, in dollars, that Alexia made to the ski resort last winter?

(A) $\frac{m+x}{l}$

(B) $\frac{m-x}{l}$

(C) $\frac{m+lx}{x}$

(D) $\frac{m+l}{mx}$

TEST⬤QUBE   Question 15 of 22 >

Section 2, Module 2: Math   Annotate ⋮

16   Mark for Review 🔖

The carbon footprint of a product is defined as the volume of total carbon dioxide emitted to make, process, and ship the product. 1kg of beef is proven to have 83 cubic meters of carbon footprint. Assuming that 1 meter is equivalent to 3.3 feet, which of the following values is closest to the carbon footprint in cubic feet that 1kg of beef has?

(A) 36

(B) 280

(C) 900

(D) $3,000$

TEST⬤QUBE   Question 16 of 22 >

Section 2, Module 2: Math   Annotate ⋮

17   Mark for Review 🔖

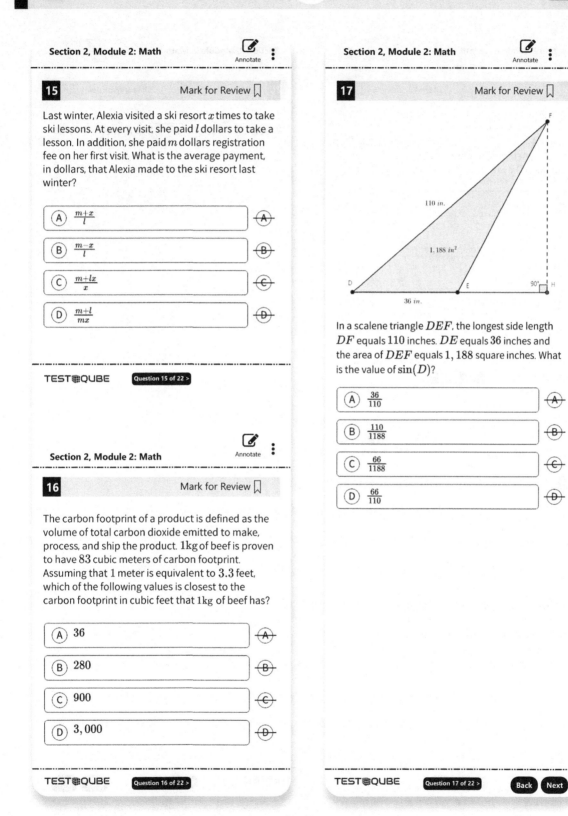

In a scalene triangle DEF, the longest side length DF equals 110 inches. DE equals 36 inches and the area of DEF equals $1,188$ square inches. What is the value of $\sin(D)$?

(A) $\frac{36}{110}$

(B) $\frac{110}{1188}$

(C) $\frac{66}{1188}$

(D) $\frac{66}{110}$

TEST⬤QUBE   Question 17 of 22 >   Back   Next

Section 2, Module 2: Math   Annotate   ⋮

18   Mark for Review 🔖

$$\begin{cases} y = x^2 + 2x + 1 \\ y = -4 \end{cases}$$

How many sets of real solutions does the given set of equations have?

(A) 0

(B) 1

(C) 2

(D) Infinitely many

TEST⬛QUBE   Question 18 of 22 >

Section 2, Module 2: Math   Annotate   ⋮

19   Mark for Review 🔖

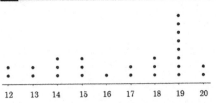

The given dot plot shows the distribution of test scores, out of 20, of 26 students in Hannah's class. What is the mode of the scores of Hannah's classmates?

TEST⬛QUBE   Question 19 of 22 >

Section 2, Module 2: Math   Annotate   ⋮

20   Mark for Review 🔖

What is the value of $\sqrt{x^2 + 3} + 3$ when $x = -1$?

TEST⬛QUBE   Question 20 of 22 >   Back   Next

21   Mark for Review 🔖

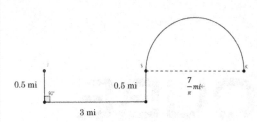

0.5 mi   0.5 mi $\frac{7}{\pi}$ mi

3 mi

Josh and Kimberly left their respective home at the same time for school S. From Josh's home, J, he drove 0.5 miles south, turned 90 degrees left, drove 3 miles, turned 90 degrees left, and drove 0.5 miles. From Kimberly's home, K, she drove along a semicircular road with a diameter of $\frac{7}{\pi}$ miles. Assuming that the average driving speeds of Josh and Kimberly are the same, who arrived at the school first?

(A) Josh

(B) Kimberly

(C) Both arrived at the same time.

(D) There is not enough information provided.

22   Mark for Review 🔖

$g(x)$ is defined as the largest possible integer that is less than or equal to x. A page of a certain academic paper contains 240 words at maximum. Which choice does the most appropriately represent the minimum number of pages of the academic paper that contains 1890 words?

(A) $g(1890)$

(B) $g(240)$

(C) $g\left(\frac{240}{1890}\right) + 1$

(D) $g\left(\frac{1890}{240}\right) + 1$ (D)

I II III IV V VI VII

TESTQUBE

Digital SAT ®

Practice Test #3

Section 1, Module 1: Reading & Writing 🕐 32:00 ✎ Annotate ⋮

In the realm of modern architecture, sustainable design has become a paramount consideration. Architects worldwide are embracing techniques that reduce carbon footprint and promote energy efficiency. This shift in focus, if adopted universally, could significantly _____ the detrimental impact of urban development on the environment.

1 Mark for Review 🔖

Which choice completes the text with the most logical and precise word or phrase?

(A) mitigate   —Ⓐ—

(B) exacerbate   —Ⓑ—

(C) venerate   —Ⓒ—

(D) trivalize   —Ⓓ—

TEST⬢QUBE   Question 1 of 27 >   Back Next

Section 1, Module 1: Reading & Writing ✎ Annotate ⋮

The new superhero movie, "Guardians of Aetheria," was an instant box-office hit, breaking records globally. However, it was not well received by all viewers. Renowned film critic Leonard Maltin argued that the film's success did not stem from its artistic merit but rather seemed to _____ the power of an aggressive marketing campaign. The disparity between the box-office figures and the critical reception, including mixed reviews on Rotten Tomatoes, sparked a debate about the influence of advertising in the film industry, with many citing the elaborate promotional collaborations with fast-food chains and toy manufacturers.

2 Mark for Review 🔖

Which choice completes the text with the most logical and precise word or phrase?

(A) embody   —Ⓐ—

(B) repudiate   —Ⓑ—

(C) vitiate   —Ⓒ—

(D) impugn   —Ⓓ—

TEST⬢QUBE   Question 2 of 27 >   Back Next

I

II

When the World Health Organization (WHO) was
gearing up for the annual Global Health Summit in
Geneva, the emergence of a recent pandemic rendered
in-person gatherings unfeasible. The organizers, led by
Dr. Tedros Adhanom Ghebreyesus, had to quickly _____
a virtual event, a Herculean task given the sheer
number of participants from different countries and the
complexity of the topics, including epidemiology and
vaccine distribution. The successful transition to a
digital platform was lauded by attendees and keynote
speakers alike, proving to be an exemplar for future
conferences.

3   Mark for Review 🔖

Which choice completes the text with the most
logical and precise word or phrase?

Ⓐ orchestrate   Ⓐ

Ⓑ extirpate   Ⓑ

Ⓒ desiccate   Ⓒ

Ⓓ mar   Ⓓ

III

TEST⬡QUBE   Question 3 of 27 >   Back Next

IV

V

In the wake of Hurricane Katrina, New Orleans
experienced an outpouring of support from its residents
and people across the nation. This _____ of goodwill took
the form of donations pouring into organizations like
the American Red Cross, an influx of volunteers helping
in rebuilding efforts, and community projects
spearheaded by local leaders. The collective response
demonstrated the city's resilience and unity in the face
of adversity, a testament to the indomitable spirit of
New Orleans.

4   Mark for Review 🔖

Which choice completes the text with the most
logical and precise word or phrase?

Ⓐ paucity

Ⓑ surfeit

Ⓒ dearth   Ⓒ

Ⓓ ennui   Ⓓ

VI

VII

TEST⬡QUBE   Question 4 of 27 >   Back Next

Section 1, Module 1: Reading & Writing

Annotate

Renowned novelist, Haruki Murakami's latest work, "The Echoing Labyrinth," is a complex narrative, woven together from multiple storylines that intersect and diverge in unexpected ways. Set in a mythical version of Tokyo, the characters journey through time, dreams, and alternate realities. The author's skillful ____ of these disparate elements, ranging from historical intrigue to surreal encounters, creates a rich and engaging tapestry that enthralls readers and critics, securing his place as a maestro of contemporary literature.

5   Mark for Review

Which choice completes the text with the most logical and precise word or phrase?

(A) amalgamation

(B) segregation

(C) trivialization

(D) dissolution

Section 1, Module 1: Reading & Writing

Annotate

Twelfth Night is a circa 1602 play by William Shakespeare. In the play, the character of Viola navigates the complex web of relationships and mistaken identities while disguised as Cesario. Viola's emotional struggle and unrequited love for Orsino are best demonstrated when she _____

6   Mark for Review

Which choice most effectively uses a quotation from Twelfth Night to illustrate the claim?

(A) confesses to Orsino, "My father had a daughter loved a man, as it might be, perhaps, were I a woman, I should your lordship."

(B) speaks to Olivia, "I am not that I play; I am the man, if it be so, as 'tis."

(C) tells the fool Feste, "This fellow is wise enough to play the fool; and to do that well craves a kind of wit."

(D) addresses Antonio, "I can no other answer make but thanks, and thanks, and ever thanks."

I

II

III

IV

V

VI

VII

Section 1, Module 1: Reading & Writing

Annotate

In 2030, the Artemis program led by NASA aimed to establish a sustainable human presence on the Moon. One significant challenge was the need to develop efficient energy sources that could operate in the harsh lunar environment. Solar energy was considered the primary option, but the Moon experiences approximately two weeks of darkness during each lunar night, making it challenging to rely solely on solar power. To address this issue, NASA developed advanced energy storage systems and utilized fuel cells in addition to solar panels, ensuring a continuous power supply during periods of darkness.

7   Mark for Review 🔖

According to the text, why is it difficult to depend exclusively on solar power for the Artemis program on the Moon?

(A) Because the Moon's surface is not suitable for solar panel installations

(B) Because the Moon has limited sunlight during its long lunar nights

(C) Because solar energy conversion technology is not advanced enough for lunar applications

(D) Because lunar dust interferes with the functioning of solar panels

TEST⬛QUBE   Question 7 of 27 >   Back   Next

Section 1, Module 1: Reading & Writing

Annotate

The following text is adapted from Edith Wharton's 1911 novella, "Ethan Frome." The narrator portrays the life of Ethan Frome in the bleak, winter-stricken rural town of Starkfield, Massachusetts.

It was there that, several years ago, I saw him for the first time; and the sight pulled me up sharp. <u>Even then he was the most striking figure in Starkfield, though he was but the ruin of a man.</u> It was not so much his great height that marked him, for the "natives" were easily singled out by their lank longitude from the stockier foreign breed: it was the careless powerful look he had, in spite of a lameness checking each step like the jerk of a chain. There was something bleak and unapproachable in his face, and he was so stiffened and grizzled that I took him for an old man and was surprised to hear that he was not more than fifty-two.

8   Mark for Review 🔖

Which choice best describes the function of the underlined sentence in the text as a whole?

(A) It introduces Ethan Frome's remarkable presence despite his physical and personal adversities.

(B) It highlights the physical deterioration of Ethan Frome in contrast to his earlier robustness.

(C) It describes Ethan Frome as a symbol of the desolation and decay pervasive in Starkfield.

(D) It underscores the narrator's initial misunderstanding about Ethan Frome's age.

TEST⬛QUBE   Question 8 of 27 >   Back   Next

Section 1, Module 1: Reading & Writing

Annotate ⋮

The following text is adapted from Fyodor Dostoevsky's 1880 novel, *The Brothers Karamazov*. The story delves into the lives of the Karamazov brothers and their father Fyodor Pavlovitch. Adelaïda Ivanovna, mentioned in this excerpt, is Fyodor Pavlovitch's second wife.

Immediately after the elopement Adelaïda Ivanovna discerned in a flash that she had no feeling for her husband but contempt. The marriage accordingly showed itself in its true colors with extraordinary rapidity. Although the family accepted the event pretty quickly and apportioned the runaway bride her dowry, the husband and wife began to lead a most disorderly life, and there were everlasting scenes between them. It was said that the young wife showed incomparably more generosity and dignity than Fyodor Pavlovitch, who, as is now known, got hold of all her money up to twenty-five thousand roubles as soon as she received it, so that those thousands were lost to her for ever.

9　　　　　　　　　　Mark for Review 🔖

Which choice best states the main purpose of the text?

(A) To illustrate the financial loss Adelaida Ivanovna suffers due to Fyodor Pavlovitch's actions

(B) To depict the deteriorating relationship between Adelaida Ivanovna and Fyodor Pavlovitch after their elopement

(C) To show the consequences of Adelaida Ivanovna's quick realization of her contempt for her husband

(D) To contrast the generosity and dignity of Adelaida Ivanovna with the greedy nature of Fyodor Pavlovitch

TEST QUBE

Back Next

Section 1, Module 1: Reading & Writing

Annotate ⋮

"No Coward Soul Is Mine" is an 1846 poem written by Emily Brontë. In the poem the author emphasizes the strength and resilience of the human spirit and that faith in one's own soul is impenetrable to despair, writing, _____

10　　　　　　　　　Mark for Review 🔖

Which quotation from "No Coward Soul Is Mine" most effectively illustrates this claim?

(A) "Vain are the thousand creeds / That move men's hearts, unutterably vain,/ Worthless as withered weeds / Or idlest froth amid the boundless main"

(B) "O God within my breast / Almighty, ever-present Deity / Life, that in me hast rest, / As I Undying Life, have power in Thee"

(C) "Though Earth and Moon were gone / And suns and universes ceased to be / And Thou wert left alone / Every Existence would exist in Thee"

(D) "No coward soul is mine / No trembler in the world's storm- troubled sphere /I see Heaven's glories shine / And Faith shines equal arming me from Fear"

TEST QUBE

Back Next

I

II

III

IV

V

VI

VII

Section 1, Module 1: Reading & Writing

 Annotate

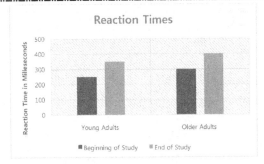

Reaction Times

Neuropsychologists are studying the effects of sleep deprivation on cognitive performance in two age groups: young adults and older adults. They have collected data on the average reaction times of participants in each age group after being sleep-deprived for 24 hours. The more sleep-deprived individuals are they posit, the greater delay they will have in reaction times. Older adults, with declining cognitive function, are at even greater risks of the consequences of sleep deprivation, the researchers argue.

11   Mark for Review 🔖

Which statement best describes the data from the graph that supports the neuropsychologists' claim?

- (A) Sleep deprivation led to faster reaction times in both age groups.

- (B) Older adults had slower reaction times at the beginning and end of the study.

- (C) Sleep deprivation had a more noticeable effect on young adults compared to older adults.

- (D) Sleep deprivation led to slower reaction times in both age groups, with older adults experiencing slower reaction times.

Section 1, Module 1: Reading & Writing

 Annotate

Oil prices are influenced by a variety of factors, including geopolitical events, natural disasters, and shifts in supply and demand. In recent years, the emergence of hydraulic fracturing, or "fracking," has contributed to a significant increase in oil production in the United States, making the country one of the world's largest oil producers. Some analysts argue that this surge in U.S. oil production has contributed to lower global oil prices by increasing the overall supply. If data shows that global oil prices have experienced a general decline since the widespread adoption of fracking in the United States, while other major oil-producing countries have maintained stable production levels, this would suggest that ____

12   Mark for Review 🔖

Which choice most logically completes the text?

- (A) hydraulic fracturing in the United States has likely played a role in contributing to lower global oil prices.

- (B) global oil prices are primarily influenced by factors unrelated to the United States' oil production.

- (C) the decline in global oil prices is solely attributable to geopolitical events and natural disasters.

- (D) oil production in other major oil-producing countries has been intentionally reduced to maintain higher global oil prices.

Section 1, Module 1: Reading & Writing

Annotate ⋮

During the Renaissance, advances in art, science, and technology flourished across Europe, with many scholars attributing the era's intellectual progress to the revival of interest in classical Greek and Roman works. In addition, various city-states, such as Florence and Venice, facilitated the spread of innovative ideas by fostering an environment that encouraged creativity and competition. Despite these favorable conditions, there is no evidence to suggest that the most significant artistic and scientific breakthroughs of the Renaissance occurred simultaneously in all European countries or that their development was solely dependent on the influence of classical works. This observation implies that ____

13   Mark for Review 🔖

Which choice most logically completes the text?

(A) the Renaissance might have been a consequence of multiple, interconnected factors, rather than solely the resurgence of classical ideas.

(B) the advancements made during the Renaissance were limited to specific geographic regions and had no lasting global impact.

(C) the Renaissance would not have occurred if the classical works of Greek and Roman scholars had been lost or destroyed.

(D) European countries that did not experience significant breakthroughs during the Renaissance were unaffected by the era's innovations.

TEST⬡QUBE   Question 13 of 27 >   Back   Next

Section 1, Module 1: Reading & Writing

Annotate ⋮

In the early 20th century, Nellie Bly—known for her groundbreaking _____ journey to travel around the world in less than 80 days, inspired by Jules Verne's famous novel. On January 25, 1890, Bly successfully completed her voyage in just 72 days, setting a new record for the fastest global circumnavigation.

14   Mark for Review 🔖

Which choice completes the text so that it conforms to the conventions of Standard English?

(A) journalism—embarked—on

(B) journalism—embarked on

(C) journalism—embarked, on

(D) journalism—embarked. On

TEST⬡QUBE   Question 14 of 27 >   Back   Next

Section 1, Module 1: Reading & Writing

Annotate ⋮

Struggling with a debilitating stutter for much of his childhood, King George VI—forced to take the throne upon his brother's abdication—became a symbol of strength and resilience _____ his country through trying times and delivering speeches that rallied the nation, despite his speech impediment. His journey to overcome his stutter was portrayed in the critically acclaimed film, "The King's Speech."

15   Mark for Review 🔖

Which choice completes the text so that it conforms to the conventions of Standard English?

(A) during World War II, leading   —Ⓐ—

(B) during World War II, he led   —Ⓑ—

(C) during World War II. Leading   —Ⓒ—

(D) during World War II; leading   —Ⓓ—

TEST❖QUBE

Question 15 of 27 >

Back   Next

Section 1, Module 1: Reading & Writing

Annotate ⋮

The small town of Greenfield has been grappling with a major pollution problem. The local river, once a vibrant ecosystem, has been severely affected by industrial waste. The townsfolk, deeply concerned about the deteriorating situation, formed a committee to address the issue. After weeks of deliberation, the committee, having thoroughly examined a comprehensive cleanup and restoration proposal that encompassed plans for waste management, water treatment, and public awareness campaigns, found _____ decision to be unanimous.

16   Mark for Review 🔖

Which choice completes the text so that it conforms to the conventions of Standard English?

(A) they're   —Ⓐ—

(B) their   —Ⓑ—

(C) it's   —Ⓒ—

(D) its   —Ⓓ—

TEST❖QUBE

Question 16 of 27 >

Back   Next

Section 1, Module 1: Reading & Writing

Annotate ⋮

Despite facing numerous challenges in his early life, Abraham Lincoln—born in a one-room log cabin in Kentucky—rose to become the 16th President of the United States, guiding the nation through one of its darkest periods, _____ ultimately working to abolish slavery with the Emancipation Proclamation. His leadership and dedication to preserving the Union are remembered as hallmarks of his presidency.

17   Mark for Review 🔖

Which choice completes the text so that it conforms to the conventions of Standard English?

(A) the Civil War. And   (A)

(B) the Civil War – and   (B)

(C) the Civil War, and   (C)

(D) the Civil War; and   (D)

TEST⬛QUBE   Question 17 of 27 >   Back Next

Section 1, Module 1: Reading & Writing

Annotate ⋮

Famous for their strength and agility, the Sherpa people of Nepal ____ as expert guides and porters for mountaineers attempting to climb the treacherous peaks of the Himalayas. Their deep understanding of the region's terrain and weather conditions makes them invaluable to climbers.

18   Mark for Review 🔖

Which choice completes the text so that it conforms to the conventions of Standard English?

(A) serves   (A)

(B) serve   (B)

(C) has served   (C)

(D) have served   (D)

TEST⬛QUBE   Question 18 of 27 >   Back Next

Section 1, Module 1: Reading & Writing

Annotate ⋮

In the world of classical music, many people admire Mozart for his prodigious talent; however, less well known is how _____ Rigorous training and a supportive family environment played a significant role in shaping his musical genius.

19   Mark for Review 🔖

Which choice completes the text so that it conforms to the conventions of Standard English?

(A) he achieved that mastery?

(B) that mastery was achieved?

(C) that mastery was achieved.

(D) was that mastery achieved.

Section 1, Module 1: Reading & Writing

Annotate ⋮

Several factors, including increased public awareness and stricter regulations, ___ a significant impact on reducing plastic pollution in the ocean. However, experts stress that more action is needed to address the remaining challenges.

20   Mark for Review 🔖

Which choice completes the text so that it conforms to the conventions of Standard English?

(A) has had

(B) had had

(C) have had

(D) were having

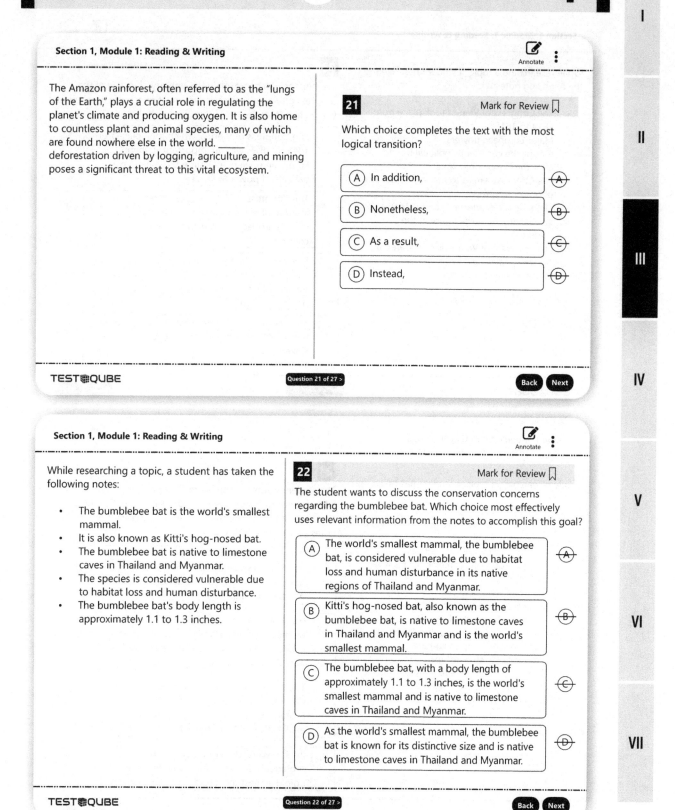

Section 1, Module 1: Reading & Writing

Annotate

The Amazon rainforest, often referred to as the "lungs of the Earth," plays a crucial role in regulating the planet's climate and producing oxygen. It is also home to countless plant and animal species, many of which are found nowhere else in the world. _____ deforestation driven by logging, agriculture, and mining poses a significant threat to this vital ecosystem.

21   Mark for Review 🔖

Which choice completes the text with the most logical transition?

(A) In addition,

(B) Nonetheless,

(C) As a result,

(D) Instead,

Section 1, Module 1: Reading & Writing

Annotate

While researching a topic, a student has taken the following notes:

- The bumblebee bat is the world's smallest mammal.
- It is also known as Kitti's hog-nosed bat.
- The bumblebee bat is native to limestone caves in Thailand and Myanmar.
- The species is considered vulnerable due to habitat loss and human disturbance.
- The bumblebee bat's body length is approximately 1.1 to 1.3 inches.

22   Mark for Review 🔖

The student wants to discuss the conservation concerns regarding the bumblebee bat. Which choice most effectively uses relevant information from the notes to accomplish this goal?

(A) The world's smallest mammal, the bumblebee bat, is considered vulnerable due to habitat loss and human disturbance in its native regions of Thailand and Myanmar.

(B) Kitti's hog-nosed bat, also known as the bumblebee bat, is native to limestone caves in Thailand and Myanmar and is the world's smallest mammal.

(C) The bumblebee bat, with a body length of approximately 1.1 to 1.3 inches, is the world's smallest mammal and is native to limestone caves in Thailand and Myanmar.

(D) As the world's smallest mammal, the bumblebee bat is known for its distinctive size and is native to limestone caves in Thailand and Myanmar.

Section 1, Module 1: Reading & Writing

Annotate

23   Mark for Review ⌑

While researching a topic, a student has taken the following notes:

- The Congress of Vienna took place from 1814 to 1815.
- Major European powers convened to redraw the continent's political boundaries after the Napoleonic Wars.
- The Congress aimed to maintain a balance of power in Europe.
- Klemens von Metternich, an Austrian statesman, was a key figure at the Congress.
- The Congress of Vienna is considered a significant event in the history of international diplomacy.

The student wants to explain the primary objective of the Congress of Vienna. Which choice most effectively uses relevant information from the notes to accomplish this goal?

(A) The Congress of Vienna, which took place from 1814 to 1815, was an important gathering of European powers that aimed to maintain a balance of power in Europe.

(B) The Congress of Vienna, a key event in international diplomacy, brought together major European powers in the early 19th century.

(C) Klemens von Metternich, an Austrian statesman, played a significant role in the Congress of Vienna, which sought to maintain a balance of power in Europe.

(D) The Congress of Vienna, a key diplomatic event, reshaped Europe's political atmosphere in the wake of the Napoleonic Wars.

Section 1, Module 1: Reading & Writing

Annotate

24   Mark for Review ⌑

While researching a topic, a student has taken the following notes:

- "The Wind-Up Bird Chronicle" is a novel by Haruki Murakami.
- The story follows Toru Okada, an unemployed man searching for his wife's missing cat.
- The novel weaves together elements of magical realism, history, and the protagonist's personal journey.
- The narrative delves into the impact of World War II on Japan and the protagonist's relationships.
- The title is a reference to a mysterious bird that seems to be connected to several events in the story.

The student wants to emphasize the novel's exploration of the interconnectedness of seemingly unrelated events. Which choice most effectively uses relevant information from the notes to accomplish this goal?

(A) "The Wind-Up Bird Chronicle" centers around Toru Okada's search for his wife's missing cat while also delving into the impact of World War II on Japan.

(B) Haruki Murakami's novel "The Wind-Up Bird Chronicle" combines magical realism, history, and personal relationships to explore the complex web of connections between disparate events.

(C) The mysterious bird in "The Wind-Up Bird Chronicle" plays a significant role in the protagonist's journey and the novel's exploration of World War II.

(D) In "The Wind-Up Bird Chronicle," the protagonist's relationships and personal journey unfold against the backdrop of Japan's history.

Section 1, Module 1: Reading & Writing

Annotate ⋮

While researching a topic, a student has taken the following notes:

- The Doppler effect is a phenomenon that causes a change in frequency and wavelength of a wave in relation to an observer who is moving relative to the wave source.
- The Doppler effect is observed in both sound and light waves.
- When the observer and the source of the wave move toward each other, the observed frequency increases, and the wavelength decreases.
- When the observer and the source of the wave move away from each other, the observed frequency decreases, and the wavelength increases.

25 Mark for Review 🔖

The student wants to describe how the Doppler effect influences the observed frequency and wavelength of a wave. Which choice most effectively uses relevant information from the notes to accomplish this goal?

(A) The Doppler effect is a phenomenon that causes a change in frequency and wavelength of a wave when the observer and the wave source are moving relative to each other, occurring in both sound and light waves. Ⓐ

(B) According to the Doppler effect, when the observer and the wave source move toward each other, the observed frequency increases and the wavelength decreases, while the opposite occurs when they move away from each other. Ⓑ

(C) The Doppler effect impacts the observed frequency and wavelength of sound and light waves, depending on the relative motion of the observer and the wave source, causing either an increase or decrease in frequency and wavelength. Ⓒ

(D) The Doppler effect, a change in frequency or wavelength experienced by an observer moving relative to the source, occurs in both sound and light waves. Ⓓ

TEST QUBE

Back Next

Section 1, Module 1: Reading & Writing

Annotate ⋮

While researching a topic, a student has taken the following notes:

- The Javan Hawk-Eagle, endemic to the island of Java in Indonesia, is a critically endangered bird species.
- This bird's population has dwindled due to deforestation and habitat fragmentation.
- The Javan Hawk-Eagle is a solitary bird that is rarely seen in groups.
- The Andean Condor, found in the Andes mountains, is a near-threatened species.
- The primary threats to the Andean Condor are habitat destruction and secondary poisoning from carcasses.
- The Andean Condor is one of the world's largest flying birds and is known to soar in groups.

26 Mark for Review 🔖

The student wants to highlight a common threat to the two bird species. Which choice most effectively uses relevant information from the notes to accomplish this goal?

(A) Both the Javan Hawk-Eagle and the Andean Condor contend with adverse environmental ramifications such as habitat degradation. Ⓐ

(B) While deforestation challenges the existence of the Javan Hawk-Eagle in Indonesia, the Andean Condor encounters its own set of ecological dilemmas in the vast Andes. Ⓑ

(C) Both the Javan Hawk-Eagle and the Andean Condor, despite their contrasting social behaviors, are indicative of the struggle for provisions faced by avian species in today's changing landscapes. Ⓒ

(D) The Javan Hawk-Eagle, deeply rooted in Indonesia's unique ecosystems, and the Andean Condor, a majestic icon of the Andes, both suffer from the lack of sustenance in their respective habitats. Ⓓ

TEST QUBE

Back Next

I

II

III

IV

V

VI

VII

Section 1, Module 1: Reading & Writing

Annotate ⋮

While researching a topic, a student has taken the following notes:

- A supermassive black hole is a type of black hole with a mass millions or billions of times greater than the Sun.
- Sagittarius A* is the supermassive black hole at the center of the Milky Way galaxy.
- Supermassive black holes are thought to reside at the centers of most galaxies.
- They are theorized to have an impact on galaxy formation and evolution.
- The Event Horizon Telescope captured the first image of a supermassive black hole in 2019.

27 Mark for Review 🔖

The student wants to discuss the role of supermassive black holes in the universe. Which choice most effectively uses relevant information from the notes to accomplish this goal?

 (A) Supermassive black holes, such as Sagittarius A* at the center of the Milky Way, are believed to reside at the centers of most galaxies and may play a role in galaxy formation and evolution. Ⓐ

 (B) A supermassive black hole is a type of black hole with a mass millions or billions of times greater than the Sun, and they can be found at the centers of most galaxies. Ⓑ

 (C) In 2019, the Event Horizon Telescope captured the first image of a supermassive black hole, providing valuable insights into these massive cosmic phenomena and their role in the universe. Ⓒ

 (D) Sagittarius A*, the supermassive black hole at the center of the Milky Way galaxy, is an example of the immense cosmic phenomena that are thought to impact the formation and evolution of galaxies. Ⓓ

Move on to the
Next Section ➤➤

Section 1, Module 2: Reading & Writing

🕐 32:00

Annotate ⋮

In an effort to conserve resources and minimize their ecological footprint, the company implemented a series of _____ measures, such as reducing energy consumption and utilizing recyclable materials in their production processes.

1   Mark for Review 🔖

Which choice completes the text with the most logical and precise word or phrase?

(A) sustainable

(B) extravagant

(C) impulsive

(D) ephemeral

TEST⬛QUBE

Question 1 of 27 >

Back Next

Section 1, Module 2: Reading & Writing

Annotate ⋮

The documentary filmmaker's unobtrusive approach allowed her subjects to speak candidly, providing a rare and intimate glimpse into their lives. Her ability to remain _____ enabled her to capture authentic moments that might otherwise have gone unnoticed.

2   Mark for Review 🔖

Which choice completes the text with the most logical and precise word or phrase?

(A) intrusive

(B) conspicuous

(C) unassuming

(D) ostentatious

TEST⬛QUBE

Question 2 of 27 >

Back Next

Section 1, Module 2: Reading & Writing

Annotate

Despite the significant advancements in medical technology, certain diseases continue to elude effective treatment options. This lack of progress only serves to _____ the importance of ongoing research and development.

3   Mark for Review

Which choice completes the text with the most logical and precise word or phrase?

- (A) undermine
- (B) underscore
- (C) trivialize
- (D) encumber

TEST❖QUBE

Back   Next

Section 1, Module 2: Reading & Writing

Annotate

The novel's protagonist, faced with seemingly insurmountable challenges, draws strength from her inner resilience and resourcefulness. Her character _____ throughout the story, ultimately leading her to overcome the obstacles in her path.

4   Mark for Review

Which choice completes the text with the most logical and precise word or phrase?

- (A) stagnates
- (B) deteriorates
- (C) flourishes
- (D) capitulates

TEST❖QUBE

Back   Next

Annotate

The following text is adapted from Henry David Thoreau's 1849 essay "Civil Disobedience."

All voting is a sort of gaming, like chequers or backgammon, with a slight moral tinge to it, a playing with right and wrong, with moral questions; and betting naturally accompanies it. The character of the voters is not staked. I cast my vote, perchance, as I think right; but I am not vitally concerned that that right should prevail. I am willing to leave it to the majority. Its obligation, therefore, never exceeds that of expediency. Even voting for the right is doing nothing for it. It is only expressing to men feebly your desire that it should prevail. A wise man will not leave the right to the mercy of chance, nor wish it to prevail through the power of the majority.

5 Mark for Review

Which choice best describes the function of the underlined sentence in the text as a whole?

(A) It elaborates on a claim about the ambivalence in voting made earlier in the text.

(B) It offers an insight into the personal disposition of voters in the democratic process discussed earlier in the text.

(C) It presents a nuanced critique of the common assumption around the efficacy of voting, as discussed earlier in the text.

(D) It sets up a counter argument for the pragmatic approach of voters discussed later in the text.

TEST QUBE

Back Next

Annotate

The following text is adapted from Sir Arthur Conan Doyle's 1903 short story "The Adventure of the Dancing Men." Sherlock Holmes is faced with a peculiar case involving coded messages.

Sherlock Holmes preserved his calm professional manner until our visitor had left us, although it was easy for me, who knew him so well, to see that he was profoundly excited. The moment that Hilton Cubitt's broad back had disappeared through the door my comrade rushed to the table, laid out all the slips of paper containing dancing men in front of him, and threw himself into an intricate and elaborate calculation. For two hours I watched him as he covered sheet after sheet of paper with figures and letters, so completely absorbed in his task that he had evidently forgotten my presence. Sometimes he was making progress and whistled and sang at his work; sometimes he was puzzled, and would sit for long spells with a furrowed brow and a vacant eye.

6 Mark for Review

Which choice best states the main purpose of the text?

(A) To demonstrate the dynamic nature of Sherlock Holmes' problem solving process

(B) To emphasize Sherlock Holmes' disregard for his surroundings when engrossed in his work

(C) To illustrate the emotional swings Sherlock Holmes experiences while deciphering clues

(D) To portray Sherlock Holmes' intense focus and dedication when solving complex cases

TEST QUBE

Back Next

Section 1, Module 2: Reading & Writing

Annotate

The following text is from T.S. Eliot's 1922 poem "The Waste Land."

April is the cruellest month, breeding
Lilacs out of the dead land, mixing
Memory and desire, stirring
Dull roots with spring rain.
Winter kept us warm, covering
Earth in forgetful snow, feeding
A little life with dried tubers.
Summer surprised us, coming over the Starnbergersee

7   Mark for Review 🔖

Which choice best describes the overall structure of the text?

(A) The speaker chronicles the passage of time, then offers a diatribe against the monotony of modern life.

(B) The speaker reflects on the impermanence of human achievements, then alludes to a personal tragedy.

(C) The speaker discusses the contradictory aspects of the seasons, then juxtaposes them with human emotions.

(D) The speaker contemplates on the transformative power of nature and then denounces its capricious character.

TEST⬛QUBE

 Back   Next

Section 1, Module 2: Reading & Writing

Annotate

The following text is adapted from John Stuart Mill's 1869 essay "On Liberty."

To prevent the weaker members of the community from being preyed upon by innumerable vultures, it was needful that there should be an animal of prey stronger than the rest, commissioned to keep them down. But as the king of the vultures would be no less bent upon preying on the flock than any of the minor harpies, it was indispensable to be in a perpetual attitude of defense against his beak and claws. The aim, therefore, of patriots, was to set limits to the power which the ruler should be suffered to exercise over the community; and this limitation was what they meant by liberty.

8   Mark for Review 🔖

Which choice best describes the function of the underlined portion in the text as a whole?

(A) It offers a rationale behind the necessity for checks and balances in governance as discussed in the previous sentence.

(B) It underscores the primary objective of patriots, delineating their role in safeguarding community freedoms.

(C) It warns against the consequences of setting limits to the power of the ruler by reiterating the importance of protection.

(D) It explains the concept of liberty by connecting it to the limitation of a ruler's power as portrayed in the analogy.

TEST⬛QUBE

 Back   Next

Section 1, Module 2: Reading & Writing

Annotate

Text 1
Galactic formations and their subsequent developments hold significant positions in our comprehensive understanding of the Universe. A prevalent hypothesis endorsed by many scientists suggests that galaxies are born out of the collapse of massive clouds of gas and dust, governed by gravitational forces. Post-formation, these celestial entities are believed to evolve by merging with other galaxies. The specific mechanics of these processes, their variations across diverse galaxy types, are topics under continuous scientific deliberation.

Text 2
Dr. Emily Sutton and her colleagues introduce an alternative lens to study galaxy formation and evolution in their recent publication. Their research highlights that the conventional theory, largely emphasizing gravitational influences and galactic merging, may overlook the intricacy of observed galactic diversity. Their proposed model encompasses a broader set of influences including stellar winds, supernova explosions, and the implications of dark matter, implying these aspects potentially play significant roles in defining a galaxy's attributes.

9   Mark for Review 🔖

Based on the texts, how would Dr. Sutton and her team (Text 2) most likely characterize the hypothesis presented in Text 1?

(A) As inconclusive, because it overlooks key factors that could play a role in galactic formation and evolution.

(B) As misguided, because it overly simplifies the complex process of galactic formation.

(C) As outdated, because it fails to consider the implications of more recent discoveries, like dark matter.

(D) As persuasive, because it effectively explains the role of gravity and merging in the formation and evolution of galaxies.

Section 1, Module 2: Reading & Writing

Annotate

Country	Internet Usage (hours/week)	Happiness Index	Mental illness Incidence
Alpha	10	70	13%
Beta	20	65	5%
Gamma	30	60	40%
Delta	40	55	30%
Epsilon	50	50	93%

The table presents data on the average internet usage per week and happiness index for five countries. The happiness index ranges from 0 (least happy) to 100 (happiest). Researchers claim that countries with higher internet usage tend to have lower happiness indices. However, researchers cite that the more happy a country is, by no means does that translate to lower incidence of mental health issues. Internet usage has a more variable, less predictable effect on the frequency of mental health problems among the population.

10   Mark for Review 🔖

Which choice best describes data from the graph that supports the researchers' conclusion?

(A) Country Alpha has the lowest internet usage, highest happiness index, and lowest mental health incidence.

(B) Country Delta, despite having a high internet usage rate, has among the highest mental health illness incidence.

(C) Country Gamma, despite having a higher happiness index than Country Delta, has higher mental health incidence.

(D) Country Epsilon has the highest internet usage and the lowest happiness index.

Section 1, Module 2: Reading & Writing

Annotate

The Hadley cell is a large-scale atmospheric circulation pattern that transports heat from the equator to higher latitudes in both hemispheres. These circulation patterns are responsible for the formation of trade winds, tropical rain belts, and subtropical deserts. A climatologist claims that changes in Hadley cell dynamics can have significant impacts on global climate and weather patterns.

11 Mark for Review

Which finding, if true, would most directly support the climatologist's claim?

(A) Hadley cells are driven by the uneven heating of Earth's surface, with warm air rising near the equator and moving poleward before cooling and sinking at higher latitudes.

(B) In a changing climate, simulations show that the edges of the Hadley cells may expand poleward, potentially altering precipitation patterns and leading to more extreme weather events in some regions.

(C) The descending branches of the Hadley cells create areas of high pressure, which are associated with clear skies and dry conditions in subtropical regions.

(D) The Coriolis effect, due to Earth's rotation, causes the trade winds to blow from east to west in both hemispheres, influencing the movement of weather systems and ocean currents.

TEST⬛QUBE

Back Next

Section 1, Module 2: Reading & Writing

Annotate

Conductivity at Various PHs

Chemists Brown and Baker investigated the relationship between the pH level of various solutions and their conductivity. They collected data on the conductivity of four solutions with different pH levels. They also applied two levels of heat to each solution. Brown and Baker argued that for higher levels of pH, the increased heat level lead to sizeable increases in the level of conductivity compared to lower levels of pH.

12 Mark for Review

Which statement best describes data from the graph that supports the chemists' claim?

(A) The conductivity of the solutions increases as the pH levels increase.

(B) At pH8, the increased heat level created a conductivity level dramatically higher than that of ph11 when given extra heat.

(C) At pH 11, the increased heat level created a conductivity level dramatically higher than that of ph2 when given extra heat.

(D) At pH2, the increased heat level created a conductivity level dramatically higher than that of ph11 when given extra heat.

TEST⬛QUBE

Back Next

Section 1, Module 2: Reading & Writing

 Annotate ⋮

Urban planners have long observed that neighborhoods with an abundance of trees and green spaces tend to exhibit lower crime rates. Jane Smith, a prominent urban planner, conducted an extensive study comparing neighborhoods with varying tree densities across several cities, taking into account various socio-economic factors. Her research concluded that the presence of more trees catalyzes increased social interaction among residents, engendering a sense of community and subsequently mitigating crime rates. Smith's analysis also considered the aesthetics of green spaces, which she hypothesized had a positive impact on residents' well-being and overall mood. Furthermore, the study investigated the effects of access to parks and other green areas on mental health and community bonds.

13   Mark for Review 🔖

Which finding, if true, would most directly undermine Smith's hypothesis?

- (A) In some tree-laden neighborhoods, crime rates remain low due to external factors, such as poverty control and drug rehab, which obfuscate the relationship between trees and crime rates.

- (B) In a few neighborhoods not included in the study, there is a surplus of trees, but crime rates remain high.

- (C) In some neighborhoods, the introduction of community gardens and various social programs had a more salient impact on crime reduction than the presence of trees.

- (D) In numerous neighborhoods within the study, there is a correlation between the proliferation of trees and increased property values.

TEST🧊QUBE

Back Next

Section 1, Module 2: Reading & Writing

 Annotate ⋮

Sojourner Truth, a prominent abolitionist and women's rights advocate, delivered powerful speeches that inspired many during the 19th century. A historian claims that Truth's famous "Ain't I a Woman?" speech, delivered at a women's rights convention in 1851, played a crucial role in uniting the causes of abolition and women's rights.

14   Mark for Review 🔖

Which finding, if correct, would most directly support the historian's assertion?

- (A) Sojourner Truth's speech emphasized the shared struggles faced by both enslaved African Americans and women, arguing for the interconnectedness of the abolition and women's rights movements.

- (B) Truth's activism facilitated encounters with eminent figures such as President Abraham Lincoln and suffragist Susan B. Anthony, demonstrating the far-reaching ramifications of her work.

- (C) After gaining her freedom. Sojourner Truth successfully sued for the return of her son, Peter, from a slave owner, making her one of the first African American women to win such a case in court.

- (D) Sojourner Truth's life and speeches were documented in her autobiography, "The Narrative of Sojourner Truth," which continues to inspire readers and activists to this day.

TEST🧊QUBE

Back Next

Section 1, Module 2: Reading & Writing

Annotate ⋮

The Gouldian finch (Erythrura gouldiae), a brightly colored bird native to Australia, is known for its remarkable head color polymorphism, with individuals exhibiting red, black, or yellow head coloration. Researchers have discovered that head color is associated with different behavioral and physiological traits, which could influence mate choice. In one study, it was found that red-headed males are more aggressive, while black-headed males have higher levels of stress tolerance. These traits could be advantageous under different environmental conditions. If female Gouldian finches are observed to show a preference for red-headed males in environments with abundant resources and low predation risk, but for black-headed males in environments with limited resources and high predation risk, this would suggest that ____

15 Mark for Review 🔖

Which choice most logically completes the text?

(A) head coloration in Gouldian finches is purely aesthetic and has no adaptive significance.

(B) female Gouldian finches are capable of adjusting their mate preferences based on environmental conditions.

(C) yellow-headed Gouldian finches are less likely to reproduce compared to red- or black-headed individuals.

(D) the relationship between head coloration and behavioral traits is not consistent across different bird species.

TEST🔲QUBE   Question 15 of 27 >   Back Next

Section 1, Module 2: Reading & Writing

Annotate ⋮

Brexit, the process of the United Kingdom (UK) leaving the European Union (EU), has had significant consequences for trade between the UK and EU member countries. One potential consequence of Brexit is the imposition of non-tariff barriers, which could increase the costs of trade and reduce the volume of goods traded between the UK and the EU. Studies have shown that non-tariff barriers can have a greater impact on trade than tariff barriers, such as import taxes. If post-Brexit trade data shows that the volume of goods traded between the UK and the EU has decreased despite no significant increase in tariff barriers, this would suggest that ____

16 Mark for Review 🔖

Which choice most logically completes the text?

(A) non-tariff barriers have likely played a significant role in reducing trade between the UK and the EU after Brexit.

(B) Brexit has had no real impact on trade between the UK and the EU.

(C) tariff barriers are more important than non-tariff barriers in determining trade patterns.

(D) trade between the UK and EU member countries was not affected by Brexit-related negotiations.

TEST🔲QUBE   Question 16 of 27 >   Back Next

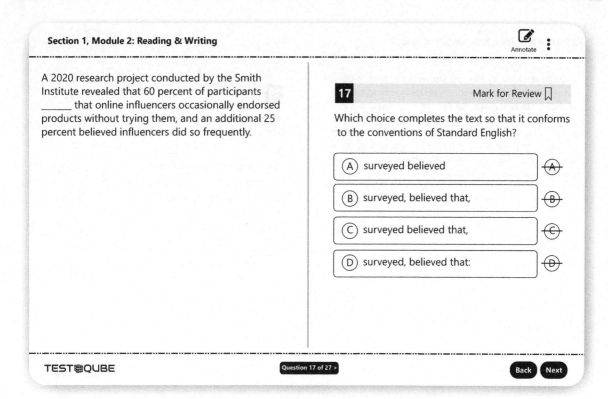

Annotate

A 2020 research project conducted by the Smith Institute revealed that 60 percent of participants _____ that online influencers occasionally endorsed products without trying them, and an additional 25 percent believed influencers did so frequently.

17   Mark for Review

Which choice completes the text so that it conforms to the conventions of Standard English?

(A) surveyed believed

(B) surveyed, believed that,

(C) surveyed believed that,

(D) surveyed, believed that:

TEST⬛QUBE   Question 17 of 27 >   Back   Next

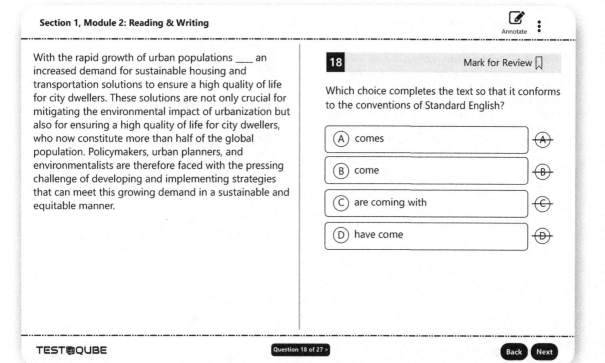

Annotate

With the rapid growth of urban populations ___ an increased demand for sustainable housing and transportation solutions to ensure a high quality of life for city dwellers. These solutions are not only crucial for mitigating the environmental impact of urbanization but also for ensuring a high quality of life for city dwellers, who now constitute more than half of the global population. Policymakers, urban planners, and environmentalists are therefore faced with the pressing challenge of developing and implementing strategies that can meet this growing demand in a sustainable and equitable manner.

18   Mark for Review

Which choice completes the text so that it conforms to the conventions of Standard English?

(A) comes

(B) come

(C) are coming with

(D) have come

TEST⬛QUBE   Question 18 of 27 >   Back   Next

I
II
III
IV
V
VI
VII

Section 1, Module 2: Reading & Writing

Annotate ⋮

A study released by Harvard University ecologist Dr. Jane Foster in 2020 provides a novel insight into the complex social behavior of African _____ networks called clans, extensive communities that emerge when multiple related family groups interact with one another, cooperate in resource sharing, and provide assistance during challenging circumstances, such as droughts or predator threats.

19   Mark for Review 🔖

Which choice completes the text so that it conforms to the conventions of Standard English?

(A) elephants intricate   Ⓐ

(B) elephants: intricate   Ⓑ

(C) elephants; intricate   Ⓒ

(D) elephants. Intricate   Ⓓ

TEST⬛QUBE   Question 19 of 27 >   Back   Next

Section 1, Module 2: Reading & Writing

Annotate ⋮

What the ancient Egyptians accomplished in the fields of art, architecture, and science ___ still a source of fascination and admiration for modern scholars. These scholars, through their meticulous research and analysis, strive to unravel the mysteries of this ancient civilization and gain insights into its profound influence on subsequent cultures and societies.

20   Mark for Review 🔖

Which choice completes the text so that it conforms to the conventions of Standard English?

(A) has been   Ⓐ

(B) are   Ⓑ

(C) is   Ⓒ

(D) have been   Ⓓ

TEST⬛QUBE   Question 20 of 27 >   Back   Next

Section 1, Module 2: Reading & Writing   Annotate ⋮

A Colorado research institution revealed that hands-on projects assist emerging innovators in cultivating a crucial _____ aptitude, that enables innovators to discern unresolved challenges that can be transformed into profitable ventures. This aptitude not only equips these innovators with the ability to identify gaps in the market but also fosters their creative problem-solving skills, thereby empowering them to devise innovative solutions that can potentially revolutionize industries, stimulate economic growth, and contribute to societal progress.

21   Mark for Review 🔖

Which choice completes the text so that it conforms to the conventions of Standard English?

- (A) ability, problem-solving   Ⓐ
- (B) ability; problem-solving   Ⓑ
- (C) ability problem-solving   Ⓒ
- (D) ability. Problem-solving   Ⓓ

TEST◉QUBE   Question 21 of 27 >   Back   Next

Section 1, Module 2: Reading & Writing   Annotate ⋮

The study's focus was the African elephant. Johnson and Thompson investigated how two _____of elephants—the smaller forest-dwelling ones and the larger savanna-dwelling ones—adapted when introduced to new environments.

22   Mark for Review 🔖

Which choice completes the text so that it confirms to the conventions of Standard English?

- (A) subspecies, or, regional populations,
- (B) subspecies or regional populations,
- (C) subspecies or, regional populations
- (D) subspecies, or regional populations,

TEST◉QUBE   Question 22 of 27 >   Back   Next

Section 1, Module 2: Reading & Writing

Annotate

⋮

In 2018, marine biologist Dr. Sylvia Earle was exploring the depths of the Coral Sea in Australia when she observed a peculiar species of bioluminescent _____ the help of advanced underwater imaging technology, she captured the stunning display of the corals, which emitted a radiant glow in a variety of colors.

23   Mark for Review 🔖

Which choice completes the text so that it conforms to the conventions of Standard English?

(A) coral, with

(B) coral. With

(C) coral so with

(D) coral with

Section 1, Module 2: Reading & Writing

Annotate

⋮

Fossil fuels, such as coal, oil, and natural gas, have been the primary sources of energy for industrialized societies. They power vehicles, generate electricity, and support manufacturing processes. _____ the combustion of fossil fuels releases greenhouse gases, contributing to global warming and air pollution.

24   Mark for Review 🔖

Which choice completes the text with the most logical transition?

(A) In addition,

(B) However,

(C) As a result,

(D) Therefore,

Section 1, Module 2: Reading & Writing

Annotate ⋮

The Internet, a global system of interconnected computer networks, has dramatically transformed the way we access and share information. It enables instant communication, facilitates research, and promotes global collaboration. _____ concerns over privacy, misinformation, and cybersecurity continue to grow as our reliance on the Internet increases.

25 Mark for Review 🔖

Which choice completes the text with the most logical transition?

- (A) Similarly,
- (B) In conclusion,
- (C) Nevertheless,
- (D) As a consequence,

TEST QUBE

Question 25 of 27 >

Back Next

Section 1, Module 2: Reading & Writing

Annotate ⋮

The Wright brothers, Orville and Wilbur, are credited with inventing the first successful airplane. Their historic flight at Kitty Hawk in 1903 marked the beginning of modern aviation. _____ advancements in aircraft design and technology have allowed for faster, safer, and more efficient air travel.

26 Mark for Review 🔖

Which choice completes the text with the most logical transition?

- (A) In contrast,
- (B) Subsequently,
- (C) However,
- (D) Regardless,

TEST QUBE

Question 26 of 27 >

Back Next

I

II

III

IV

V

VI

VII

Section 1, Module 2: Reading & Writing

Annotate

While researching a topic, a student has taken the following notes:

- The Balfour Declaration of 1917 expressed British support for the establishment of a "national home for the Jewish people" in Palestine.
- The declaration was made during World War I, at a time when Britain and its allies were seeking Jewish support for the war effort.
- The declaration was controversial among Palestinians, who constituted the majority population in Palestine at the time.
- The declaration is viewed by some as a primary cause of the ongoing Israeli-Palestinian conflict.

27   Mark for Review

The student wants to discuss the possible ramifications of the Balfour Declaration. Which choice most effectively uses relevant information from the notes to accomplish this goal?

(A) The Balfour Declaration was made during World War I to gather Jewish support for the war effort.

(B) The Balfour Declaration's statement of support for a Jewish national home in Palestine is viewed by some as a primary cause of the Israeli-Palestinian conflict.

(C) The Balfour Declaration was controversial due to its timing during World War I.

(D) The Balfour Declaration was made to establish Palestine as a national home for the Jewish people, which was controversial among the Palestinian majority.

TEST◈QUBE   **End of Test 3 Reading/Writing Section**   Back Next

Upcoming Math Section: Reference Formula Sheet

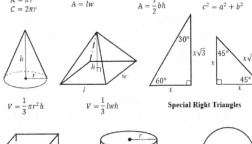

$A = \pi r^2$
$C = 2\pi r$

$A = lw$

$A = \frac{1}{2}bh$

$c^2 = a^2 + b^2$

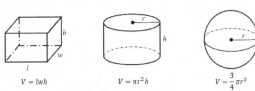

$V = \frac{1}{3}\pi r^2 h$

$V = \frac{1}{3}lwh$

Special Right Triangles

$V = lwh$

$V = \pi r^2 h$

$V = \frac{3}{4}\pi r^3$

The number of degrees of arc in a circle is 360.
The number of radians of arc in a circle is 2π.
The sum of the measures in degrees of the angles of a triangle is 180.

Directions for Student-Produced Response

- **TEST QUBE** recommends students to use decimals for most answers but suggests using fractions only in cases where the answers involve repeating decimals (e.g., 0.333 = 1/3)
- For cases with more than one answer, enter **just one of the answers.**
- You can enter up to 5 characters for your answer. (For negative answers, the **negative sign** does not count as one character)
- For **fractions** that don't fit the answer box, enter the decimal equivalent (Unless advised to do otherwise)
- For **decimals** that exceed the answer box, round to the fourth digit. (Unless advised to do otherwise)
- For mixed number (such as $4\frac{1}{4}$), enter it as an improper fraction ($17/4$) or its decimal equivalent (4.25)
- For all answers, you may omit the symbols and units such as $.%, cm^3, m^2, etc.

Acceptable vs Non-Acceptable Answers

Answer	Acceptable ways to receive credit	Ways you WON'T receive credit
4.25	4.25 , 17/4	41/4 , 4 1/4
4/6	2/3 .6666 , .6667 0.666 , 0.667	0.66 , .66 0.67 , .67
-1/6	-1/6 -0.166 , -0.167 -.1666 , -.1667	-0.16 , -.16 -0.17, -.167

Move on to the
Next Section

Section 2, Module 1: Math   ✎ Annotate ⋮

1   Mark for Review 🔖

$f(x)$ is defined by $f(x) = 2x - 12$. What is the value of x when $f(x) = 2$?

Ⓐ -12 Ⓐ

Ⓑ -8 Ⓑ

Ⓒ 2 Ⓒ

Ⓓ 7 Ⓓ

TEST⬢QUBE   Question 1 of 22 >

Section 2, Module 1: Math   ✎ Annotate ⋮

2   Mark for Review 🔖

Stephanie is planning to hold a party. She intends to spend no more than 140 dollars on decorating the party room and preparing the food. The room decoration costs 38 dollars regardless of the number of guests, and food preparation costs 9 dollars per guest. Which of the following expressions is most appropriate to find the maximum number of guests, g?

Ⓐ $38 - 9g \leq 140$ Ⓐ

Ⓑ $38 + 9g \geq 140$ Ⓑ

Ⓒ $9 + 39g \leq 140$ Ⓒ

Ⓓ $38 + 9g \leq 140$ Ⓓ

TEST⬢QUBE   Question 2 of 22 >

Section 2, Module 1: Math   ✎ Annotate ⋮

3   Mark for Review 🔖

Which of the following is a common factor of $x(x + 2)$ and $x^2 + 4x + 4$?

Ⓐ x Ⓐ

Ⓑ x^2 Ⓑ

Ⓒ $x + 2$ Ⓒ

Ⓓ $x + 4x + 4$ Ⓓ

TEST⬢QUBE   Question 3 of 22 >

Section 2, Module 1: Math   ✎ Annotate ⋮

4   Mark for Review 🔖

Note: Figure Not Drawn to Scale

Line a intersects with parallel lines l and m in the diagram shown above. What is the value of x?

[   ]

TEST⬢QUBE   Question 4 of 22 >   Back   Next

  Annotate   ⋮

5   Mark for Review 🔖

What is the sum of two distinct real solutions for $x^2 - 6x - 16$?

TEST◆QUBE

  Annotate   ⋮

6   Mark for Review 🔖

Each side of a right hexagon H whose area is $24\sqrt{3}$ is 4 units long. What is the area of a right hexagon J that has a side length of 2?

- (A) $3\sqrt{3}$
- (B) $6\sqrt{3}$
- (C) $12\sqrt{3}$
- (D) $48\sqrt{3}$

TEST◆QUBE

  Annotate   ⋮

7   Mark for Review 🔖

Light travels at a constant speed of $300,000$ kilometers per second in a vacuum. However, the speed of light is halved in water. How long, in kilometers, would light travel in 10 seconds underwater?

- (A) $3,000,000 km$
- (B) $1,500,000 km$
- (C) $750,000 km$
- (D) $300,000 km$

TEST◆QUBE

  Annotate   ⋮

8   Mark for Review 🔖

$y = -4x + 4$
$x - 1 = 16$
(x, y) is a solution for the given system of equations. What is the value of y?

- (A) -1
- (B) -4
- (C) -16
- (D) -64

TEST◆QUBE   Back   Next

9   Mark for Review 🔖

$11, 9, 17, 15, 3$

Data set S consists of five values as shown above. What is the mean value of data set S?

11   Mark for Review 🔖

Which of the following expressions is equivalent to $2ab$?

- (A) $\frac{a^2b^2}{2ab}$ Ⓐ
- (B) $\frac{2a^{-1}b}{b}$ Ⓑ
- (C) $\frac{2a}{b}$ Ⓒ
- (D) $\frac{2a^2}{ab^{-1}}$ Ⓓ

10   Mark for Review 🔖

The graphs of $y = \sqrt{x} - 2$ and $x = 4$ intersect at exactly one point $P(x, y)$. What is the value of y?

- (A) -3 Ⓐ
- (B) 0 Ⓑ
- (C) 3 Ⓒ
- (D) 6 Ⓓ

12   Mark for Review 🔖

Nutrient	Calories per gram
Carbohydrate	4 kcal/g
Fat	9 kcal/g
Protein	4 kcal/g

The table above shows the calories for each nutrient: carbohydrate, fat, and protein. For example, 1 gram of protein contains 4 kcal. A serving of certain food consists of 30 grams of fat and carbohydrates together and contains no protein. If the food contains 210 kcal per serving, how many calories, in kcal, in a serving of the food are from fat?

Section 2, Module 1: Math

Annotate

13   Mark for Review 🔖

1 foot equals 12 inches. How much is 1 cubic foot (ft^3) in cubic inches?

(A) 12

(B) 144

(C) 1,728

(D) 20,736

Section 2, Module 1: Math

Annotate

14   Mark for Review 🔖

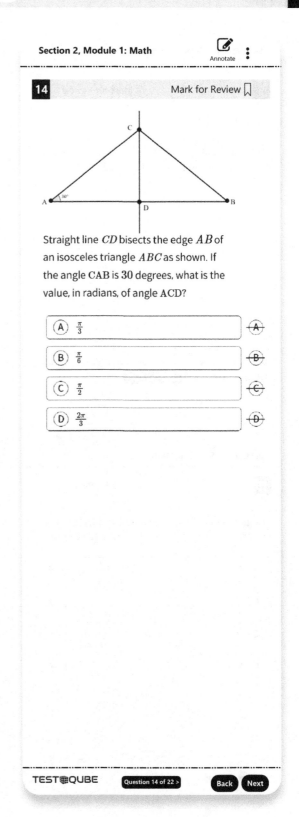

Straight line CD bisects the edge AB of an isosceles triangle ABC as shown. If the angle CAB is 30 degrees, what is the value, in radians, of angle ACD?

(A) $\frac{\pi}{3}$

(B) $\frac{\pi}{6}$

(C) $\frac{\pi}{2}$

(D) $\frac{2\pi}{3}$

15   Mark for Review 🔖

$S(t) = 30 + 2t$
The formula above models the speed of a car t seconds after passing the speed enforcement camera in $\frac{miles}{hour}$. Find the speed of the car, in $\frac{miles}{hour}$, 3 seconds after the event.

16   Mark for Review 🔖

Function g is defined by $g(x) = 1.5^x$. What is the value of x if $g(x) = 1.5$?

- (A) 0
- (B) 1
- (C) 1.5
- (D) 2

17   Mark for Review 🔖

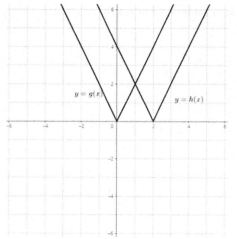

The graph of $g(x) = |2x|$ on the xy-plane is given. The graph of $h(x)$ is generated by pushing the graph of $g(x)$ by 2 units to the right. Which of the following correctly defines $h(x)$?

- (A) $h(x) = |2x| + 2$
- (B) $h(x) = |2(x + 2)|$
- (C) $h(x) = |2(x - 2)|$
- (D) $h(x) = |2x| - 2$

18 Mark for Review 🔖

Function f is defined by $f(x) = x^2 - 7$. What is the minimum value of $f(x)$?

19 Mark for Review 🔖

Data set X
$12, 9, 5, 5, 1, 1, 1, 9, 1, 8$

Restaurant B replaces the knife when the durability of the knife reaches below 95%. Durability is defined as the proportion of the knife's original strength or effectiveness that remains after a certain period of use. The formula $D(w) = 100(0.99)^w$ models the durability of a knife in Restaurant B, w weeks after the purchase. Data set X represents the period of use of all 10 knives in Restaurant B in weeks. How many knives in Restaurant B are subject to replacement?

20 Mark for Review 🔖

What is a solution for an equation $x^3 - 27 = 0$?

(A) -3

(B) 0

(C) 3

(D) 9

21   Mark for Review 🔖

The median payment of 21 employees of Company A is 49,000 dollars per year. Which of the following changes in Company A cannot possibly change the median payment?

- (A) The company hires 2 more interns each of who receives 32,000 dollars per year.   ~~(A)~~
- (B) The company decides to cut down every employee's annual payment by 1,000 dollars.   ~~(B)~~
- (C) The company pays an extra 2,000 dollars for an employee who receives the top payment.   ~~(C)~~
- (D) The company doubles all employee payments.   ~~(D)~~

22   Mark for Review 🔖

The density of a certain steel is 0.25 pounds per cubic inch. Which of the following answer choices most accurately shows the mass, in pounds, of a metal sphere with a diameter of 6 inches?

- (A) 13 pounds   ~~(A)~~
- (B) 28 pounds   ~~(B)~~
- (C) 113 pounds   ~~(C)~~
- (D) 339 pounds   ~~(D)~~

Move on to the Next Section »

Section 2, Module 2: Math

1   Mark for Review 🔖

GDP Per Capita

The given graph represents the four-year change in a particular country's Gross Domestic Product per capita, in dollars per capita. In which year in the four years did the country have the highest GDP per capita?

(A) 2018

(B) 2019

(C) 2020

(D) 2021

Section 2, Module 2: Math

2   Mark for Review 🔖

Various dating systems call a year differently. For example, the year 2023 in Gregorian Calendar equals the year 2567 in Buddhist Calendar. Assuming the starting date and length of a year are the same, the year in Gregorian Calendar G can be modeled in a linear function $f(B)$ where B is the year in Buddhist Calendar, such that $f(B) = B + c$ where c is constant. What is the value of c?

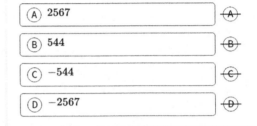

(A) 2567

(B) 544

(C) -544

(D) -2567

Section 2, Module 2: Math

3   Mark for Review 🔖

Which of the following expressions is equivalent to $xy + 2x^2y^2 - xy^3$?

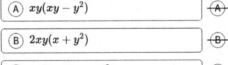

(A) $xy(xy - y^2)$

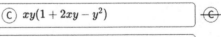

(B) $2xy(x + y^2)$

(C) $xy(1 + 2xy - y^2)$

(D) $y(xy + 2x^2 - y)$

Section 2, Module 2: Math   Annotate ⋮

4   Mark for Review 🔖

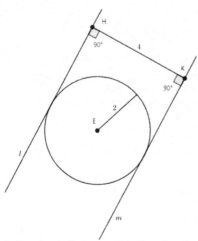

In the shown figure, straight lines l and m are tangent to a circle with a radius of 2 units. HK is perpendicular to both lines l and m and is 4 units long. At how many points do lines l and m intersect?

- (A) 0   A̶
- (B) 1   B̶
- (C) 2   C̶
- (D) Infinitely many   D̶

Section 2, Module 2: Math   Annotate ⋮

5   Mark for Review 🔖

Emily has 21 chairs in her office. Some of the chairs have four legs each, while the others have three legs each. If there are a total of 72 legs, how many three-legged chairs does Emily have in her office?

[   ]

Section 2, Module 2: Math   Annotate ⋮

6   Mark for Review 🔖

Function f is defined by $f(x) = \frac{1}{x} + 2$. What is the value of $f(\frac{1}{2})$?

- (A) $\frac{5}{2}$ A̶
- (B) 3   B̶
- (C) $\frac{7}{2}$ C̶
- (D) 4   D̶

I
II
III
IV
V
VI
VII

7   Mark for Review 🔖

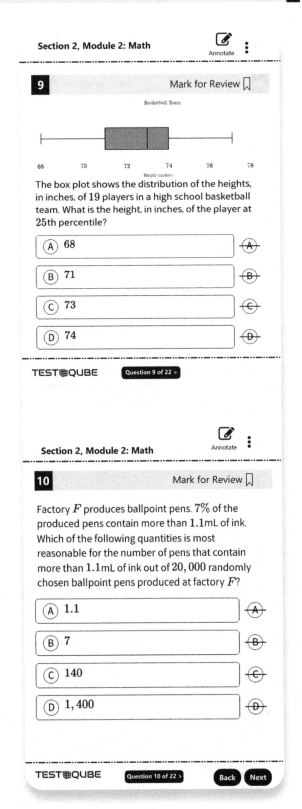

In a given figure, LO and MN are parallel sides of trapezoid $LMNO$. The mean of the lengths LO and MN is 8 units. If the area of trapezoid $LMNO$ is 32 square units, what is the height of the trapezoid $LMNO$?

TEST◉QUBE   Question 7 of 22 >

8   Mark for Review 🔖

Which of the following statements is true for a circle that is defined by $(x + 2)^2 + (y - 1)^2 = 4$?

(A) It has a radius of 4 units.   Ⓐ

(B) It is tangent to the y-axis.   Ⓑ

(C) Its center is $(1, 2)$.   Ⓒ

(D) It has a diameter of 2 units.   Ⓓ

TEST◉QUBE   Question 8 of 22 >

9   Mark for Review 🔖

Basketball Team

68   70   72   74   76   78
Height (inches)

The box plot shows the distribution of the heights, in inches, of 19 players in a high school basketball team. What is the height, in inches, of the player at 25th percentile?

(A) 68   Ⓐ

(B) 71   Ⓑ

(C) 73   Ⓒ

(D) 74   Ⓓ

TEST◉QUBE   Question 9 of 22 >

10   Mark for Review 🔖

Factory F produces ballpoint pens. 7% of the produced pens contain more than 1.1mL of ink. Which of the following quantities is most reasonable for the number of pens that contain more than 1.1mL of ink out of $20,000$ randomly chosen ballpoint pens produced at factory F?

(A) 1.1 Ⓐ

(B) 7 Ⓑ

(C) 140 Ⓒ

(D) $1,400$ Ⓓ

TEST◉QUBE   Question 10 of 22 >   Back   Next

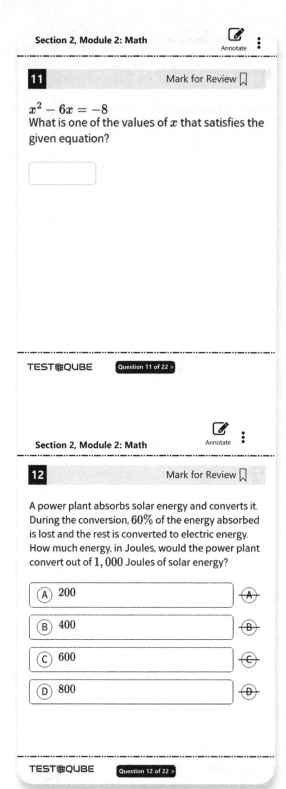

11 Mark for Review 🔖

$x^2 - 6x = -8$

What is one of the values of x that satisfies the given equation?

12 Mark for Review 🔖

A power plant absorbs solar energy and converts it. During the conversion, 60% of the energy absorbed is lost and the rest is converted to electric energy. How much energy, in Joules, would the power plant convert out of $1,000$ Joules of solar energy?

(A) 200

(B) 400

(C) 600

(D) 800

13 Mark for Review 🔖

Which of the following expressions has the same value as $2\sqrt{2}$?

(A) 2^2

(B) $\frac{8}{2}$

(C) $\sqrt{8}$

(D) $\sqrt{4}$

14 Mark for Review 🔖

When a printer starts printing, it loads document data from a computer and prints out the document. Amma's printer always takes 12 seconds to load data and prints 10 pages per minute. Which of the following functions correctly models the time T, in seconds, it takes for Amma's printer to start loading a document and complete printing p pages?

(A) $T(p) = 12 + 6p$

(B) $T(p) = 6 + \frac{1}{12}p$

(C) $T(p) = 12 + 10p$

(D) $T(p) = 12 + \frac{1}{10}p$

Annotate

15
Mark for Review

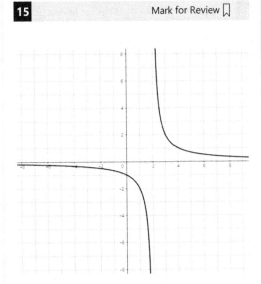

The graph of $y = \frac{2}{x-2}$ is shown. Which of the following values of x does not have a corresponding y value?

(A) 1

(B) 2

(C) 3

(D) 4

  Annotate

16
Mark for Review

Which of the equations represents a line that has a slope of -1 and a y-intercept of 6?

(A) $y = x + 6$

(B) $y = x - 6$

(C) $y = -x + 6$

(D) $y = -x - 6$

  Annotate

17
Mark for Review

$x = y(y^2 - 11y - 20) + 1$
$(a, 0)$ is one of the solution sets for the given equation. What is the value of a?

Section 2, Module 2: Math

 Annotate :

18   Mark for Review 🔖

What is the area of a square with a perimeter of 12?

(A) 16   (A)

(B) 9   (B)

(C) 8   (C)

(D) 4   (D)

Section 2, Module 2: Math

 Annotate :

19   Mark for Review 🔖

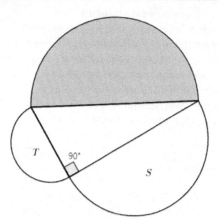

In the given figure, each of the three semicircles has a diameter that equals a corresponding side length of a right triangle. S and T are the area of two smaller semicircles. What is the area of the largest semicircle in terms of S and T?

(A) $S + T$ (A)

(B) $S^2 + T^2$ (B)

(C) ST (C)

(D) $\sqrt{ST}$ (D)

20 Mark for Review 🔖

A bicycle lock consists of a three digit password. Each digit of the password can have an integer value from 0 to 6, where the same number may appear more than once. A different order of the same combination sets a different password. For example, 656 and 566 are two different valid passwords. What is the number of different passwords that can be set for the lock?

(A) 3^6

(B) 6^3

(C) 3^7

(D) 7^3

21 Mark for Review 🔖

Factory A produces 12-ounce packs of breakfast cereal in four parallel production lanes. The owner conducted research to find if the production lanes are operating as intended. She randomly selected a production lane and measured the masses of 5 consecutively produced packs from the lane. She found the mean value of 13.5 ounces per pack of breakfast cereal. She concluded that Factory A has a defect in all production lanes. Which of the following strategy is most appropriate for the owner to apply in order to improve her research?

(A) Measuring the mass of just one pack instead of 5.

(B) Using pounds as a unit instead of ounces.

(C) Examining 50 randomly selected packs from Factory A.

(D) Comparing the result of the same research from another factory.

Annotate

22 Mark for Review

The clock marks the time $2:00$. The angle between the hour hand and the minute hand is $\frac{\pi}{d}$ radians. What is the value of d?

I
II
III
IV
V
VI
VII

TEST QUBE   Question 22 of 22 >

135

Move on to the Next Section »

TEST◻QUBE

Digital SAT ®

Practice Test #4

Section 1, Module 1: Reading & Writing   ⏱ 32:00   ✎ Annotate ⋮

Influential Japanese animator Hayao Miyazaki often _____ traditional gender roles in his films: this subversion is evident in the movie Princess Mononoke, which features a strong, independent female lead who defies expectations and displays courage and leadership.

1   Mark for Review 🔖

Which choice completes the text with the most logical and precise word or phrase?

(A) satirizes   Ⓐ

(B) emboldens   Ⓑ

(C) undermines   Ⓒ

(D) corroborates   Ⓓ

TEST⬢QUBE   Question 1 of 27 >   Back   Next

Section 1, Module 1: Reading & Writing   ✎ Annotate ⋮

In the world of finance, high-frequency trading has been a controversial topic, as it is often criticized for _____ market volatility and potentially undermining the stability of financial systems. However, some argue that it can also provide liquidity and reduce transaction costs for other market participants.

2   Mark for Review 🔖

Which choice completes the text with the most logical and precise word or phrase?

(A) exacerbarting   Ⓐ

(B) mitigating   Ⓑ

(C) diversifying   Ⓒ

(D) stabilizing   Ⓓ

TEST⬢QUBE   Question 2 of 27 >   Back   Next

Section 1, Module 1: Reading & Writing

Annotate

The British artist Michelle Reader's unique sculptures were created using an assemblage of found objects, repurposing discarded materials such as old buttons, plastic bottles, and worn-out clothing in unexpected and innovative ways. Her work, featured in exhibitions at the Saatchi Gallery and the Victoria and Albert Museum, explored the concept of _____ by transforming ordinary items into extraordinary works of art. Through her artistic endeavors, Reader breathes new life into what was once considered waste, prompting viewers to contemplate themes of sustainability, consumerism, and the transformative power of creativity.

3 Mark for Review

Which choice completes the text with the most logical and precise word or phrase?

A stagnation

B alchemy

C convergence

D disparity

TEST⬛QUBE   Question 3 of 27 >   Back Next

Section 1, Module 1: Reading & Writing

Annotate

The Golden Ratio, an irrational mathematical constant often found in nature and art, is believed to be aesthetically pleasing. This proportion has been used in various works, such as the Parthenon and Leonardo da Vinci's "Vitruvian Man." In nature, the Golden Ratio can be observed in the _____ of a nautilus shell's spiral.

4 Mark for Review

Which choice completes the text with the most logical and precise word or phrase?

A disarray

B congruence

C turpitude

D configuration

TEST⬛QUBE   Question 4 of 27 >   Back Next

Section 1, Module 1: Reading & Writing

Annotate ⋮

The Gutenberg Bible, printed in the mid-15th century, marked a major turning point in the history of printing as the first substantial book produced using movable type. This technological innovation paved the way for the dissemination of knowledge, enabling the _____ of information on an unprecedented scale.

5   Mark for Review 🔖

Which choice completes the text with the most logical and precise word or phrase?

(A) ossification   —Ⓐ—

(B) proliferation   —Ⓑ—

(C) generalization   —Ⓒ—

(D) obfuscation   —Ⓓ—

TEST⬛QUBE   Question 3 of 27 >   Back Next

Section 1, Module 1: Reading & Writing

Annotate ⋮

The following text is adapted from William Blake's 1789 poem "The Lamb."

Little Lamb who made thee
Dost thou know who made thee
Gave thee life & bid thee feed.
By the stream & o'er the mead;
Gave thee clothing of delight,
Softest clothing wooly bright;
Gave thee such a tender voice,
Making all the vales rejoice!

6   Mark for Review 🔖

Which choice best describes the overall structure of the text?

(A) The speaker questions the lamb's origins, then ponders the mystery of creation.

(B) The speaker interrogates the lamb, then extols its various qualities and attributes.

(C) The speaker contemplates the innocence of the lamb, then juxtaposes it with human experience.

(D) The speaker marvels at the lamb's beauty, then enumerates the gifts bestowed upon it by its creator.

TEST⬛QUBE   Question 4 of 27 >   Back Next

Section 1, Module 1: Reading & Writing

 Annotate

Following the successful development of the Mars helicopter, Amelia Quon and her team at NASA faced the challenge of integrating it into a rover mission for deployment on the Martian surface. The Mars helicopter, dubbed Ingenuity, had to be lightweight and compact enough to be attached to the Perseverance rover, while still being robust enough to withstand the harsh conditions on Mars. Engineers carefully designed Ingenuity's systems to ensure it could endure the extreme temperature fluctuations, dusty environment, and potential wind gusts. Upon landing on Mars in February 2021, Ingenuity made history by performing the first powered flight on another planet, proving the viability of aerial exploration as a valuable tool to complement future Mars missions and expand our understanding of the Red Planet.

7 Mark for Review

According to the text, why was it difficult to integrate the Mars helicopter into a rover mission for deployment on the Martian surface?

(A) Because ensuring power supply compatibility and energy sufficiency was difficult.

(B) Because improving communication technologies between helicopter and rover was complex.

(C) Because reaching a compromise between a versatile propulsion system and durability was demanding.

(D) Because balancing the helicopter's size, weight, and durability posed challenges.

TEST❖QUBE

Back Next

Section 1, Module 1: Reading & Writing

 Annotate

In a study conducted by Alexandra Horowitz, a cognitive scientist specializing in dog behavior, dogs were tested for their ability to understand and imitate human actions using a method known as "Do as I do." This approach involved the dog's owner performing a specific action, such as touching a cone, sitting on a chair, or opening a box, before giving their dog the command "Do it!" The dogs participating in the study were of various breeds and ages, and they had varying levels of prior training. The study aimed to evaluate how well dogs could learn to imitate their owners' actions under these conditions and whether the "Do as I do" method was effective in teaching dogs new behaviors. The results showed that many dogs were indeed capable of imitating their owners' actions, demonstrating a level of social cognition that was previously thought to be limited to humans and certain other primates.

8 Mark for Review

According to the text, how did the researchers assess the dogs' ability to imitate their owners' actions in this study?

(A) They focused on the dogs' emotional responses to the training method.

(B) They observed whether dogs could reproduce the actions performed by their owners after hearing the "Do it!" command.

(C) They compared the dogs' imitative skills to those of other animals in similar experiments.

(D) They timed how quickly the dogs mimicked the new behaviors during the experiment.

TEST❖QUBE

Back Next

Section 1, Module 1: Reading & Writing

Annotate

During the Great Migration, nearly six million African Americans left the South in search of better lives in the North and West. This mass relocation, which spanned the 1910s to the 1970s, was the largest internal migration in U.S. history. The migrants fled from the Jim Crow laws and racial violence of the South, but they also sought economic opportunity in the industrial cities of the North and West. They transformed the cultural and political landscape of their new homes, shaping the development of 20th-century America. Yet, despite their dreams and aspirations, they faced challenges and hardships in their new lives.

9   Mark for Review

Which choice best describes the main idea of the text?

(A) The impact of the Great Migration on the lives of African Americans

(B) The reasons behind the massive relocation of African Americans during the Great Migration

(C) The cultural and political contributions of African Americans to the North and West

(D) The challenges and opportunities faced by African Americans during the Great Migration

Section 1, Module 1: Reading & Writing

Annotate

In Emily Dickinson's 1863 poem "I felt a Funeral, in my Brain," the speaker vividly describes the experience of succumbing to an unrelenting, overwhelming sensation in her mind, writing,

_____

10   Mark for Review

Which quotation from "I felt a Funeral, in my Brain" most effectively illustrates the claim?

(A) "And then a Plank in Reason, broke, / And I dropped down, and down— /And hit a World, at every plunge, / And Finished knowing—then—"

(B) "And when they all were seated, / A Service, like a Drum— / Kept beating—beating—till I thought / My mind was going numb—"

(C) "And then I heard them lift a Box / And creak across my Soul / With those same Boots of Lead, again, / Then Space—began to toll,"

(D) "As all the Heavens were a Bell, / And Being, but an Ear, / And I, and Silence, some strange Race / Wrecked, solitary, here—"

1

Module 1

1

Section 1, Module 1: Reading & Writing

Annotate

The Venus flytrap, Dionaea muscipula, is a carnivorous plant native to subtropical wetlands in the southeastern United States. It is known for its unique trapping mechanism that involves modified leaves that snap shut when triggered by the movement of an insect or other small prey. The rapid closure of the trap is a result of the plant's cells undergoing rapid turgor pressure changes, which cause the cells to expand or contract. Interestingly, the plant has evolved to prevent false alarms by requiring two stimulations of the trigger hairs within a short period to initiate the trapping mechanism. Given the high energy cost of closing the trap and the potential risk of damaging the leaves, this adaptation likely serves to ____

11　　　　　　　　Mark for Review 🔖

Which choice most logically completes the text?

- (A) increase the plant's ability to capture larger prey in a more prompt fashion.
- (B) reduce the likelihood of capturing prey that is too small to provide adequate nutritional benefits. Ⓑ
- (C) minimize the chances of the trap closing in response to non-prey stimuli, such as raindrops or debris. Ⓒ
- (D) enhance the visual appeal of the plant to attract more prey. Ⓓ

TEST⬛QUBE　　　　Question 11 of 27 >　　　　Back　Next

Section 1, Module 1: Reading & Writing

Annotate

The 18th-century Scottish economist and philosopher Adam Smith is often regarded as the father of modern economics due to his influential work, "The Wealth of Nations." Smith's central argument was in favor of free markets and the concept of the "invisible hand," which posits that individuals pursuing their self-interest will unintentionally promote the collective good. This idea has had a lasting impact on economic theory and policy, shaping the development of capitalism and free trade. However, critics argue that unfettered markets can lead to significant wealth inequality, environmental degradation, and the exploitation of workers. Considering the ongoing debates surrounding economic systems, if a policymaker wants to address some of these concerns without abandoning Smith's core ideas, they could ____

12　　　　　　　　Mark for Review 🔖

Which choice most logically completes the text?

- (A) implement regulations and social policies that strike a balance between free markets and equitable outcomes.
- (B) reject the notion of the invisible hand and adopt a centrally planned economic system.
- (C) abolish bureaucratic forms of government intervention in the economy.
- (D) disregard the potential negative consequences of free markets and prioritize individual self-interest.

TEST⬛QUBE　　　　Question 12 of 27 >　　　　Back　Next

I

II

III

IV

V

VI

VII

142

Section 1, Module 1: Reading & Writing

Annotate

In an effort to reduce traffic congestion in major cities, urban planners have proposed the implementation of congestion pricing, which charges drivers a fee for entering high-traffic areas during peak hours. Proponents argue that this system would encourage the use of public transportation and carpooling, reducing the number of vehicles on the road. Critics, however, argue that congestion pricing disproportionately affects low-income individuals. To address this concern, planners could _____

13   Mark for Review

Which choice most logically completes the text?

(A) eliminate all public transportation fees to compensate for congestion pricing.

(B) provide exemptions or discounts for low-income drivers.

(C) charge higher fees for luxury vehicles to discourage their use in high-traffic areas.

(D) lower public transportation fares to offset the costs of congestion pricing.

TEST QUBE   Question 13 of 27 >   Back   Next

Section 1, Module 1: Reading & Writing

Annotate

Delving into the complex dynamics that shaped the second half of the 20th century, historian John Lewis Gaddis observed in his book *The Cold War* that "The United States and _____ fascism, went on to construct an international order designed to prevent its resurgence."

14   Mark for Review

Which choice completes the text so that it conforms to the conventions of Standard English?

(A) the Soviet Union had defeated

(B) the Soviet Union defeated

(C) the Soviet Union, have defeated

(D) the Soviet Union, having defeated

TEST QUBE   Question 14 of 27 >   Back   Next

Section 1, Module 1: Reading & Writing

Annotate ⋮

Based on recent astronomical data, scientists believe that there is a ninth planet in our solar system beyond Neptune. However, since analyzing the unusual orbits of distant objects in the Kuiper Belt, _____ may actually exist.

15   Mark for Review 🔖

Which choice completes the text so that it conforms to the conventions of Standard English?

(A) astronomer Mike Brown has suggested that Planet Nine

(B) astronomer Mike Brown's suggestion is that Planet Nine

(C) Planet None, astronomer Mike Brown has suggested,

(D) the suggestion astronomer Mike Brown has made is that Planet Nine

TEST⬛QUBE   Back   Next

Section 1, Module 1: Reading & Writing

Annotate ⋮

The Metropolitan Museum of Art in New York City and the Louvre Museum in Paris are two of many art museums around the world dedicated to preserving significant works of art; showcasing various artistic _____ and inspiring appreciation and understanding of human creativity and history.

16   Mark for Review 🔖

Which choice completes the text so that it conforms to the conventions of Standard English?

(A) styles, both foreign and domestic,

(B) styles; both foreign and domestic,

(C) styles both foreign and domestic,

(D) styles, both foreign and domestic;

TEST⬛QUBE   Back   Next

Each coral reef functions as a biodiversity hotspot in the marine ecosystem, and the symbiotic relationships within these underwater habitats play a pivotal role in this fact. The survival of many endangered species, such as the hawksbill sea turtle (Eretmochelys imbricata), depends on the health and vitality of these coral communities. Hawksbill sea turtles rely on coral reefs for food and shelter, and the decline of these ecosystems due to factors such as climate change, pollution, and overfishing, _____ their already precarious existence further at risk. By preserving and protecting coral reefs, we can help safeguard the future of these critically endangered species and maintain the delicate balance of marine ecosystems.

17   Mark for Review 🔖

Which choice completes the text so that it conforms to the conventions of Standard English?

(A) puts   Ⓐ

(B) put   Ⓑ

(C) putting   Ⓒ

(D) have put   Ⓓ

The mimic octopus (Thaumoctopus mimicus), a remarkable species found in the tropical waters of Southeast Asia, possesses an extraordinary ability to camouflage and impersonate other marine creatures. Discovered in the late 1990s off the coast of Indonesia, the mimic octopus is known for its incredible _____ shape, and movement, it can mimic a wide range of marine animals, such as lionfish, jellyfish, and sea snakes, to evade predators and even lure prey. This remarkable skill, unlike any other cephalopod's, highlights the mimic octopus's unique place in the marine ecosystem and underscores the importance of studying and protecting such a diverse and complex species.

18   Mark for Review 🔖

Which choice completes the text so that it conforms to the conventions of Standard English?

(A) adaptability; by adjusting its color,   Ⓐ

(B) adaptability by adjusting its color,   Ⓑ

(C) adaptability, by adjusting its color,   Ⓒ

(D) adaptability and by adjusting its color,   Ⓓ

I
II
III
IV
V
VI
VII

Section 1, Module 1: Reading & Writing

Annotate

By investing in cutting-edge recycling technologies, _____ and decrease the demand for nonrenewable resources. However, securing adequate funding for these environmentally friendly initiatives often proves to be an uphill battle, as many communities grapple with competing budgetary priorities.

19   Mark for Review

Which choice completes the text so that it conforms to the conventions of Standard English?

- (A) municipalities can significantly reduce landfill waste
- (B) landfill waste can be significantly reduced
- (C) a significant reduction in landfill waste can be achieved
- (D) municipalities' significantly reduced landfill waste

TEST⬛QUBE

Back   Next

Section 1, Module 1: Reading & Writing

Annotate

A steaming bowl of ramen, a popular Japanese dish, can be found in various forms, such as shoyu ramen, which features a soy sauce-based broth, and tonkotsu ramen, known for its rich, pork bone broth. There are also regional preferences when it comes to this versatile noodle _____ Tokyo-style ramen typically incorporates a lighter, soy-based broth, the version from Sapporo, a city on the northern island of Hokkaido, is characterized by its miso-infused broth and generous toppings, such as corn and butter. These distinct interpretations of the classic dish reflect the diverse culinary landscape of Japan, showcasing the country's rich food culture and regional pride.

20   Mark for Review

Which choice completes the text so that it conforms to the conventions of Standard English?

- (A) soup: while
- (B) soup; while
- (C) soup, while
- (D) soup — while

TEST⬛QUBE

Back   Next

Section 1, Module 1: Reading & Writing   Annotate   ⋮

The French Revolution, a period of radical social and political upheaval, profoundly influenced the course of modern history, reshaping both France's internal structure and its foreign relations. It led to the decline of the Bourbon monarchy, notably Louis XVI and Marie Antoinette, and the rise of radical political factions like the Jacobins. _____ the revolution set the stage for Napoleon Bonaparte's ascent to power, ultimately crowning him as the Emperor of the French.

21   Mark for Review 🔖

Which choice completes the text with the most logical transition?

- (A) In summary,
- (B) Consequently,
- (C) Despite this,
- (D) Similarly,

Section 1, Module 1: Reading & Writing   Annotate   ⋮

The Roaring Twenties, a decade marked by economic prosperity and cultural dynamism in the United States, saw the rise of consumerism and mass entertainment. Jazz music flourished, and the film industry boomed. _____ the stock market crash of 1929 marked the end of this era, plunging the country into the Great Depression.

22   Mark for Review 🔖

Which choice completes the text with the most logical transition?

- (A) In conclusion,
- (B) Nevertheless,
- (C) Similarly,
- (D) Meanwhile,

Section 1, Module 1: Reading & Writing

Annotate

Photosynthesis, the process by which plants convert sunlight, carbon dioxide, and water into glucose and oxygen, is essential for life on Earth. It provides energy for plants and oxygen for other organisms. _____ the process also plays a vital role in mitigating climate change by removing carbon dioxide from the atmosphere.

23   Mark for Review

Which choice completes the text with the most logical transition?

- Ⓐ In contrast,
- Ⓑ Furthermore,
- Ⓒ On the other hand,
- Ⓓ As a consequence,

Section 1, Module 1: Reading & Writing

Annotate

While researching a topic, a student has taken the following notes:

- The Industrial Revolution was a period of rapid industrialization from the mid-18th to mid-19th century.
- It began in Great Britain and later spread to other parts of the world.
- The revolution was marked by the development of new technologies, such as the steam engine and spinning jenny.
- Urbanization increased as people moved to cities in search of jobs in factories.
- The Industrial Revolution had significant social, economic, and environmental consequences.

24   Mark for Review

The student wants to discuss the impact of the Industrial Revolution on society. Which choice most effectively uses relevant information from the notes to accomplish this goal?

- Ⓐ The Industrial Revolution, characterized by rapid industrialization and technological advancements, led to increased urbanization and significant social, economic, and environmental changes.
- Ⓑ The steam engine and spinning jenny were among the groundbreaking technologies developed during the Industrial Revolution, which began in Great Britain and later spread globally.
- Ⓒ As people moved to cities for factory jobs, the Industrial Revolution drove urbanization and altered the social and economic landscape of the world.
- Ⓓ Despite the many technological innovations of the Industrial Revolution, its impact on society included both positive and negative consequences, such as urbanization and environmental degradation.

Section 1, Module 1: Reading & Writing

Annotate ⋮

While researching a topic, a student has taken the following notes:

- Sigmund Freud was the founder of psychoanalysis.
- Freud's theory of personality includes the id, ego, and superego.
- The id is the unconscious part of the mind that seeks immediate gratification.
- The ego is the conscious part that mediates between the id and the superego.
- The superego represents the moral values and standards of society.

25 Mark for Review 🔖

The student wants to explain the function of the ego in Freud's theory. Which choice most effectively uses relevant information from the notes to accomplish this goal?

(A) Freud's theory of personality focuses on the unconscious mind, where the id seeks immediate gratification and conflicts with societal standards represented by the superego.

(B) Sigmund Freud's psychoanalysis is centered around the id, ego, and superego, with the ego serving as the conscious mediator between the id's desires and the superego's moral values.

(C) As the founder of psychoanalysis, Freud's work on the id, ego, and superego has shaped modern understanding of the human mind and personality development.

(D) The id, ego, and superego are central components of Freud's theory, with the id representing unconscious desires and the superego representing moral values.

TEST QUBE

Back Next

Section 1, Module 1: Reading & Writing

Annotate ⋮

While researching a topic, a student has taken the following notes:

- Dr. Jane Cooke Wright (1919-2013) was an African American pioneer in oncology.
- She was instrumental in developing chemotherapy treatment techniques.
- In 1967, she became the highest-ranking African American woman in a US medical institution.
- She served as the president of the New York Cancer Society in 1971.
- In the 1970s, she led delegations of oncologists to China, the USSR, and Africa.
- Dr. Wright's work has contributed significantly to the field of cancer research.

26 Mark for Review 🔖

The student wants to highlight Dr. Wright's accomplishments and significant impact in the field of oncology. Which choice most effectively uses relevant information from the notes to accomplish this goal?

(A) Dr. Jane Cooke Wright was a well-respected figure in oncology and led delegations of oncologists to various parts of the world in the 1970s.

(B) Dr. Jane Cooke Wright was a pioneer in the field of oncology, contributing significantly to cancer research and the development of chemotherapy treatment techniques.

(C) Dr. Jane Cooke Wright, an African American woman, was the highest-ranking individual in a US medical institution in 1967.

(D) As the president of the New York Cancer Society in 1971, Dr. Jane Cooke Wright made a significant impact in the field of oncology.

TEST QUBE

Back Next

I

II

III

IV

V

VI

VII

Annotate

While researching a topic, a student has taken the following notes:

- The Silk Road was a network of trade routes connecting the East and the West.
- It was established during the Han Dynasty of China (206 BCE - 220 CE).
- The Silk Road facilitated the exchange of goods, ideas, and cultural practices.
- Key goods traded included silk, spices, and precious metals.
- The spread of religions like Buddhism and Christianity was also facilitated by the Silk Road.

27   Mark for Review 🔖

The student wants to emphasize the cultural significance of the Silk Road. Which choice most effectively uses relevant information from the notes to accomplish this goal?

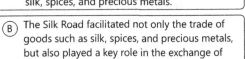

(A) The Silk Road was a trade network established during the Han Dynasty, connecting the East and the West for the exchange of goods like silk, spices, and precious metals.

(B) The Silk Road facilitated not only the trade of goods such as silk, spices, and precious metals, but also played a key role in the exchange of ideas and cultural practices between different regions.

(C) The Silk Road, established during the Han Dynasty, contributed to the spread of religions like Buddhism and Christianity across Asia and beyond.

(D) The network of trade routes known as the Silk Road connected the East and the West, fostering economic and cultural exchange for centuries.

Move on to the
Next Section ≫

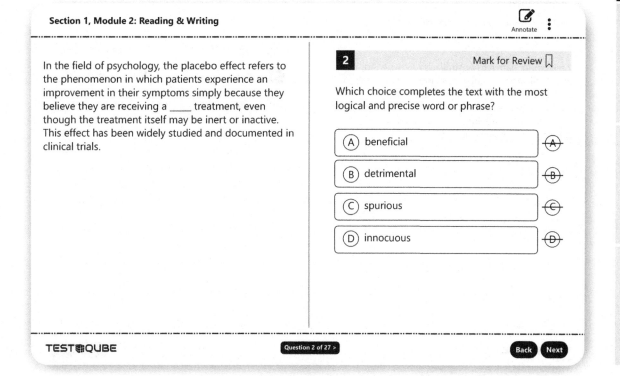

Section 1, Module 2: Reading & Writing　　🕐 **32:00**　　　📝 Annotate　⋮

Coral reefs are often referred to as the "rainforests of the sea" due to their ____ biodiversity. They provide a home to a vast array of marine species, many of which are not found anywhere else on Earth. This makes coral reef conservation a top priority for marine biologists and environmentalists.

1　　　　　　　　　　　Mark for Review 🔖

Which choice completes the text with the most logical and precise word or phrase?

(A) intrinsic　　　Ⓐ

(B) labyrinthine　　Ⓑ

(C) remarkable　　Ⓒ

(D) insipid　　　　Ⓓ

TEST QUBE　　　Question 1 of 27 >　　　Back　Next

Section 1, Module 2: Reading & Writing　　　　📝 Annotate　⋮

In the field of psychology, the placebo effect refers to the phenomenon in which patients experience an improvement in their symptoms simply because they believe they are receiving a ____ treatment, even though the treatment itself may be inert or inactive. This effect has been widely studied and documented in clinical trials.

2　　　　　　　　　　　Mark for Review 🔖

Which choice completes the text with the most logical and precise word or phrase?

(A) beneficial　　　Ⓐ

(B) detrimental　　Ⓑ

(C) spurious　　　Ⓒ

(D) innocuous　　Ⓓ

TEST QUBE　　　Question 2 of 27 >　　　Back　Next

Section 1, Module 2: Reading & Writing

Annotate ⋮

The fabled city of Timbuktu, located in present-day Mali, was once a _____ hub of trade and learning during the height of the Mali Empire. Scholars and traders from across Africa and the Middle East would travel there to exchange goods, ideas, and knowledge. The city's rich history continues to captivate historians and archaeologists today.

3   Mark for Review 🔖

Which choice completes the text with the most logical and precise word or phrase?

(A) lackluster   Ⓐ

(B) peripheral   Ⓑ

(C) vibrant   Ⓒ

(D) inscrutable   Ⓓ

TEST⬛QUBE   Question 3 of 27 >   Back   Next

Section 1, Module 2: Reading & Writing

Annotate ⋮

The lyrebird, native to Australia, is renowned for its remarkable ability to mimic an array of sounds, from other birds' calls to man-made noises such as chainsaws and camera shutters. This astonishing vocal _____ makes the lyrebird one of the most intriguing species in the animal kingdom.

4   Mark for Review 🔖

Which choice completes the text with the most logical and precise word or phrase?

(A) dissonance   Ⓐ

(B) versatility   Ⓑ

(C) deception   Ⓒ

(D) monotony   Ⓓ

TEST⬛QUBE   Question 4 of 27 >   Back   Next

Annotate ⋮

The following text is adapted from Edgar Allan Poe's 1843 short story *The Tell-Tale Heart*. The narrator, feeling disturbed and anxious, is describing the old man's eye that has haunted him.

It is impossible to say how first the idea entered my brain; but once conceived, it haunted me day and night. Object there was none. Passion there was none. I loved the old man. He had never wronged me. He had never given me insult. For his gold I had no desire. I think it was his eye! yes, it was this! He had the eye of a vulture—a pale blue eye, with a film over it. The thought of it <u>consumed</u> me, unsettling my every moment. Whenever it fell upon me, my blood ran cold; and so by degrees—very gradually—I made up my mind to take the life of the old man, and thus rid myself of the eye forever.

5 Mark for Review 🔖

As used in the text, what does the word "consumed" most nearly mean?

(A) Devoured — Ⓐ

(B) Engrossed — Ⓑ

(C) Purchased — Ⓒ

(D) Destroyed — Ⓓ

TEST🌐QUBE Question 5 of 27 > Back Next

Annotate ⋮

The following text is adapted from Henry David Thoreau's 1849 essay, "Civil Disobedience." In this philosophical work, Thoreau critiques various aspects of governance, especially the implications of majority rule.

After all, the practical reason why, when the power is once in the hands of the people, a majority are permitted, and for a long period continue, to rule, is not because they are most likely to be in the right, nor because this seems fairest to the minority, but because they are physically the strongest. But a government in which the majority rule in all cases cannot be based on justice, even as far as men understand it. Can there not be a government in which majorities do not virtually decide right and wrong, but conscience?—in which majorities decide only those questions to which the rule of expediency is applicable?

6 Mark for Review 🔖

Which choice best states the main purpose of the text?

(A) To question the fairness of majority rule in democratic governance

(B) To propose a government based on the rule of conscience rather than majority decision

(C) To critique the concept of physical strength as the basis for majority rule

(D) To suggest the application of the rule of expediency in governmental decision-making

TEST🌐QUBE Question 6 of 27 >   Back Next

I
II
III
IV
V
VI
VII

I

II

III

IV

Annotate

The following text is an excerpt from Ralph Waldo Emerson's 1841 essay "Self-Reliance."

There is a time in every man's education when he arrives at the conviction that envy is ignorance; that imitation is suicide; that he must take himself for better or worse as his portion; that though the wide universe is full of good, no kernel of nourishing corn can come to him but through his toil bestowed on that plot of ground which is given to him to till. <u>The power which resides in him is new in nature, and none but he knows what that is which he can do, nor does he know until he has tried.</u> Not for nothing one face, one character, one fact, makes much impression on him, and another none. It is not without preestablished harmony, this sculpture in the memory.

7   Mark for Review

Which choice best describes the function of the underlined sentence in the text as a whole?

(A) It underscores the philosophy of individualism by highlighting the unique potential within each person.

(B) It provides an example of the dangers of imitation, emphasizing the importance of personal trials.

(C) It contradicts the idea that a man's worth is determined by his social standing or material wealth.

(D) It introduces the concept of preestablished harmony, linking personal experiences and memory.

TEST QUBE   Back   Next

V

VI

VII

Annotate

The following excerpt is from Sigmund Freud's 1920 book, *Beyond the Pleasure Principle*.

An organism we judge to be living strives to maintain its own organic substance constant against the decomposing influences of external forces. <u>Consequently, its goal becomes to die only its own way, by avoiding or damping down as much as possible the more intense and rapid chemical processes in its environment.</u> The course of its decomposition is a slow process known as aging.

8   Mark for Review

Which choice best describes the function of the underlined sentence in the text as a whole?

(A) It emphasizes the organism's desire to control the circumstances of its death.

(B) It explains the role of environmental factors in an organism's survival.

(C) It provides insight into the organism's strategy for prolonging its life.

(D) It highlights the significance of the organism's ability to adapt to its surroundings.

TEST QUBE   Back   Next

Section 1, Module 2: Reading & Writing

Annotate

Text 1

The evolution of the bristlecone pine, with its ability to survive in the harsh climate of the White Mountains, is an exceptional study in adaptation. With a life span of up to 5,000 years, these trees thrive where few others can, adapting to severe temperature shifts, nutrient-poor soil, and high altitudes. Scientists speculate that one secret to their longevity is their capacity to increase the density of their wood in response to such challenging environmental conditions.

Text 2

Botanist Amelia Vasquez and her team argue that the secret to the bristlecone pine's resilience lies in its seemingly unremarkable bark. Given the tree's exposure to the arid, high-altitude environment, it would appear to be at the mercy of these conditions. Yet, according to Vasquez, the tree's bark is its first line of defense, containing unique compounds that enable the bristlecone pine to resist the intense solar radiation and dehydration that come with its habitat.

9   Mark for Review 🔖

How would Vasquez and her team (Text 2) most likely interpret the information presented in Text 1?

(A) They would acknowledge it as an additional explanation for the bristlecone pine's longevity, noting the interplay between internal and external factors.

(B) They would reject it, asserting that it overemphasizes the tree's internal adjustments and disregards the vital role of its external defenses.

(C) They would consider it outdated, as their findings have demonstrated the paramount importance of the tree's bark.

(D) They would concur with it, positing that a denser wood composition could potentially support a more resilient bark.

TEST🎲QUBE

Back   Next

Section 1, Module 2: Reading & Writing

Annotate

GDP Growth Rates and Unemployment Rates in Four Countries

Country	GDP Growth Rate (%)	Unemployment Rate (%)
Pania	3.5	5.0
Qalia	2.0	8.0
Rovia	4.0	4.5
Sovia	1.5	9.0

The table presents GDP growth rates and unemployment rates in four countries. GDP growth rate measures the change in the value of goods and services produced by a country over a period of time, while the unemployment rate measures the percentage of the labor force that is unemployed. Researchers claim that there is a negative correlation between GDP growth rates and unemployment rates.

10   Mark for Review 🔖

Which choice best describes data from the table that support the researchers' claim?

(A) Pania has the second-highest GDP growth rate and the second-lowest unemployment rate.

(B) Qualia has a lower GDP growth rate and a higher unemployment rate than Pania.

(C) Rovia has the highest GDP growth rate and the lowest unemployment rate.

(D) Sovia has the lowest GDP growth rate and the highest unemployment rate.

TEST🎲QUBE

Back   Next

Section 1, Module 2: Reading & Writing

Annotate

The Milankovitch cycles are a set of periodic variations in Earth's orbit and axial tilt that influence the planet's climate over tens of thousands of years. These cycles affect the distribution of sunlight on Earth, contributing to the onset and retreat of ice ages. A paleoclimatologist claims that the Milankovitch cycles play a crucial role in shaping long-term climate changes.

11 Mark for Review

Which finding, if true, would most directly support the paleoclimatologist's claim?

(A) The Milankovitch cycles consist of three main components: eccentricity, axial tilt, and precession, each with different periodicities and effects on Earth's climate.

(B) Geological and climatic records, such as ice cores and ocean sediments, provide evidence of past climate changes that correspond to variations in the Milankovitch cycles.

(C) The Milankovitch cycles are named after Milutin Milankovitch, a Serbian scientist who mathematically described their effects on Earth's climate in the early 20th century.

(D) The Milankovitch cycles have been incorporated into climate models to better understand the complex interactions between Earth's orbit, axial tilt, and climate system.

TEST⬛QUBE Question 11 of 27 > Back Next

Section 1, Module 2: Reading & Writing

Annotate

Emily Johnson, a renowned historian, contends that the extensive deployment of the printing press in the 15th century was the primary impetus behind the rapid dissemination of new ideas and the subsequent success of the Renaissance. Her research examined the spread of printed materials, the accessibility of new ideas to different social classes, and the role of influential patrons in promoting intellectual development. Johnson's work also explored the impact of the printing press on the standardization of written language and the preservation of cultural heritage.

12 Mark for Review

Which finding, if true, would most directly undermine Johnson's hypothesis?

(A) In some regions, the Renaissance's success was largely attributable to the largesse of affluent and influential patrons, who supported artists and intellectuals.

(B) In some instances, fastidious handwritten manuscripts played an indispensable role in propagating new ideas and fostering cultural growth during the Renaissance.

(C) The printing press was frequently utilized to produce materials that bolstered extant beliefs and traditions, rather than fomenting new ideas and challenging the status quo.

(D) In several areas where the printing press was not ubiquitously employed, the Renaissance still flourished due to other factors, such as burgeoning trade and cultural exchange.

TEST⬛QUBE Question 12 of 27 > Back Next

Section 1, Module 2: Reading & Writing   Annotate

Rain Levels on Species Growth

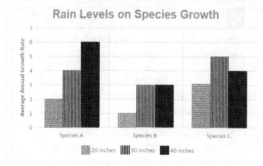

Environmental scientists are analyzing the relationship between the amount of annual precipitation and the growth rate of three tree species. They have collected data on the average annual growth rate at three different precipitation levels. In the process of acquiring the data, scientists noticed that certain species experienced unusual levels of a bacteria called Zylonova that dehydrates a tree, hindering its ability to grow properly. This bacteria can colonate with higher levels of rainfall, leading to even more stunted growth.

13 Mark for Review 🔖

Which statement best describes data from the graph that supports the scientists' claim?

(A) Species B's average annual growth remained the same at 30 inches and 40 inches of rainfall.

(B) Species C experienced greater levels of annual growth at 30 inches compared to 20 inches.

(C) Species C experienced greater levels of annual growth at 30 inches compared to 40 inches.

(D) Species A had higher levels of annual growth at all levels of rainfall compared to Species B.

TEST❖QUBE
Back Next

Section 1, Module 2: Reading & Writing   Annotate

The Taming of the Shrew is a circa 1594 play by William Shakespeare. In the play, Petruchio's unconventional tactics to "tame" his wife, Katherine, eventually lead to a profound change in her attitude. Katherine's transformation is best illustrated when she _____

14 Mark for Review 🔖

Which choice most effectively uses a quotation from The Taming of the Shrew to illustrate the claim?

(A) argues with Petruchio, "If I be waspish, best beware my sting."

(B) admits to Petruchio, "I see a woman may be made a fool if she had not a spirit to resist."

(C) tells the other wives, "Thy husband is thy lord, thy life, thy keeper, thy head, thy sovereign; one that cares for thee."

(D) speaks to Bianca, "I'll not budge an inch, boy. Let him come, and kindly."

TEST❖QUBE
Back Next

Section 1, Module 2: Reading & Writing

Annotate

Photosynthesis Rates and Chlorophyll Concentrations in Three Plant Species

Plant Species	Photosynthesis Rate (μmol CO2/m²/s)	Chlorophyll Concentration (μg/cm²)
Xylophyta	15	35
Yuccoides	25	50
Zostera	30	40

The table displays photosynthesis rates and chlorophyll concentrations in three plant species. Photosynthesis rate is the rate at which plants convert carbon dioxide into glucose using sunlight, and chlorophyll concentration refers to the amount of chlorophyll found in the plants' leaves. Researchers claim that higher chlorophyll concentrations are associated with increased photosynthesis rates.

15 Mark for Review

Which choice best describes data from the table that support the researchers' claim?

(A) Xylophyta has the lowest photosynthesis rate and chlorophyll concentration.

(B) Yuccoides has a higher photosynthesis rate and chlorophyll concentration than Xylophyta.

(C) Zostera has the highest photosynthesis rate but not the highest chlorophyll concentration.

(D) All plant species have the same photosynthesis rate and chlorophyll concentration.

TEST QUBE

Question 15 of 27 >

Back Next

Section 1, Module 2: Reading & Writing

Annotate

The following text is adapted from Joseph Conrad's 1900 novel, *Lord Jim*. The novel follows the life of a young British seaman, Jim, who suffers a lapse of judgment during a crisis and is publicly censured for his actions.

To the white men in the waterside business and to the captains of ships he was just Jim--nothing more. He had, of course, another name, but he was anxious that it should not be pronounced. His incognito, which had as many holes as a sieve, was not meant to hide a personality but a fact. When the fact broke through the incognito he would leave suddenly the seaport where he happened to be at the time and go to another--generally farther east. He kept to seaports because he was a seaman in exile from the sea, and had Ability in the abstract, which is good for no other work but that of a water-clerk.

16 Mark for Review

According to the text what is true about Jim?

(A) He is comfortable with his true identity and enjoys the recognition from the white men in the waterside business and ship captains.

(B) Jim's incognito is flawless and effectively hides the truth about him from others.

(C) Despite his exile, he has abandoned his connection to the sea completely and is seeking to start a new profession.

(D) He is seeking to conceal a specific aspect of his past and moves from port to port when his secret is close to being revealed.

TEST QUBE

 Question 16 of 27 >

Back Next

The global bee population has been declining at an alarming rate, posing a significant threat to agricultural systems and food security, as bees play a crucial role in pollination. Factors contributing to the decline include habitat loss, pesticide exposure, and climate change. In order to reverse this trend and safeguard the vital services provided by bees, it is necessary to _____

17 Mark for Review 🔖

Which choice most logically completes the text?

(A) implement comprehensive conservation strategies to protect bee populations and their habitats. Ⓐ

(B) develop alternative, artificially-engineered pollinators to replace the dwindling bee population. Ⓑ

(C) focus solely on reducing pesticide use, as it is the primary driver of bee population decline. Ⓒ

(D) rely on the natural adaptation of bee species to overcome the challenges they currently face. Ⓓ

TEST⬛QUBE

Back Next

II

III

IV

Science fiction stories—the most captivating ones, at_____ on the potential consequences of technological advancements and the exploration of the human condition, and the futuristic-setting-versus-current-societal-issues dynamic had been a vehicle to provoke such profound musings.

18 Mark for Review 🔖

Which choice completes the text so that it conforms to the conventions of Standard English?

(A) least—dwell Ⓐ

(B) least, dwell Ⓑ

(C) least dwell— Ⓒ

(D) least dwell Ⓓ

V

VI

VII

TEST⬛QUBE

Back Next

Section 1, Module 2: Reading & Writing

Annotate ⋮

In the early years of her political career, Eleanor Anderson stood on the steps of the city hall, overlooking the bustling streets of her hometown, a vibrant urban landscape that would come to define her legacy. Anderson championed progressive policies and social welfare initiatives, relentlessly advocating for the betterment of her constituents. She didn't always follow _____ she first entered politics, she adhered to more conservative principles, reflecting the predominant political climate of the time.

19   Mark for Review 🔖

Which choice completes the text so that it conforms to the conventions of Standard English?

(A) this path, however; when   Ⓐ

(B) this path; however, when   Ⓑ

(C) this path, however, when   Ⓒ

(D) this path. However, when   Ⓓ

TEST🔲QUBE

Back   Next

Section 1, Module 2: Reading & Writing

Annotate ⋮

During his formative years, Michael Thompson _____ on the worn basketball court situated in the heart of his childhood neighborhood, a place where dreams were born and passions ignited. Thompson honed his skills and talents, eventually rising to prominence as a world-class athlete. He didn't always play basketball, though. When he was younger, he dabbled in various sports, searching for the one that would ignite his passion and dedication. It wasn't until he stumbled upon the game of basketball that he found his true calling, dedicating himself to mastering the sport and etching his name in the annals of athletic history.

20   Mark for Review 🔖

Which choice completes the text so that it conforms to the conventions of Standard English?

(A) practiced relentlessly,

(B) practiced relentlessly;

(C) practiced relentlessly—

(D) practiced relentlessly   Ⓓ

TEST🔲QUBE

Back   Next

Section 1, Module 2: Reading & Writing

Annotate

In Haruki Murakami's novel *Kafka on the Shore*, the protagonist Kafka Tamura embarks on a surreal journey where reality and dreams intersect. Meanwhile, an elderly man named Nakata, who possesses unique abilities, also sets out on his own quest. Throughout the novel, their stories intertwine as they _____ a world filled with mysterious events and supernatural occurrences.

21   Mark for Review 🔖

Which choice completes the text so that it conforms to the conventions of Standard English?

- (A) navigated
- (B) had navigated
- (C) navigate
- (D) will be navigating

TEST QUBE

Back   Next

Section 1, Module 2: Reading & Writing

Annotate

An iconic Spanish dish, paella, varies considerably depending on the region and local ingredients. For instance, the Valencian paella, hailing from the eastern coast of Spain, traditionally comprises rabbit, chicken, and a variety of _____ the seafood paella, found in coastal areas, brims with an assortment of shellfish and fish. There are also specific customs surrounding the preparation and consumption of this vibrant rice dish: in Spain, paella is traditionally cooked and enjoyed outdoors, often during social gatherings and celebrations, fostering a sense of camaraderie and togetherness among family and friends.

22   Mark for Review 🔖

Which choice completes the text so that it confirms to the conventions of Standard English?

- (A) beans—while
- (B) beans; while
- (C) beans, while
- (D) beans: while

TEST QUBE

Back   Next

Greek philosopher Socrates, known for his Socratic method of questioning, had a profound influence on Western philosophy. His teachings emphasized the importance of critical thinking and self-examination. _____ Socrates never wrote down his ideas, and much of our knowledge about him comes from the writings of his student Plato.

23 Mark for Review 🔖

Which choice completes the text with the most logical transition?

(A) In addition,

(B) As a result,

(C) Nonetheless,

(D) Conversely,

While researching a topic, a student has taken the following notes:

- CRISPR-Cas9 is a gene-editing technology.
- It allows for precise editing of DNA sequences in living organisms.
- This technology has the potential to revolutionize medicine and agriculture.
- However, ethical concerns have been raised about the possible misuse of CRISPR-Cas9.
- Future applications of CRISPR-Cas9 could include the correction of genetic diseases and the creation of drought-resistant crops.

24 Mark for Review 🔖

The student wants to emphasize the potential benefits and concerns of CRISPR-Cas9 technology. Which choice most effectively uses relevant information from the notes to accomplish this goal?

(A) CRISPR-Cas9 is a gene-editing technology that enables precise DNA sequence editing in living organisms, revolutionizing medicine and agriculture.

(B) With the potential to cure genetic diseases and create drought-resistant crops, CRISPR-Cas9 also poses grave threats to genetic intervention.

(C) CRISPR-Cas9 has revolutionized medicine and agriculture, but its future applications are a subject of debate due to ethical concerns surrounding gene editing.

(D) The gene-editing technology CRISPR-Cas9 holds great promise for the fields of medicine and agriculture, but it also raises important ethical questions about its potential misuse.

Annotate

While researching a topic, a student has taken the following notes:

- The Battle of Thermopylae took place in 480 BC.
- It was fought between an alliance of Greek city-states and the Persian Empire, led by Xerxes I.
- The Greeks, led by King Leonidas I of Sparta, made a stand at the narrow coastal pass of Thermopylae.
- The battle was part of the larger Greco-Persian Wars.
- Although the Greeks were ultimately defeated, their resistance inspired future Greek military efforts.

25   Mark for Review

The student wants to highlight the significance of the Battle of Thermopylae in the context of the Greco-Persian Wars. Which choice most effectively uses relevant information from the notes to accomplish this goal?

(A) The Battle of Thermopylae, which took place in 480 BC, was a conflict between an alliance of Greek city- states and the Persian Empire, and it marked a crucial moment in the larger Greco-Persian Wars.   (A)

(B) Fought in 480 BC, the Battle of Thermopylae was led by King Leonidas I of Sparta and Xerxes I of the Persian Empire, and it became a symbol of Greek resistance in the Greco-Persian Wars.   (B)

(C) The Battle of Thermopylae, a part of the Greco-Persian Wars, saw King Leonidas I of Sparta and his Greek allies make a courageous stand against the Persian Empire at the narrow coastal pass of Thermopylae.   (C)

(D) Despite being ultimately defeated in the Battle of Thermopylae, the Greeks' resistance against the Persian Empire, led by King Leonidas I of Sparta, served as an inspiration for future Greek military efforts.   (D)

Annotate

While researching a topic, a student has taken the following notes:

- The Paris Commune was a radical socialist government that ruled Paris from March 18 to May 28, 1871.
- Karl Marx (1818-1883) was a philosopher, economist, and socialist revolutionary.
- Marx's book "The Civil War in France" (1871) provides an analysis of the Paris Commune.
- He argued that the Paris Commune was an example of the dictatorship of the proletariat.
- Marx believed the Commune demonstrated how workers could seize political power.

26   Mark for Review

The student wants to emphasize Marx's interpretation of the Paris Commune. Which choice most effectively uses relevant information from the notes to accomplish this goal?

(A) The Paris Commune, which ruled Paris in 1871, was the subject of Karl Marx's book "The Civil War in France."   (A)

(B) Karl Marx, in his book "The Civil War in France," saw the Paris Commune as an example of how workers could seize political power.   (B)

(C) Karl Marx, a philosopher and economist, wrote about the Paris Commune in his book "The Civil War in France."   (C)

(D) The Paris Commune, according to Karl Marx, demonstrated the potential for a democracy of the proletariat.   (D)

I
II
III
IV
V
VI
VII

Section 1, Module 2: Reading & Writing

Annotate

While researching a topic, a student has taken the following notes:

- Cubism is an early 20th-century art movement.
- It was pioneered by artists Pablo Picasso and Georges Braque.
- Cubism involves breaking objects into geometric shapes and depicting them from multiple perspectives.
- The movement is divided into two phases: Analytic Cubism and Synthetic Cubism.
- Cubism had a significant influence on the development of modern art.

27   Mark for Review

The student wants to explain the artistic innovations of Cubism. Which choice most effectively uses relevant information from the notes to accomplish this goal?

(A) Cubism, an early 20th-century art movement pioneered by Pablo Picasso and Georges Braque, involves breaking objects into geometric shapes and depicting them from multiple perspectives.

(B) As an art movement, Cubism had a significant influence on the development of modern art, and it was characterized by the depiction of objects as geometric shapes from various perspectives.

(C) Pioneered by artists Pablo Picasso and Georges Braque, Cubism is divided into two phases: Analytic Cubism and Synthetic Cubism, both of which involve depicting objects as geometric shapes.

(D) The early 20th-century art movement of Cubism, led by artists like Pablo Picasso and Georges Braque, is known for its unique approach to object representation and its influence on modern art.

TEST QUBE

End of Test 4 Reading/Writing Section

Back | Next

Upcoming Math Section: Reference Formula Sheet

$A = \pi r^2$
$C = 2\pi r$

$A = lw$

$A = \frac{1}{2}bh$

$c^2 = a^2 + b^2$

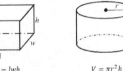

$V = \frac{1}{3}\pi r^2 h$

$V = \frac{1}{3}lwh$

Special Right Triangles

$V = lwh$

$V = \pi r^2 h$

$V = \frac{3}{4}\pi r^3$

The number of degrees of arc in a circle is 360.
The number of radians of arc in a circle is 2π.
The sum of the measures in degrees of the angles of a triangle is 180.

Directions for Student-Produced Response

- TEST QUBE recommends students to use decimals for most answers but suggests using fractions only in cases where the answers involve repeating decimals (e.g., 0.333 = 1/3)
- For cases with more than one answer, enter **just one of the answers.**
- You can enter up to 5 characters for your answer. (For negative answers, the **negative sign** does not count as one character)
- For **fractions** that don't fit the answer box, enter the decimal equivalent (Unless advised to do otherwise)
- For **decimals** that exceed the answer box, round to the fourth digit. (Unless advised to do otherwise)
- For mixed number (such as $4\frac{1}{4}$), enter it as an improper fraction $(17/4)$ or its decimal equivalent (4.25)
- For all answers, you may omit the symbols and units such as $,%, cm^3, m^2, etc.

Acceptable vs Non-Acceptable Answers

Answer	Acceptable ways to receive credit	Ways you **WON'T** receive credit
4.25	4.25 , 17/4	41/4 , 4 1/4
4/6	2/3 .6666 , .6667 0.666 , 0.667	0.66 , .66 0.67 , .67
-1/6	-1/6 -0.166 , -0.167 -.1666 , -.1667	-0.16 , -.16 -0.17 , -.167

Move on to the Next Section

1 Mark for Review 🔖

How do the mean and standard deviation of Class A compare to those of Class B based on the scores of their students given in the list below?

Class A	60	70	65	78	62
Class B	78	35	45	50	40

(A) Class A has a greater mean but lower standard deviation than Class B.

(B) Class A has a greater mean and standard deviation than Class B.

(C) Class A has a lower mean but greater standard deviation than Class B.

(D) Class A has a lower mean and lower standard deviation than Class B.

2 Mark for Review 🔖

What is the most appropriate function to describe the graph depicted below?

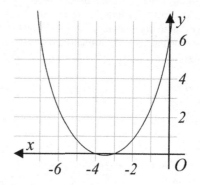

(A) $(x+4)(x+3)$

(B) $(x+4)(x+3)+6$

(C) $0.5(x+4)(x+3)$

(D) $2(x+4)(x+3)$

I

II

III

IV

V

VI

VII

3 Mark for Review 🔖

Out of 300 residents in a town, a sample was randomly selected and asked if they were satisfied with the air quality. 30% of those surveyed responded positively. Based on this result, what is the most accurate estimate of the total number of residents in the town who are satisfied with the air quality?

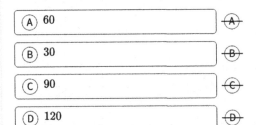

(A) 60

(B) 30

(C) 90

(D) 120

4 Mark for Review 🔖

Which equation provides the best estimate for the slope of the line of best fit for the given graph below?

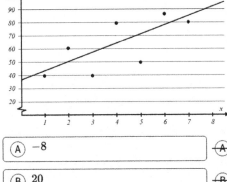

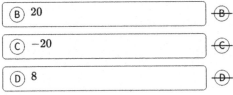

(A) -8

(B) 20

(C) -20

(D) 8

Annotate

5 Mark for Review

Which expression is equivalent to $(a^4b^3c^{-1})(b^2c^{-3})$, where $a, b,$ and c are positive?

(A) $a^8b^{-9}c^3$

(B) $a^4b^5c^{-4}$

(C) $a^4b^6c^3$

(D) $a^8b^3c^{-2}$

TEST QUBE   Question 5 of 22 >

Annotate

6 Mark for Review

The function g represents the distance, in miles, from home to school after driving m miles. Based on this model, what is the initial distance in miles from home to school?

$$g(m) = -0.5m + 20$$

(A) 15

(B) 10

(C) 20

(D) None of the above

TEST QUBE   Question 6 of 22 >

Annotate

7 Mark for Review

Given that a table provides the distribution of favorite classes and grade levels of 100 students, what is the likelihood of randomly selecting a student who is a sophomore and has Math as their favorite class?

Grade	Favorite Class			
	Math	English	Science	Total
Freshman	9	8	5	22
Sophomore	8	9	12	29
Junior	4	10	8	22
Senior	9	13	5	27
Total	30	40	30	100

(A) 2/25

(B) 3/10

(C) 29/100

(D) 1/2

TEST QUBE   Question 7 of 22 >   Back   Next

Section 2, Module 1: Math Annotate ⋮

8 Mark for Review 🔖

A right triangle ABC is similar to right triangle DEF, where angle B corresponds to angle E and angle A corresponds to angle D. If, the length of AB is 3, BC is 4, and DE is 6, what is the length of DF? (Angles B and E are right angles.)

(A) 12 — Ⓐ

(B) 5 — Ⓑ

(C) 10 — Ⓒ

(D) 8 — Ⓓ

TEST⬛QUBE Question 8 of 22 >

Section 2, Module 1: Math Annotate ⋮

9 Mark for Review 🔖

Which of the following would be the **approximate** value of James' house after a year if it is currently worth $200,000$ and its value increases by 25 percent every three months?

(A) $250,000$ — Ⓐ

(B) $390,625$ — Ⓑ

(C) $312,500$ — Ⓒ

(D) $488,281$ — Ⓓ

TEST⬛QUBE Question 9 of 22 >

Section 2, Module 1: Math Annotate ⋮

10 Mark for Review 🔖

What is the y-coordinate of the y-intercept of function g if it is perpendicular to $h(x) = 0.5x + 48$ and passes through the x-intercept at $(3, 0)$?

(A) 6 — Ⓐ

(B) -2 — Ⓑ

(C) 48 — Ⓒ

(D) -6 — Ⓓ

TEST⬛QUBE Question 10 of 22 >

Section 2, Module 1: Math Annotate ⋮

11 Mark for Review 🔖

On the election ballot, there was a proposal for a new grading policy. The results showed that there were twice as many students who voted in favor of the proposal as those who voted against it. If there were $2,000$ students who voted against the proposal, how many students voted in favor of it?

(A) 1000 — Ⓐ

(B) 2000 — Ⓑ

(C) 4000 — Ⓒ

(D) 6000 — Ⓓ

TEST⬛QUBE Question 11 of 22 > Back Next

12   Mark for Review 🔖

What is the volume, in cubic centimeters, of a rectangular prism with a length of $10cm$, a width of $6cm$, and a height of $8cm$?

[   ]

13   Mark for Review 🔖

How many real solutions does the equation below have?
$$8x^2 + 17x + 3 = 0$$

(A) Exactly one   (A)

(B) Zero   (B)

(C) Infinitely many   (C)

(D) Exactly two   (D)

14   Mark for Review 🔖

Which equation among the options below best represents the line of best fit in the scatterplot displaying the relationship between variables x and y? (Note: The graph below does not illustrate $x = 0$.)

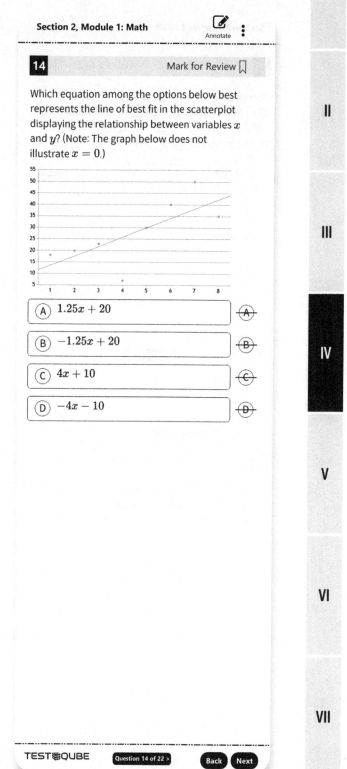

(A) $1.25x + 20$ (A)

(B) $-1.25x + 20$ (B)

(C) $4x + 10$ (C)

(D) $-4x - 10$ (D)

I   II   III   IV   V   VI   VII

15   Mark for Review 🔖

Bob bought a phone that was on sale at a store. The phone was on 70% discount but included a 20% tax which ended up costing Bob 900 dollars. What was the original price of the phone?

Ⓐ $1000   A̶

Ⓑ $1500   B̶

Ⓒ $2500   C̶

Ⓓ $3000   D̶

TEST⬛QUBE   Question 15 of 22 >

Annotate ⋮

16   Mark for Review 🔖

What is the area, in square meters, of a rectangular garden that has a perimeter of 100 meters and where the length is 10 meters more than the width?

TEST⬛QUBE   Question 16 of 22 >

17   Mark for Review 🔖

The bar graph below shows the scores for each student in Mr.Jackson's math class where each student spent different amounts of time preparing for the exam. What is the average score of the students based on the bar graph?

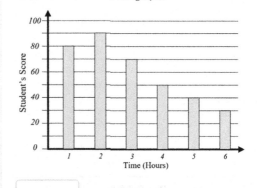

TEST⬛QUBE   Question 17 of 22 >   Back Next

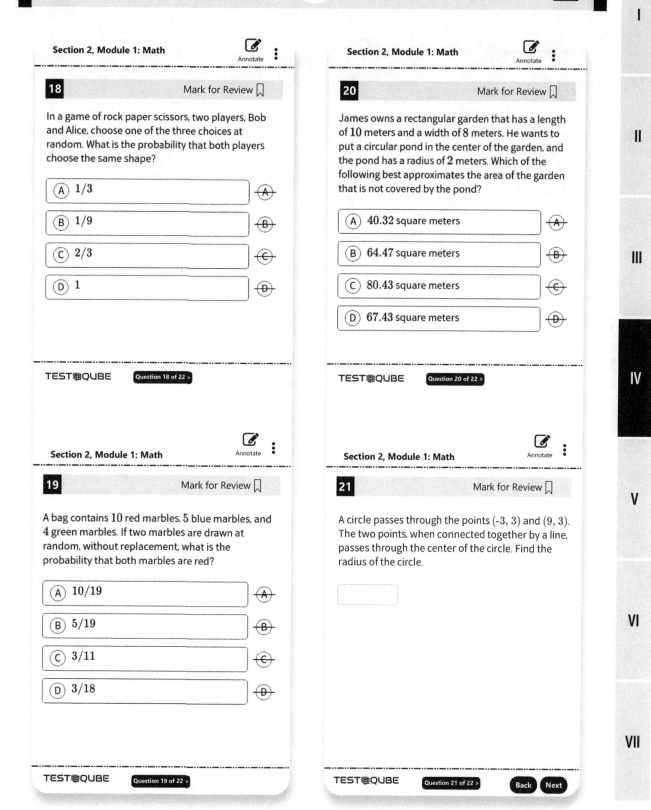

18 Mark for Review 🔖

In a game of rock paper scissors, two players, Bob and Alice, choose one of the three choices at random. What is the probability that both players choose the same shape?

- (A) 1/3 — Ⓐ
- (B) 1/9 — Ⓑ
- (C) 2/3 — Ⓒ
- (D) 1 — Ⓓ

TEST⬚QUBE   Question 18 of 22 >

19 Mark for Review 🔖

A bag contains 10 red marbles, 5 blue marbles, and 4 green marbles. If two marbles are drawn at random, without replacement, what is the probability that both marbles are red?

- (A) 10/19 — Ⓐ
- (B) 5/19 — Ⓑ
- (C) 3/11 — Ⓒ
- (D) 3/18 — Ⓓ

TEST⬚QUBE   Question 19 of 22 >

20 Mark for Review 🔖

James owns a rectangular garden that has a length of 10 meters and a width of 8 meters. He wants to put a circular pond in the center of the garden, and the pond has a radius of 2 meters. Which of the following best approximates the area of the garden that is not covered by the pond?

- (A) 40.32 square meters — Ⓐ
- (B) 64.47 square meters — Ⓑ
- (C) 80.43 square meters — Ⓒ
- (D) 67.43 square meters — Ⓓ

TEST⬚QUBE   Question 20 of 22 >

21 Mark for Review 🔖

A circle passes through the points (-3, 3) and (9, 3). The two points, when connected together by a line, passes through the center of the circle. Find the radius of the circle.

TEST⬚QUBE   Question 21 of 22 >   Back Next

I

II

III

IV

V

VI

VII

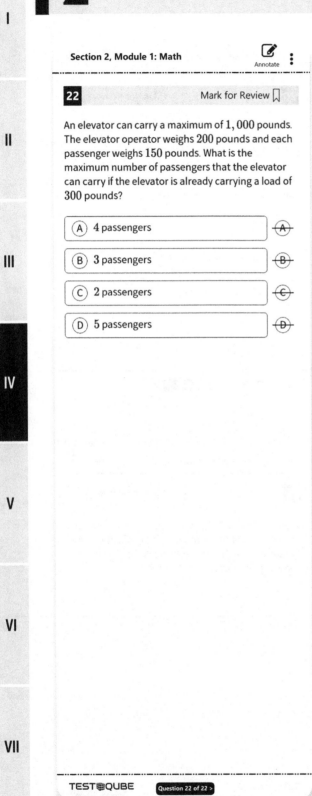

Annotate

22 Mark for Review

An elevator can carry a maximum of $1,000$ pounds. The elevator operator weighs 200 pounds and each passenger weighs 150 pounds. What is the maximum number of passengers that the elevator can carry if the elevator is already carrying a load of 300 pounds?

(A) 4 passengers

(B) 3 passengers

(C) 2 passengers

(D) 5 passengers

TEST QUBE Question 22 of 22 >

172

Move on to the
Next Section

⏱ 35:00

1   Mark for Review 🔖

What is the value of x that satisfies the two systems of equations given below? $(x \geq 0)$

$$x^2 - y = 18$$
$$x = 2y + 8$$

(A) -4

(B) -2

(C) 2

(D) 4

TEST◉QUBE

2   Mark for Review 🔖

Elizabeth is participating in a quiz show. For every question she gets correct, she earns 2 points. For every question she gets incorrect, she loses 1 point. If there are a total of 20 questions and she earned 19 points in total, how many questions did she answer incorrectly?

(A) 6

(B) 7

(C) 8

(D) 9

TEST◉QUBE

3   Mark for Review 🔖

If $6x - 3 = 15$, what is the value of $15x - 35$?

TEST◉QUBE

4   Mark for Review 🔖

Rectangle A has a width $3cm$ shorter than the length. If the perimeter of rectangle A is 26, what is the width of rectangle A?

(A) $5cm$

(B) $6cm$

(C) $7cm$

(D) $8cm$

TEST◉QUBE   Back   Next

I   II   III   IV   V   VI   VII

Annotate

5   Mark for Review 🔖

A travel agency is selling two types of tickets, Ticket A and Ticket B, for the observatory deck. Ticket A costs $15 each, and Ticket B costs $25 each. In one day, the travel agency sold a total of 57 tickets and earned a total revenue of $1,065. How many Ticket B's were sold that day?

(A) 7

(B) 14

(C) 21

(D) 28

TEST⬛QUBE   Question 5 of 22 >

Annotate

6   Mark for Review 🔖

In the given equation below, b is a constant. The equation has one real solution. What is the value of b when $b > 0$?

$$3x^2 - bx + 3 = 0$$

TEST⬛QUBE   Question 6 of 22 >

Annotate

7   Mark for Review 🔖

Which of the following is not a factor of $2x^3 + 7x^2 - 19x - 60$?

(A) -4

(B) 3

(C) $-5/2$

(D) $2/3$

TEST⬛QUBE   Question 7 of 22 >

Annotate

8   Mark for Review 🔖

Which of the following expressions is equivalent to $a^6 \div a^4$?

(A) a^{6+4}

(B) a^{6-4}

(C) $a^{6\times4}$

(D) $a^{6/4}$

TEST⬛QUBE   Question 8 of 22 >   Back   Next

9 Mark for Review 🔖

In the xy-plane, what is the area of a polygon that satisfies the condition of the three inequalities shown below?

$y \leq \frac{4}{3}x + 4$

$y \leq -x + 4$

$y \geq 0$

10 Mark for Review 🔖

What is the x-intercept of the graph below?

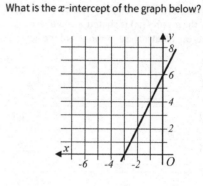

(A) $(-3, 0)$

(B) $(3, 0)$

(C) $(0, 6)$

(D) $(6, 0)$

I

II

III

IV

V

VI

VII

I

II

III

IV

V

VI

VII

11 Mark for Review 🔖

The function f is defined by $f(x) = 2x - 5$. In the xy-plane, the graph $f(x)$ is shifted 1 unit to the left and 4 units up. What is the x-intercept of the new function?

(A) -1

(B) -0.5

(C) 0.5

(D) 1

12 Mark for Review 🔖

The graph of $y = g(x)$ is shown below. For how many values of x does $g(x) = 0$?

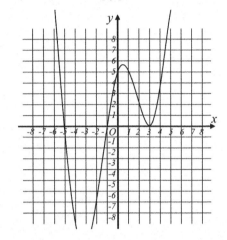

(A) 0

(B) 1

(C) 2

(D) 3

Section 2, Module 2: Math   ⋮

13   Mark for Review 🔖

Which of the following graphs correctly represents the function $f(x) = x(x - 3)(x + 5)$?

 Ⓐ

 Ⓑ

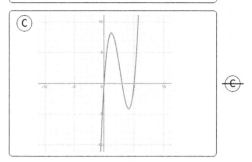 Ⓒ

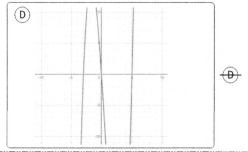 Ⓓ

Section 2, Module 2: Math   ⋮

14   Mark for Review 🔖

The equation below defines the function g. What is the maximum value of $g(x)$?

$$g(x) = \frac{-5}{3}x^2 - 10x + 9$$

Section 2, Module 2: Math   ⋮

15   Mark for Review 🔖

For a particular factory that manufactures pens, 6 out of every 100 pens are defective. If this machine produces 500 pens a day, how many defects in total are expected to be found in a <u>week</u>? (The machine produces all seven days a week from Monday to Sunday.)

16   Mark for Review 🔖

Alex is depositing his money at a bank. Alex estimates that, starting from present, the value of money will increase by 0.5 percent every 10 years. If the present amount of money deposited is $\$7,500$, which of the following represents the estimate of the amount of money, in dollars, x years from now?

(A) $7,500(1.05)^{x/10}$ (A)

(B) $7,500(1.005)^{x/10}$ (B)

(C) $7,500(1.05)^{10/x}$ (C)

(D) $7.500(1.005)^{10/x}$ (D)

17   Mark for Review 🔖

The line graph below shows the price of semiconductor A over the years from 2019 to 2022. Which time interval, spanning from 2019 to 2022, exhibits the largest difference in the price of semiconductor A?

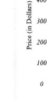

Price of Semiconductor 'A' Over the Years

(A) 2019 to 2020   (A)

(B) 2020 to 2021   (B)

(C) 2021 to 2022   (C)

(D) None of the above   (D)

18   Mark for Review

There is a 12-sided die which is labeled with a number from 1 to 12, with a different number on each side. If the die is rolled once, what is the probability the number is either an odd or even number?

(A) 0

(B) $1/12$

(C) $1/2$

(D) 1

19   Mark for Review

In the diagram below, the lines l and m run parallel to each other. What is the measure of angle x in degrees?

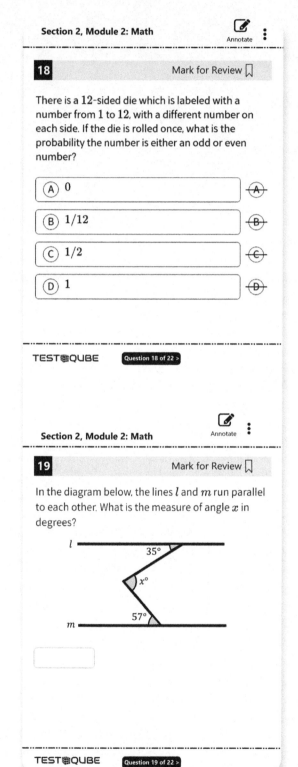

20   Mark for Review

A circle has an equation of $x^2 + 6x + y^2 - 10y + 18 = 0$. What is the radius of this circle?

(A) 2

(B) 4

(C) 8

(D) 16

21   Mark for Review

What is the circumference of a circle with an area of 16π?

(A) 2π

(B) 4π

(C) 8π

(D) 16π

Section 2, Module 2: Math

Annotate

22 Mark for Review 🔖

Find the area of a regular hexagon with each side length of 4. Round your answer to the nearest tenth.

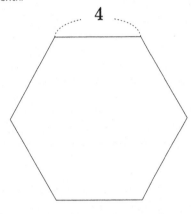

4

TESTQUBE

Digital SAT ®

Practice Test #5

Section 1, Module 1: Reading & Writing ⏱ 32:00 Annotate ⋮

Renowned composer John Williams, revered for his contributions to the film industry and his ability to capture the essence of a movie through music, frequently _____ leitmotifs in his film scores: this technique is particularly evident in the Star Wars saga. For instance, the menacing "Imperial March" is synonymous with Darth Vader, while the heroic "Force Theme" is often associated with Luke Skywalker and moments of hope. Furthermore, Princess Leia has her own poignant and memorable theme.

1 Mark for Review 🔖

Which choice completes the text with the most logical and precise word or phrase?

(A) eschews

(B) suppresses

(C) harnesses

(D) refutes

Section 1, Module 1: Reading & Writing Annotate ⋮

The proliferation of smartphones and social media platforms, such as Facebook, Twitter, and Instagram, has facilitated an era of unprecedented connectivity, enabling people from around the globe to communicate with ease. However, critics like Nicholas Carr, author of "The Shallows: What the Internet Is Doing to Our Brains", argue that the constant barrage of notifications and updates can lead to _____ attention spans and hinder meaningful face-to-face interactions. The debate around the impact of technology on human cognition and social skills continues to be a topic of scholarly discussion and public concern.

2 Mark for Review 🔖

Which choice completes the text with the most logical and precise word or phrase?

(A) fractured

(B) emboldened

(C) ephemeral

(D) laconic

I

II

III

IV

V

VI

VII

Section 1, Module 1: Reading & Writing

Annotate

⋮

The process of extracting honey from beehives, a practice dating back to ancient times, has remained relatively unchanged for centuries, involving a labor-intensive and time-consuming method that often disturbs the bees. However, a groundbreaking invention by father-son duo Stuart and Cedar Anderson, called the Flow Hive, has emerged, making honey extraction more _____ and less disruptive to the bees, thereby revolutionizing beekeeping practices. The Flow Hive allows honey to be harvested directly from the hive without opening it up and has been widely acclaimed for its innovation and sustainability.

3   Mark for Review 🔖

Which choice completes the text with the most logical and precise word or phrase?

(A) meticulous   A̶

(B) ephemeral   B̶

(C) efficient   C̶

(D) convoluted   D̶

TEST◉QUBE   Question 3 of 27 >   Back   Next

Section 1, Module 1: Reading & Writing

Annotate

⋮

In Margaret Atwood's celebrated novel "The Handmaid's Tale," the protagonist, Offred, faced with seemingly insurmountable challenges in a dystopian society, draws strength from her inner resilience and resourcefulness. Her character _____ throughout the story, as she navigates a repressive regime that subjugates women. Through acts of defiance and determination, Offred's development illustrates the indomitable human spirit, ultimately leading her to overcome the obstacles in her path and inspiring readers with her courage and fortitude.

4   Mark for Review 🔖

Which choice completes the text with the most logical and precise word or phrase?

(A) stagnates

(B) deteriorates

(C) flourishes

(D) capitulates   D̶

TEST◉QUBE   Question 4 of 27 >   Back   Next

Section 1, Module 1: Reading & Writing

Annotate ⁝

New York City's public transportation system, historically regarded as one of the most extensive and efficient in the United States, has unfortunately become increasingly unpredictable and sluggish due to a chronic lack of maintenance and upgrades. The aged subway trains often experience breakdowns, and the bus services have been plagued by delays. The need for a comprehensive _____ of the system is now more apparent than ever.

5 Mark for Review 🔖

Which choice completes the text with the most logical and precise word or phrase?

(A) overhaul ──Ⓐ──

(B) detriment ──Ⓑ──

(C) stagnation ──Ⓒ──

(D) dilution ──Ⓓ──

TEST🧊QUBE   Question 3 of 27 >   Back Next

Section 1, Module 1: Reading & Writing

Annotate ⁝

The following text is adapted from Henry James' 1903 novel *The Ambassadors*. The novel centers around Lambert Strether, a man in the midst of a European journey.

Strether's first question, when he reached the hotel, was about his friend; yet on his learning that Waymarsh was apparently not to arrive till evening he was not wholly disconcerted. A telegram from him bespeaking a room 'only if not noisy,' reply paid, was produced for the enquirer at the office, so that the understanding they should meet at Chester rather than at Liverpool remained to that extent sound. The same secret principle, however, that had prompted Strether not absolutely to desire Waymarsh's presence at the dock, that had led him thus to postpone for a few hours his enjoyment of it, now operated to make him feel he could still wait without disappointment.

6 Mark for Review 🔖

Which choice best describes the overall structure of the text?

(A) It uses a sequence of events to highlight the complexities of Strether's relationship with Waymarsh.

(B) It presents Strether's anticipation of Waymarsh's arrival, elaborates on the delay, and concludes with Strether's acceptance of the situation.

(C) It introduces a setting and follows it with the protagonist's reaction to changes in his planned meeting with Waymarsh.

(D) It details Strether's actions, then explores the reasons behind them and ends with a reflection on his emotional state.

TEST🧊QUBE   Question 4 of 27 >   Back Next

Section 1, Module 1: Reading & Writing

Annotate ⋮

The following text is adapted from Elizabeth Barrett Browning's 1850 poem "Sonnets from the Portuguese 43: How do I love thee? Let me count the ways." The poem is a passionate expression of affection.

How do I love thee? Let me count the ways.
I love thee to the depth and breadth and height
My soul can reach, when feeling out of sight
For the ends of Being and ideal Grace.
I love thee to the level of every day's
Most quiet need, by sun and candle-light.
I love thee freely, as men strive for Right;
I love thee purely, as they turn from Praise.

7 Mark for Review 🔖

What is the main idea of the text?

(A) The speaker is questioning the nature of love and its impact on their life.

(B) The speaker is expressing regret for not having loved deeply enough in the past.

(C) The speaker is conveying the intensity and totality of their love for the person they address.

(D) The speaker is reflecting on the fickleness of love and the potential for betrayal.

TEST◉QUBE

Back Next

Section 1, Module 1: Reading & Writing

Annotate ⋮

Believing that connecting with the natural world can strengthen community bonds and spiritual well-being, the Nuu-chah-nulth tribe of the Pacific Northwest has practiced traditional sea-hunting and wood-carving for centuries. These activities are deeply embedded in the tribe's culture; for instance, they carve intricate totem poles and craft sturdy canoes. Their connection with the sea is so profound that a young member, upon catching his first fish, is celebrated through a communal feast. This kinship with nature is believed to have fostered a sense of belonging and tranquility among the tribe members.

8 Mark for Review 🔖

Which choice best states the main idea of the text?

(A) As a sea-hunting community, the Nuu-chah-nulth tribe has been influential in promoting sustainable fishing practices among other Native American tribes.

(B) Through traditional sea-hunting and wood-carving, the Nuu-chah-nulth tribe maintains a deep connection with nature, which strengthens community bonds and well-being.

(C) The Nuu-chah-nulth tribe has perfected the art of sea-hunting and wood-carving, making them the most skilled craftsmen among Native American tribes.

(D) Although engaging in sea-hunting and wood-carving is an integral part of the Nuu-chah-nulth tribe's culture, it is slowly fading due to modernization.

TEST◉QUBE

Back Next

Section 1, Module 1: Reading & Writing

Annotate

The following text is adapted from Elizabeth von Arnim's 1898 novel *Elizabeth and Her German Garden*. The novel, inspired by the author's own life, tells the story of Elizabeth as she navigates her marriage and life in rural Germany.

Elizabeth, a woman of keen horticultural predilections, sought refuge in her cherished garden from the exigencies of domestic life. The verdant sanctuary offered her solace and respite from her quotidian responsibilities, allowing her to cultivate not only her prized flora, but also her sense of self. As the seasons progressed, her garden flourished, each bloom an affirmation of her perseverance and dedication. While her marriage was often a source of consternation, Elizabeth's unwavering devotion to her garden served as an anchor in the tempestuous seas of her life.

9   Mark for Review 🔖

According to the text, what is true about Elizabeth?

(A) She dislikes gardening and prefers indoor activities.

(B) Elizabeth's marriage is a harmonious and fulfilling partnership.

(C) Her garden serves as a source of happiness and stability.

(D) She is indifferent to the challenges of her domestic life.

Section 1, Module 1: Reading & Writing

Annotate

Macbeth is a circa 1623 play by William Shakespeare. In the play, Lady Macbeth's descent into guilt-ridden madness becomes evident as the play progresses. Her unraveling state of mind is best illustrated when she

_____

10   Mark for Review 🔖

Which choice most effectively uses a quotation from Macbeth to illustrate the claim?

(A) encourages Macbeth, "Art thou afeard to be the same in thine own act and valor as thou art in desire?

(B) advises Macbeth, "Look like the innocent flower, but be the serpent under't. Who dares do more is none."

(C) tells Macbeth, "We fail? But screw your courage to the sticking-place, and we'll not fail. When Duncan is asleep."

(D) speaks to herself, "Out, damned spot! Out, I say! One, two; why then, 'tis time to do't. Hell is murky!"

Section 1, Module 1: Reading & Writing

Annotate

In 2009, Dr. Felicia Martinez and her team began a research project to develop a solar cell that can efficiently harness energy from the sun even during cloudy weather. Traditional solar cells have a low efficiency in diffused sunlight, which limits their performance under cloudy conditions. Dr. Martinez's team worked on designing solar cells with a broader light-absorption spectrum and a nanostructured surface that improves their efficiency in capturing light from different angles. As a result, the new solar cells can generate electricity more effectively under cloudy skies compared to standard solar cells.

11   Mark for Review 🔖

According to the text why are traditional solar cells less efficient in cloudy weather?

- (A) Because they have a narrow light-absorption spectrum
- (B) Because they can only generate electricity under direct sunlight
- (C) Because they have a nanostructured surface that absorbs light poorly
- (D) Because they are not designed to capture light from different angles

TEST🧊QUBE

Back   Next

Section 1, Module 1: Reading & Writing

Annotate

The Chinese social structure has historically been influenced by the teachings of Confucius, a philosopher who lived during the Zhou Dynasty (1046-256 BCE). Confucianism emphasizes the importance of familial relationships, social harmony, and personal virtue. The concept of filial piety, or "xiao" in Chinese, is a key tenet of Confucianism, which entails the idea that children should demonstrate unwavering respect, obedience, and loyalty towards their parents and ancestors. In the context of traditional Chinese society, the principle of filial piety would likely ____

12   Mark for Review 🔖

Which choice most logically completes the text?

- (A) promote the importance of individualism and self-expression.
- (B) ease tensions between different social classes.
- (C) incite resistance to established social hierarchies.
- (D) reinforce the deference to authority figures.

TEST🧊QUBE

Back   Next

Section 1, Module 1: Reading & Writing

Annotate

The concept of time dilation, as described by Albert Einstein's theory of relativity, states that time passes at different rates depending on an observer's relative speed or proximity to a gravitational mass. In practical terms, this means that a person traveling at a significant fraction of the speed of light or living near a massive object, such as a black hole, would experience time at a slower rate compared to someone in a different situation. This phenomenon has been experimentally confirmed through the use of atomic clocks placed on aircraft and satellites, which have shown that their timekeeping deviates from those on Earth. Given this understanding, if an astronaut were to embark on a long journey at near-light speed and then return to Earth, they would find that ____

13   Mark for Review 🔖

Which choice most logically completes the text?

A) they have aged more than people who remained on Earth.

B) they have aged less than people who remained on Earth.

C) their aging process has been entirely halted during the journey.

D) their experience of time has not been affected by their journey.

TEST●QUBE   Question 13 of 27 >   Back   Next

Section 1, Module 1: Reading & Writing

Annotate

The organization's primary goal is to empower young people through education and skill development. The _____ success in achieving this objective has transformed countless lives.

14   Mark for Review 🔖

Which choice completes the text so that it conforms to the conventions of Standard English?

A) nonprofit's

B) nonprofits

C) nonprofit

D) nonprofits'

TEST●QUBE   Question 14 of 27 >   Back   Next

Section 1, Module 1: Reading & Writing

Annotate ⋮

Whether the proposed "Green Living Initiative," championed by Mayor Sophie Anderson, will achieve its intended goals _____ yet to be determined. The program, aimed at reducing carbon footprints and promoting sustainable living, has recently been passed by the city council of Newport. Despite the enthusiastic support from environmental advocacy groups like Green Horizon, its long-term effects on the Newport community remain unclear.

15   Mark for Review 🔖

Which choice completes the text so that it conforms to the conventions of Standard English?

(A) have

(B) are

(C) have been

(D) is

Section 1, Module 1: Reading & Writing

Annotate ⋮

The widespread use of smartphones and social media in recent years _____ a considerable influence on the way people communicate and access information. This shift has led to new opportunities and challenges for individuals, businesses, and governments alike.

16   Mark for Review 🔖

Which choice completes the text so that it conforms to the conventions of Standard English?

(A) has had

(B) have had

(C) have

(D) are having

Acclaimed composer Ludwig van Beethoven's music evolved dramatically throughout his career. In his early period, Beethoven composed piano sonatas that showcased his virtuosic skills; _____ in his late period, he composed complex, introspective works like the Ninth Symphony, which introduced choral elements and revolutionized the genre.

17 Mark for Review 🔖

Which choice completes the text so that it conforms to the conventions of Standard English?

(A) however later,   (A)

(B) however   (B)

(C) however,   (C)

(D) however, later,   (D)

In the animal kingdom, the mantis shrimp is known for its incredible striking speed and vibrant _____ being an anomaly, these features have evolved for specific purposes. Scientists have discovered that the mantis shrimp's punch, which can reach speeds of up to 50 mph, is used not only for hunting but also for breaking open the shells of its prey. Besides having one of the fastest strikes in nature, the mantis shrimp also possesses an extraordinary visual system, with 16 color-receptive cones compared to humans' three. This remarkable vision allows the creature to see a vast array of colors that humans cannot even comprehend, which helps it navigate the complex environments of coral reefs.

18 Mark for Review 🔖

Which choice completes the text so that it conforms to the conventions of Standard English?

(A) colors; rather than

(B) colors, rather than

(C) colors rather than   (C)

(D) colors — rather than

I

Section 1, Module 1: Reading & Writing

Annotate ⋮

Egyptian doctors were known for their comprehensive knowledge of the human body and utilized a wide range of natural remedies _____ the ancient Egyptians also had a rudimentary understanding of geometry, which was essential for their construction projects. They developed a system of measurements and standardized units, allowing them to create monumental structures with impressive precision. This combination of practical knowledge and artistic vision has left a lasting legacy that continues to fascinate modern scholars.

19   Mark for Review 🔖

Which choice completes the text so that it conforms to the conventions of Standard English?

- (A) for various ailments — besides   Ⓐ
- (B) for various ailments. Besides   Ⓑ
- (C) for various ailments, besides   Ⓒ
- (D) for various ailments. Besides,   Ⓓ

TEST⬛QUBE   Question 19 of 27 >   Back Next

II

III

IV

Section 1, Module 1: Reading & Writing

Annotate ⋮

A large number of people have doubts about the credibility of online health advice from unverified sources and often find themselves swamped by the countless, frequently contradictory _____ there is an increased need for reliable, expert guidance offered by a certified medical professional or platform.

20   Mark for Review 🔖

Which choice completes the text so that it conforms to the conventions of Standard English?

- (A) recommendations,   Ⓐ
- (B) recommendations; now that   Ⓑ
- (C) recommendations, so   Ⓒ
- (D) recommendations, therefore,   Ⓓ

TEST⬛QUBE   Question 20 of 27 >   Back Next

V

VI

VII

Section 1, Module 1: Reading & Writing

Annotate

In a paper published in the American Economic Review, economists Daron Acemoglu and Pascual Restrepo examined the relationship between automation and labor markets. They found that while automation can increase productivity and reduce the need for human labor in certain tasks, it can also create new tasks that require human skills. This dynamic process, in which tasks are constantly being automated and new tasks are being created, can lead to significant adjustments in labor markets ____.

21   Mark for Review

Which choice completes the text so that it conforms to the conventions of Standard English?

(A) itself

(B) themselves

(C) them

(D) it

Section 1, Module 1: Reading & Writing

Annotate

As the scientists observed, quadrupeds with shorter necks typically have a greater range of motion. The giraffes, in contrast, possess remarkably elongated necks, which enable them to access foliage at higher elevations, providing a distinct ecological advantage. This unique adaptation has allowed giraffes to perform tasks in ____ other herbivores may struggle, such as reaching nutritious leaves in the uppermost branches of tall trees, thereby reducing competition for resources and promoting their survival in various African savannah ecosystems.

22   Mark for Review

Which choice completes the text so that it conforms to the conventions of Standard English?

(A) whom

(B) which

(C) what

(D) that

Section 1, Module 1: Reading & Writing

Annotate

The human brain, often referred to as the epicenter of human consciousness and an astoundingly intricate organ, isn't merely an assembly of neurons suspended in empty space. According to Dr. Sandra Aamodt, a renowned neuroscientist and author of "Welcome to Your Brain," it is composed of approximately 75% water, which plays a crucial role in various brain functions. How _____ Water facilitates chemical reactions, provides a medium for nutrients to travel, and helps in waste removal from the brain.

23   Mark for Review 🔖

Which choice completes the text so that it conforms to the conventions of Standard English?

- (A) it maintains this composition!
- (B) does it maintain this composition.
- (C) it maintains this composition.
- (D) does it maintain this composition?

TEST QUBE

Back   Next

Section 1, Module 1: Reading & Writing

Annotate

Commonly referred to as the "father of modern genetics," _____ made groundbreaking discoveries in the field of heredity through his experiments with pea plants, laid the foundation for our understanding of genes, inheritance, and genetic variation.

24   Mark for Review 🔖

Which choice completes the text so that it conforms to the conventions of Standard English?

- (A) Gregor Mendel, whose work
- (B) it was Gregor Mendel's work that
- (C) the work of Gregor Mendel
- (D) Gregor Mendel and his work

TEST QUBE

Back   Next

I

II

III

IV

V

VI

VII

Section 1, Module 1: Reading & Writing

Annotate

The invention of the steam engine in the 18th century revolutionized transportation and industry. It powered trains, ships, and factories, enabling the rapid movement of goods and people. _____ the widespread adoption of steam power marked the beginning of the Industrial Revolution, which transformed economies and societies worldwide.

25   Mark for Review

Which choice completes the text so that it conforms to the conventions of Standard English?

(A) For instance,   Ⓐ

(B) As a consequence,   Ⓑ

(C) On the contrary,   Ⓒ

(D) Despite this,   Ⓓ

Section 1, Module 1: Reading & Writing

Annotate

While researching a topic, a student has taken the following notes:

- A political system is the set of institutions, rules, and processes that determine how a government functions.
- Common types of political systems include democracies, autocracies, and oligarchies.
- In a democracy, power is vested in the people, who elect representatives to make decisions on their behalf.
- Autocracies are characterized by a single individual or small group holding significant power, often with limited checks and balances.
- Oligarchies involve a small group of individuals or families controlling the government, often for their own benefit.

26   Mark for Review

The student wants to compare the distribution of power in democracies and autocracies. Which choice most effectively uses relevant information from the notes to accomplish this goal?

(A) Democracies and autocracies are both types of political systems, with democracies characterized by power being vested in the people, while autocracies involve a single individual or small group holding significant power.

(B) Political systems, such as democracies and autocracies, determine the institutions, rules, and processes that govern how a country is run, influencing the distribution of power within the government.

(C) In a democracy, power is distributed among the people who elect representatives to make decisions, whereas in an autocracy, the centralized power is devoid of checks and balances.

(D) Oligarchies are a type of political system that can be contrasted with democracies and autocracies, as they involve a small group of individuals or families controlling the government for their own benefit.

Section 1, Module 1: Reading & Writing

Annotate

While researching a topic, a student has taken the following notes:

- Climate change refers to long-term shifts in temperature, precipitation, and other weather patterns.
- Human activities, particularly the burning of fossil fuels, contribute to climate change through greenhouse gas emissions.
- Climate change can lead to various consequences, such as rising sea levels, extreme weather events, and species extinction.
- Mitigation strategies aim to reduce greenhouse gas emissions, while adaptation strategies focus on coping with the impacts of climate change.
- International agreements, such as the Paris Agreement, aim to address climate change on a global scale.

27   Mark for Review

The student wants to stress the primary human activity contributing to climate change. Which choice most effectively uses relevant information from the notes to accomplish this goal?

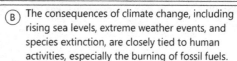

(A) Climate change, characterized by long-term shifts in weather patterns, is primarily driven by human activities, such as the burning of fossil fuels, which leads to greenhouse gas emissions.

(B) The consequences of climate change, including rising sea levels, extreme weather events, and species extinction, are closely tied to human activities, especially the burning of fossil fuels.

(C) Mitigation strategies aimed at reducing greenhouse gas emissions are necessary to address the primary human activity contributing to climate change: the burning of fossil fuels.

(D) International agreements like the Paris Agreement seek to combat climate change by addressing its primary cause: human activities such as the burning of fossil fuels that lead to greenhouse gas emissions.

I

II

III

IV

V

VI

VII

Move on to the Next Section ≫

Section 1, Module 2: Reading & Writing

🕐 32:00

Annotate ⋮

In the heated realm of academic competitions, the debate team from Lexington High School in Massachusetts was working tirelessly to sharpen their skills for the approaching 2021 National Speech & Debate Tournament. Guided by their coach Sara Sanchez, these prodigious teenagers, including standout performer Lavanya Singh, spent endless nights honing their argumentative skills. Their success hinged on their capability to tackle the trickiest part of a debate - addressing counter-arguments. Hence, their ability to adroitly _____ opposing viewpoints was key to their success.

1 Mark for Review 🔖

Which choice completes the text with the most logical and precise word or phrase?

- (A) rebut — Ⓐ
- (B) endorse — Ⓑ
- (C) emulate — Ⓒ
- (D) baffle — Ⓓ

TEST⬚QUBE

Question 1 of 27 >

Back Next

Section 1, Module 2: Reading & Writing

Annotate ⋮

The visionary independent film director, Penelope Alvarez, was lavishly praised by both critics and audiences for her distinctive artistic vision and unflinching willingness to tackle challenging, often controversial themes. Her films, "Fragments of Shadows" and "The Woven Tapestry", audaciously _____ traditional storytelling norms. She deftly employs nonlinear narratives, multifaceted characters, and evocative cinematography to craft compelling stories that push the boundaries of what is customarily seen in mainstream cinema. Her bold choices have sparked myriad discussions and breathed fresh air into an industry that often leans towards formulaic blockbusters.

2 Mark for Review 🔖

Which choice completes the text with the most logical and precise word or phrase?

- (A) appeases — Ⓐ
- (B) advocates —
- (C) subverts —
- (D) mollifies —

TEST⬚QUBE

Question 2 of 27 >

Back Next

Section 1, Module 2: Reading & Writing

Annotate ⋮

The veteran journalist, Daniel Rodriguez, was known for his ability to remain calm under pressure, particularly when reporting from conflict zones such as Syria and Afghanistan. His _____ demeanor, which had earned him the nickname 'The Eye of the Storm' among his peers, helped him deliver clear, unbiased reports even in the most tumultuous situations, making him a reliable source of information for millions of viewers around the world.

3 Mark for Review 🔖

Which choice completes the text with the most logical and precise word or phrase?

- Ⓐ impulsive
- Ⓑ stoic
- Ⓒ volatile
- Ⓓ insipid

TEST⬛QUBE

Back Next

Section 1, Module 2: Reading & Writing

Annotate ⋮

Dr. Amelia Thompson's groundbreaking study on neuroplasticity, published in the prestigious journal Nature Neuroscience, has had far-reaching implications for the field of neuroscience. Her pioneering work, which involved years of meticulous research at the University of Cambridge's Brain Research Centre, _____ the understanding of how the human brain adapts and changes over time. This has opened new avenues in the development of treatments for brain injuries and neurological disorders.

4 Mark for Review 🔖

Which choice completes the text with the most logical and precise word or phrase?

- Ⓐ undermined
- Ⓑ revolutionized
- Ⓒ diluted
- Ⓓ obliterated

TEST⬛QUBE

Back Next

Section 1, Module 2: Reading & Writing

Annotate

The following text is adapted from Henry James's novella *Daisy Miller*.

One of the hotels at Vevey, however, is famous, even classical, being distinguished from many of its upstart neighbors by an air both of luxury and of maturity. In this region, in the month of June, American travelers are extremely numerous; it may be said, indeed, that Vevey <u>assumes</u> at this period some of the characteristics of an American watering place. There are sights and sounds which evoke a vision, an echo, of Newport and Saratoga. There is a flitting hither and thither of "stylish" young girls, a rustling of muslin flounces, a rattle of dance music in the morning hours, a sound of high-pitched voices at all times.

5 Mark for Review

As used in the text, what does the word "assumes" most nearly mean?

(A) Adopts

(B) Surmises

(C) Conjecture

(D) Pretends

Section 1, Module 2: Reading & Writing

Annotate

The following text is adapted from Sarah Orne Jewett's 1896 collection of short stories, *The Country of the Pointed Firs*. The stories are set in a small coastal town in Maine, and are largely characterized by the relationships formed between the narrator and the town's interesting inhabitants, like the local herbalist, Mrs. Todd.

For some days after this, Mrs. Todd's customers came and went past my windows, and, haying-time being nearly over, strangers began to arrive from the inland country, such was her widespread reputation. Sometimes I saw a pale young creature like a white windflower left over into midsummer, upon whose face consumption had set its bright and wistful mark; but oftener two stout, hard-worked women from the farms came together, and detailed their symptoms to Mrs. Todd in loud and cheerful voices, combining the satisfactions of a friendly gossip with the medical opportunity. They seemed to give much from their own store of therapeutic learning.

6 Mark for Review

Which choice best states the main idea of the text?

(A) Mrs. Todd receives various kinds of customers, some of whom are seriously ill.

(B) The end of haying-time brings more visitors to Mrs. Todd from inland regions.

(C) Visitors to Mrs. Todd often share their own knowledge about remedies and treatments.

(D) Mrs. Todd's medical knowledge is greatly respected in her community.

Section 1, Module 2: Reading & Writing

Annotate ⋮

The following text is adapted from Max Weber's 1905 work, *The Protestant Ethic and the Spirit of Capitalism*.

In order that a manner of life well adapted to the peculiarities of the capitalism... could come to dominate others, it had to originate somewhere, and not in isolated individuals alone. <u>It had to become the dominant form of life for whole groups of people and impress its specific style on the highest spheres of human activity.</u> This specific style included a disciplined, rational approach to economic life.

7 Mark for Review 🔖

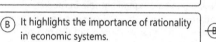

Which choice best describes the function of the underlined sentence in the text as a whole?

- (A) It explains the process by which capitalism became dominant. Ⓐ
- (B) It highlights the importance of rationality in economic systems. Ⓑ
- (C) It emphasizes the collective nature of the capitalist spirit. Ⓒ
- (D) It introduces the concept of the Protestant work ethic. Ⓓ

Section 1, Module 2: Reading & Writing

Annotate ⋮

The following text is adapted from William Wordsworth's 1807 poem "Daffodils" (I Wandered Lonely as a Cloud).

The waves beside them danced, but they
Out-did the sparkling waves in glee:
A poet could not be but gay,
In such a jocund company:
I gazed'and gazed'but little thought
What wealth the show to me had brought:

<u>For oft, when on my couch I lie
In vacant or in pensive mood.</u>
They flash upon that inward eye
Which is the bliss of solitude;
And then my heart with pleasure fills,
And dances with the daffodils.

8 Mark for Review 🔖

Which choice best describes the function of the underlined sentence in the text as a whole?

- (A) It establishes the setting and emotional state in which the speaker reflects on the daffodils.
- (B) It underscores the importance of physical restand relaxation in appreciating nature's beauty.
- (C) It portrays the speaker's inner turmoil and desire for solace and relaxation. Ⓒ
- (D) It introduces the idea that daydreaming and imagination are essential for mental well-being.

I

II

III

IV

Annotate ⋮

The Treaty of Tordesillas, signed in 1494, was an agreement between the Spanish and Portuguese monarchies to divide newly discovered lands outside Europe along a meridian in the Atlantic Ocean. This agreement aimed to resolve conflicts between the two nations over the colonization and exploration of the New World, following Christopher Columbus's voyages. The Pope played a significant role in mediating the negotiations, which ultimately resulted in the division of territories, with lands to the west of the meridian belonging to Spain and those to the east belonging to Portugal. The Treaty of Tordesillas proved influential in shaping the colonial landscape of the Americas, with Spain gaining control over most of South and Central America, while Portugal established a foothold in Brazil.

9   Mark for Review 🔖

Which of the following best describes the primary purpose of the Treaty of Tordesillas?

(A) To establish a trade alliance between Spain and Portugal

(B) To facilitate the joint exploration of newly discovered lands by both nations

(C) To remedy problems between Spain and Portugal over the colonization of the New World

(D) To create a unified European effort to colonize the Americas

---

Annotate ⋮

V

Text 1
"Duality of Light," a comprehensive review by Dr. Anton Llewellyn, brings to the fore a lesser-known aspect of light's nature - its particle-wave duality. In the domain of physics, light is often seen as a mere electromagnetic wave, but Dr. Llewellyn contests this perspective. His work, borrowing from quantum mechanics, argues that light behaves both as a particle and a wave. This particle-wave duality, as per his argument, has profound implications for our understanding of fundamental physics and the natural world.

VI

Text 2
In her exploration of the cosmos, astrophysicist Dr. Cara Rodriguez often employs the concept of light as a wave in her models. Rodriguez's research primarily focuses on cosmic phenomena like star formations, galaxy evolutions, and dark matter, phenomena that are better understood when light is treated as a wave. Her work affirms the importance of the wave theory of light, especially in understanding astronomical observations and elucidating the mysteries of the cosmos.

VII

10   Mark for Review 🔖

Considering both texts, how might Dr. Rodriguez perceive Dr. Llewellyn's stance on the nature of light?

(A) By appreciating the duality concept but maintain that in her field, the wave theory remains paramount.

(B) By rejecting the duality argument, asserting that light, in her astrophysical studies, behaves solely as a wave.

(C) By being intrigued by the duality perspective but argue that its relevance to cosmic phenomena is yet to be established.

(D) By endorsing the duality theory, incorporating it into her astrophysical models to refine her understanding.

Section 1, Module 2: Reading & Writing

Annotate ⋮

Milk Type	Fat (g/100ml)	Protein (g/100ml)	Calcium (mg/100ml)
Whole	3.3	3.3	120
Semi-Skim	1.8	3.4	125
Skim	0.1	3.4	130
Soy	2.5	3.5	50
Almond	2.8	1.0	40

The table presents data on the fat, protein, and calcium content of five types of milk. Researchers looked for the type of milk that had the least amount of fat, while maximizing protein and calcium content. Upon examining the contents of milk, the researchers identified ____

11   Mark for Review 🔖

Which choice most effectively uses data from the table to complete the statement?

- (A) Whole milk because it has the highest fat content and lower calcium levels compared to skim milk.
- (B) Semi-skim milk because it has a lower fat content but higher protein content than whole milk.
- (C) Skim milk because it has the lowest fat content higher calcium levels than soy milk, and higher protein levels than almond milk.
- (D) Skim milk because it has the lowest fat content and lower protein levels than soy milk, while having higher calcium levels than almond milk.

Section 1, Module 2: Reading & Writing

Annotate ⋮

Temperature vs Cases

(Scatter plot: Number of Cases on y-axis (0 to 400) vs Temperature (F) on x-axis (0 to 80). ◇ Cases)

Biostatisticians at a renowned health institute are studying the correlation between average daily temperature and the number of cases of a specific respiratory disease in a city over the course of 6 months. The city, known for its wide temperature swings between seasons, has recently experienced an uptick in cases of this disease. The research team concluded that there exists a general pattern between temperature variations and disease incidence.

12   Mark for Review 🔖

Which choice best describes data from the graph that support the researchers' conclusion?

- (A) There is a negative correlation between the number of cases and temperature as observed by the points in the graph following roughly a linear negative slope.
- (B) There is a positive correlation between the number of cases and temperature as observed by the points in the graph following roughly a linear positive slope.
- (C) Partially, for non-extreme temperatures, the data tends to reflect a linear trend.
- (D) There is no trend whatsoever, as evidenced by the scattered nature of the points.

Section 1, Module 2: Reading & Writing

The Arctic fox (Vulpes lagopus) is a small carnivorous mammal that has evolved an array of adaptations to thrive in the inhospitable conditions of the tundra. These adaptations include a thick fur coat that provides insulation against frigid temperatures and a keen olfactory sense that enables them to detect prey beneath the snow. Researchers have observed that Arctic foxes primarily feed on lemmings and voles, which are abundant in the tundra. These observations have led some scientists to posit that Arctic foxes rely exclusively on these small mammals for sustenance, citing evidence of their hunting strategies, such as excavating tunnels in the snow to access subnivean prey. This purported specialization, they argue, could make the Arctic foxes susceptible to fluctuations in lemming and vole populations.

13   Mark for Review 🔖

Which finding, if true, would most directly weaken the scientists' claim?

(A) Evidence emerges that Arctic foxes also consume a variety of other food sources in addition to lemmings and voles as part of a more diverse and adaptable diet.

(B) A specific population of Arctic foxes is observed to have a predilection for voles over lemmings, despite the availability of both prey species.

(C) An examination of Arctic foxes' fecal matter unveils a trace amount of lemming and vole bones, indicating their behavior adaptability in response to changing environments.

(D) The method for determining the dietary preferences of Arctic foxes is discovered to be less effective when analyzing other carnivorous mammals in the tundra.

TEST◼QUBE   Question 13 of 27 >   Back Next

Section 1, Module 2: Reading & Writing

Born in 1936 in St. Louis, Missouri, Katherine Dunham was a pioneer in the use of folk and ethnic choreography and one of the founders of the anthropological dance movement. In a dissertation for a Dance Studies course, a graduate student posits that Dunham's dance techniques served not just as artistic expression but as a sociocultural commentary— through her choreography, Dunham was able to depict diverse aspects of African and Caribbean cultures, representing them with both vibrancy and respect.

14   Mark for Review 🔖

Which finding, if true, would most directly support the student's claim?

(A) Dunham choreographed dances for Hollywood movies and Broadway shows, but she also created hundreds of routines based on the traditional dances, rituals, and customs of African and Caribbean communities.

(B) Dunham's choreography demonstrates a high level of technical skill, as seen in her innovative use of rhythm and movement to evoke emotional responses.

(C) During her lifetime, Dunham was acclaimed both within and outside her native United States, as her work was performed in places like France, Brazil, and Canada.

(D) Some of the cultures and dances Dunham portrayed had long been popular subjects for American choreographers.

TEST◼QUBE   Question 14 of 27 >   Back Next

Section 1, Module 2: Reading & Writing

Annotate

In recent years, scientists have discovered that certain species of plants exhibit a type of communication through the release of volatile organic compounds (VOCs). These compounds can alert nearby plants to potential dangers, such as herbivore attacks, encouraging them to increase their production of defensive chemicals. However, research has also shown that some insects have evolved to exploit these VOCs as cues to locate their preferred host plants. This information suggests that ____

15   Mark for Review

Which choice most logically completes the text?

- (A) volatile organic compounds are harmful to all plant species.

- (B) the use of VOCs for communication between plants is completely ineffective.

- (C) plant communication through VOCs might also inadvertently benefit herbivorous insects.

- (D) insects have no role in the evolution of plant communication systems.

TEST⬛QUBE

Back   Next

Section 1, Module 2: Reading & Writing

Annotate

When it comes to renewable energy sources, hydroelectric power is an essential component, making use of water to generate electricity. The Three Gorges Dam in China, the world's largest hydroelectric power station, _____ by harnessing the water flow from the Yangtze River, thereby supplying a significant amount of clean energy to millions of people.

16   Mark for Review

Which choice completes the text so that it conforms to the conventions of Standard English?

- (A) operates

- (B) had operated

- (C) would operate

- (D) was operating

TEST⬛QUBE

Back   Next

Section 1, Module 2: Reading & Writing

Annotate ⋮

The diverse approaches to addressing climate change ___ the various priorities and interests of the stakeholders involved in the debate. These differing opinions highlight the complexity of finding effective strategies to mitigate the impact and transition to a more sustainable future.

17   Mark for Review 🔖

Which choice completes the text so that it conforms to the conventions of Standard English?

(A) stem from   Ⓐ

(B) stems from   Ⓑ

(C) stemmed from   Ⓒ

(D) have stemmed from   Ⓓ

TEST⬛QUBE   Back   Next

Section 1, Module 2: Reading & Writing

Annotate ⋮

The intricate network of relationships between predators and prey in an ecosystem ___ the delicate balance necessary for the survival of all species involved. Disruptions to these relationships can have profound consequences on the overall health of the environment.

18   Mark for Review 🔖

Which choice completes the text so that it conforms to the conventions of Standard English?

(A) maintain   Ⓐ

(B) maintains   Ⓑ

(C) maintained   Ⓒ

(D) have maintained   Ⓓ

TEST⬛QUBE   Back   Next

Section 1, Module 2: Reading & Writing

Annotate

As the experience of Dr. Susan _____ who dedicated over 30 years to environmental research at Green Foundation, a prominent conservation organization — illustrates, the sector is perfect for individuals eager to apply their knowledge to protect natural resources and contribute to ecological sustainability.

19   Mark for Review 🔖

Which choice completes the text so that it conforms to the conventions of Standard English?

- Ⓐ Taylor,   Ⓐ
- Ⓑ Taylor   Ⓑ
- Ⓒ Taylor —   Ⓒ
- Ⓓ Taylor;   Ⓓ

TEST QUBE   Question 19 of 27 >   Back   Next

Section 1, Module 2: Reading & Writing

Annotate

As the career of Michael Johnson — who spent 15 years as a data privacy expert at Secure Solutions, a top cybersecurity firm _____ the industry is well-suited for professionals looking to use their skills to safeguard sensitive information while staying abreast of cutting-edge security developments.

20   Mark for Review 🔖

Which choice completes the text so that it conforms to the conventions of Standard English?

- Ⓐ firm – demonstrates,   Ⓐ
- Ⓑ firm demonstrates,   Ⓑ
- Ⓒ firm, demonstrates;   Ⓒ
- Ⓓ firm – demonstrates: Ⓓ

TEST QUBE   Question 20 of 27 >   Back   Next

I

II

III

IV

Section 1, Module 2: Reading & Writing   Annotate   ⋮

With the assumption that the Rosetta Stone contained the key to deciphering Egyptian hieroglyphs, _____ demonstrated that this artifact was indeed crucial for understanding ancient Egyptian texts. Through his painstaking efforts and linguistic expertise, Champollion deciphered the hieroglyphs and laid the foundation for modern Egyptology. His work provided invaluable insights into the culture, religion, and history of ancient Egypt.

21   Mark for Review 🔖

Which choice completes the text so that it conforms to the conventions of Standard English?

(A) it was French scholar Jean-François Champollion who   Ⓐ

(B) the deciphering by French scholar Jean-François Champollion   Ⓑ

(C) French scholar Jean-François Champollion's deciphering   Ⓒ

(D) French scholar Jean-François Champollion   Ⓓ

TEST🎲QUBE   Back   Next

V

VI

VII

Section 1, Module 2: Reading & Writing   Annotate   ⋮

A burgeoning field of study in environmental science is the examination of the effects of climate change on various ecosystems. One of the research focuses is the ____ over the last few decades, which scientists believe might be contributing to shifts in migration patterns of various animal species.

22   Mark for Review 🔖

Which choice completes the text so that it confirms to the conventions of Standard English?

(A) ecosystems' average temperature changes   Ⓐ

(B) ecosystem's average temperature change's   Ⓑ

(C) ecosystems average temperature changes   Ⓒ

(D) ecosystems average temperature changes'   Ⓓ

TEST🎲QUBE   Back   Next

Section 1, Module 2: Reading & Writing

Annotate ⋮

The Panama Canal, an artificial waterway connecting the Atlantic and Pacific Oceans, greatly facilitates international maritime trade. Completed in 1914, the canal significantly reduced the time and distance required for ships to travel between the oceans. _____ the construction of the canal presented numerous engineering challenges and required significant labor and resources.

23   Mark for Review ⬚

Which choice completes the text with the most logical transition?

- (A) In contrast,   —Ⓐ—
- (B) Consequently,   —Ⓑ—
- (C) Meanwhile,   —Ⓒ—
- (D) Nonetheless,   —Ⓓ—

TEST⬚QUBE

Back Next

Section 1, Module 2: Reading & Writing

Annotate ⋮

The development of antibiotics has saved countless lives by treating bacterial infections. Penicillin, discovered by Alexander Fleming in 1928, was the first antibiotic to be widely used. _____ the overuse and misuse of antibiotics have led to the emergence of antibiotic-resistant bacteria, posing a significant public health threat.

24   Mark for Review ⬚

Which choice completes the text with the most logical transition?

- (A) Similarly,   —Ⓐ—
- (B) In conclusion,   —Ⓑ—
- (C) However,   —Ⓒ—
- (D) In addition,   —Ⓓ—

TEST⬚QUBE

Back Next

Section 1, Module 2: Reading & Writing

Annotate

While researching a topic, a student has taken the following notes:

- Nellie Bly, born in 1864, was a groundbreaking journalist known for her investigative and undercover reporting.
- In 1887, she feigned insanity to investigate reports of brutality and neglect at the Women's Lunatic Asylum on Blackwell's Island.
- Her report, later published as "Ten Days in a Mad-House," caused a sensation and brought her lasting fame.
- In 1889, Bly undertook a journey around the world, inspired by Jules Verne's "Around the World in Eighty Days."
- She completed the trip in 72 days, setting a world record.

25   Mark for Review

The student wants to emphasize the daring acts Bly undertook during her journalism career. Which choice most effectively uses relevant information from the notes to accomplish this goal?

(A) Nellie Bly, known for her investigative reporting, undertook a record- breaking journey around the world in 1889.

(B) Nellie Bly's report on the Women's Lunatic Asylum brought her lasting fame and highlighted her role as a groundbreaking journalist.

(C) Nellie Bly's work, characterized by exploits such as feigning insanity to investigate an asylum and traveling around the world, had a significant impact on journalism.

(D) In 1887 and 1889, Nellie Bly undertook high-profile projects that showcased her commitment to investigative journalism.

Section 1, Module 2: Reading & Writing

Annotate

While researching a topic, a student has taken the following notes:

- Plato was a classical Greek philosopher and student of Socrates.
- Plato's philosophy is often known for the theory of Forms, which argues that non-physical forms (or ideas) represent the most accurate reality.
- Plato's Allegory of the Cave is a metaphor for human perception and knowledge.
- His works, written as dialogues, often feature Socrates as a main character.
- The Academy, founded by Plato, was an important institution for philosophical and scientific education in the ancient world.

26   Mark for Review

The student wants to articulate the core idea of Plato's philosophy. Which choice most effectively uses relevant information from the notes to accomplish this goal?

(A) Plato's philosophical perspective underscores the supremacy of abstract concepts, or forms, as constituting the fundamental nature of reality.

(B) Plato, a student of Socrates, emphasized the importance of dialogue in his philosophical treatises, which often highlighted Socrates as a protagonist.

(C) The Allegory of the Cave, an essential metaphor in Plato's philosophy, illustrates the human quest for knowledge and understanding.

(D) The Academy, founded by Plato, epitomizes his commitment to the proliferation of philosophical and scientific knowledge in the ancient world.

Section 1, Module 2: Reading & Writing ✎ Annotate ⋮

While researching a topic, a student has taken the following notes:

- Elizabeth Loftus is a cognitive psychologist known for her work on memory.
- She conducted a study where participants were shown a film of a car accident.
- Participants were asked how fast the cars were going when they "smashed into" each other, or "hit" each other.
- Those who heard "smashed into" estimated higher speeds than those who heard "hit."
- This study suggested that the phrasing of a question can influence a person's memory of an event.

27 Mark for Review 🔖

The student wants to summarize the main findings of Loftus's study. Which choice most effectively uses relevant information from the notes to accomplish this goal?

(A) Loftus conducted an experiment showing a car accident film to participants and asked them about the speed of the cars.

(B) Elizabeth Loftus's research revealed that the terminology used in questioning can alter an individual's recollection of an incident.

(C) The study by Loftus indicated that participants who heard the phrase "smashed into" estimated higher speeds for the cars.

(D) Loftus's work in cognitive psychology mainly revolves around memory and how it can be influenced by external factors.

TEST◼QUBE **End of Test 5 Reading/Writing Section** Back Next

---

Upcoming Math Section: Reference Formula Sheet

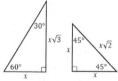

$A = \pi r^2$
$C = 2\pi r$

$A = lw$

$A = \frac{1}{2}bh$

$c^2 = a^2 + b^2$

$V = \frac{1}{3}\pi r^2 h$

$V = \frac{1}{3}lwh$

Special Right Triangles

$V = lwh$

$V = \pi r^2 h$

$V = \frac{3}{4}\pi r^3$

The number of degrees of arc in a circle is 360.
The number of radians of arc in a circle is 2π.
The sum of the measures in degrees of the angles of a triangle is 180.

Directions for Student-Produced Response

- **TEST QUBE** recommends students to use decimals for most answers but suggests using fractions only in cases where the answers involve repeating decimals (e.g., 0.333 = 1/3).
- For cases with more than one answer, enter **just one of the answers.**
- You can enter up to 5 characters for your answer. (For negative answers, the **negative sign** does not count as one character)
- For **fractions** that don't fit the answer box, enter the decimal equivalent (Unless advised to do otherwise)
- For **decimals** that exceed the answer box, round to the fourth digit. (Unless advised to do otherwise)
- For mixed number (such as $4\frac{1}{4}$), enter it as an improper fraction (17/4) or its decimal equivalent (4.25)
- For all answers, you may omit the symbols and units such as $,%, cm^3, m^2, etc.

Acceptable vs Non-Acceptable Answers

Answer	Acceptable ways to receive credit	Ways you **WON'T** receive credit
4.25	4.25 , 17/4	41/4 , 4 1/4
4/6	2/3 .6666 , .6667 0.666 , 0.667	0.66 , .66 0.67 , .67
-1/6	-1/6 -0.166 , -0.167 -.1666 , -.1667	-0.16 , -.16 -0.17 , -.167

Move on to the Next Section ≫

I
II
III
IV
V
VI
VII

⏱ 35:00

Annotate ⋮

1   Mark for Review 🔖

Which of the following points represent the intersections of the function
$f(x) = 3x^2 + 36x + 96$ with the x axis?

Ⓐ $(4, 0)$

Ⓑ $(0, -4)$

Ⓒ $(-8, 0)$

Ⓓ $(0, 0)$

TEST🟦QUBE   Question 1 of 22 >

Annotate ⋮

2   Mark for Review 🔖

Jimmy is booking a hotel which costs $80 per night and a $100 one-time fee. Considering Jimmy's budget of $1200, what is the maximum number of days Jimmy can stay at the hotel?

Ⓐ 12

Ⓑ 13

Ⓒ 14

Ⓓ 15

TEST🟦QUBE   Question 2 of 22 >

Annotate ⋮

3   Mark for Review 🔖

James created a unique shape by combining without overlapping three identical equilateral triangles. If each triangle has a side length of 10 centimeters, what is the **closest** total area of this special shape?

Ⓐ 140 cm²

Ⓑ 43.30 cm²

Ⓒ 129.90 cm²

Ⓓ 229.90 cm²

TEST🟦QUBE   Question 3 of 22 >

Annotate ⋮

4   Mark for Review 🔖

A bag contains 18 marbles, 13 of which are red and 5 of which are blue. Three marbles are drawn at random, without replacement. What is the probability that all three marbles are red?

Ⓐ $1/18$

Ⓑ $143/408$

Ⓒ $13/126$

Ⓓ $1/4$

TEST🟦QUBE   Question 4 of 22 >   Back   Next

I

II

III

IV

V

VI

VII

Section 2, Module 1: Math   Annotate   ⋮

5   Mark for Review 🔖

In a random selection of 230 voters, they were asked about their satisfaction with a policy. Out of these voters, 80 expressed dissatisfaction. If a total of $17,250$ people were to vote for the policy, what is the best estimate of votes that indicate satisfaction with the policy?

(A) 11250   (A)

(B) 6000   (B)

(C) 16470   (C)

(D) 8000   (D)

TEST🎲QUBE   Question 5 of 22 >

Section 2, Module 1: Math   Annotate   ⋮

6   Mark for Review 🔖

In triangle ABC, the following information is given: Angle B measures 90 degrees, and Angle C measures 30 degrees. If the length of side AB is 20, what is the length of side AC?

(A) $20\sqrt{3}$ (A)

(B) 40   (B)

(C) 60   (C)

(D) 15   (D)

TEST🎲QUBE   Question 6 of 22 >

Section 2, Module 1: Math   Annotate   ⋮

7   Mark for Review 🔖

What is the product of the solutions for x in the given equation?

$$x(x+8) = 4x^2 + 45x + 20$$

(A) 37/3   (A)

(B) 37   (B)

(C) 20/3   (C)

(D) 20   (D)

TEST🎲QUBE   Question 7 of 22 >   Back   Next

8   Mark for Review 🔖

Based on the dot plot provided, which of the following descriptions best characterizes the distribution of data sets A and B?

Data set A:

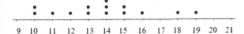

Data set B:

(A) Data set A has greater mean and standard deviation than Data set B.   (A)

(B) Data set A has greater mean but lower standard deviation than Data set B.   (B)

(C) Data set A has smaller mean but greater standard deviation than Data set B.   (C)

(D) Data set A has smaller mean and standard deviation than Data set B.   (D)

---

9   Mark for Review 🔖

The given function $f(x) = (x+4)(x+3)$ is translated up by 3 units. At which y-coordinate does this graph intersect $x = 3$?

(A) 45   (A)

(B) 48   (B)

(C) 50   (C)

(D) 52   (D)

10   Mark for Review 🔖

If $2x + 4 = 12$, what is the value of $x + 9$?

11   Mark for Review 🔖

What is the y-intercept for the given graph below?

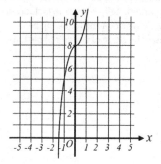

(A)   8

(B)   7

(C)   1

(D) -1

12   Mark for Review 🔖

Chris rides his bicycle at a constant speed of 30 feet per minute. How long, in seconds, does it approximately take him to reach a point that is 70 feet away?

(A)   125

(B)   130

(C)   140

(D)   160   (D)

13   Mark for Review 🔖

The length of the garden is 20 meters, and it is 20% longer than its width. What is the approximate width of the garden in meters? (Round your answer to the nearest tenth.)

Section 2, Module 1: Math Annotate ⋮

14 Mark for Review 🔖

James boards a train leaving a station at $10:00$ AM and observes that the train is traveling at a speed of 60 miles per hour. Meanwhile, Eve boards another train from the same station, departing one hour later, and her train travels in the same direction at a speed of 70 miles per hour. What time will Eve's train catch up to James' train?

(A) $1:00$ PM ⊘A

(B) $2:30$ PM ⊘B

(C) $4:00$ PM ⊘C

(D) $5:00$ PM ⊘D

TEST⬛QUBE Question 14 of 22 >

Section 2, Module 1: Math Annotate ⋮

15 Mark for Review 🔖

The store is selling a shirt for $20. The store is offering a 20% discount on the shirt. If there is a sales tax of 5% on the discounted price, what will be the final price of the shirt?

(A) $15.00 ⊘A

(B) $15.20 ⊘B

(C) $16.00 ⊘C

(D) $16.80 ⊘D

TEST⬛QUBE Question 15 of 22 >

Section 2, Module 1: Math Annotate ⋮

16 Mark for Review 🔖

The scatter plot provided illustrates the relationship between hours of exercise and the corresponding weight loss. Additionally, the graph includes a line of best fit as well. Which of the following best approximates the slope of the line of best fit?

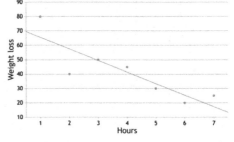

(A) 8 ⊘A

(B) -8 ⊘B

(C) 10 ⊘C

(D) -10 ⊘D

TEST⬛QUBE Question 16 of 22 > Back Next

I

II

III

IV

V

VI

VII

17   Mark for Review 🔖

For the quadratic function $f(x)$,
$f(1) = 4$, $f(2) = 7$
Which equation could define $f(x)$?

- (A) $f(x) = x^2 + 3$
- (B) $f(x) = 2x^2 - 1$
- (C) $f(x) = x^2 + x + 3$
- (D) $f(x) = 3x^2 - 2$

TEST⬛QUBE   Question 17 of 22 >

18   Mark for Review 🔖

A hotel has a rectangular swimming pool with dimensions 20 meters in length and 15 meters in width. The manager fills the pool with water to a depth of 2 meters. What is the volume of water in the pool, measured in cubic meters?

- (A) 450 cubic meters
- (B) 400 cubic meters
- (C) 300 cubic meters
- (D) 600 cubic meters

TEST⬛QUBE   Question 18 of 22 >

19   Mark for Review 🔖

With the given system of equations
$$2x + 3y = 25$$
$$x = 2y$$

What is the value of x?

TEST⬛QUBE   Question 19 of 22 >   Back   Next

20
Mark for Review 🔖

The table provided displays the preference distribution of students from three classes. If a student is chosen randomly from the total student population, what is the probability that the selected student prefers Math class?

	Math	English	Science	Total
Class A	40	20	15	75
Class B	80	50	30	160
Class C	30	10	20	60
Total	150	80	65	295

(A) 160/295   ~~(A)~~

(B) 60/295   ~~(B)~~

(C) 80/295   ~~(C)~~

(D) 150/295   ~~(D)~~

21
Mark for Review 🔖

Considering the given function $f(x) = 1.5x + 30$, if there exists a linear function g that is parallel to function f and intersects at the point $(-4, 2)$, what is the y-intercept of function g?

22
Mark for Review 🔖

Alice is trying to determine the optimal allocation of hours between her two jobs. She aims to work a total of 30 hours per week while earning $300 in total. The first job offers a pay rate of $5 per hour, and the second job pays $15 per hour. How many hours should Alice work for the first job in order to achieve her desired earnings and total hours?

(A) 20 hours   ~~(A)~~

(B) 15 hours   ~~(B)~~

(C) 10 hours   ~~(C)~~

(D) 30 hours   ~~(D)~~

Move on to the Next Section ≫

⏱ 35:00

1   Mark for Review 🔖

What value of x is the solution for the following equation below?

$$6x - 3x - 15 = 75$$

TEST⬡QUBE   Question 1 of 22 >

2   Mark for Review 🔖

The solution to the given system of equations is (m, n). What is the value of $m - n$?

$$3m + 4n = 7$$
$$4m + 3n = 10$$

(A) -3

(B) -1

(C) 1

(D) 3

TEST⬡QUBE   Question 2 of 22 >

3   Mark for Review 🔖

Alex takes a tram and bicycle from home to his workplace. The tram travels at a constant speed of 15 miles per hour and the bicycle at 10 miles per hour. The distance between his home and workplace is 10 miles and it takes 45 minutes for him to travel one-way. How long did Alex travel on the tram?

(A) 12 minutes

(B) 15 minutes

(C) 24 minutes

(D) 30 minutes

TEST⬡QUBE   Question 3 of 22 >

4   Mark for Review 🔖

Which of the systems of equations have infinitely many solutions?

(A) $2x + 4y = 3$ and $6x + 12y = 9$

(B) $-x - y = 5$ and $x - y = 5$

(C) $4x - y = -2$ and $4x - y = 2$

(D) $3x + 3y = 1$ and $3x - 3y = -1$

TEST⬡QUBE   Question 4 of 22 >   Back   Next

I
II
III
IV
V
VI
VII

Annotate

5 Mark for Review

The function g is defined by $g(x) = 3x^2 - 6x + 4$. For what value of x does $g(x) = 28$?

- (A) -4
- (B) -2
- (C) 3
- (D) 5

TEST█QUBE Question 5 of 22 >

Annotate

6 Mark for Review

What value of b would result in no real solution for the given equation below?

$$3x^2 - bx + 2 = 0$$

- (A) 4
- (B) 5
- (C) 6
- (D) 7

TEST█QUBE Question 6 of 22 >

Annotate

7 Mark for Review

The given equation relates the numbers a, b, and c. Which of the following correctly expresses b in terms of a and c?

$$c = 3a^2 - 2b$$

- (A) $b = \frac{3a^2 + c}{2}$
- (B) $b = \frac{3}{2a^2 - c}$
- (C) $b = \frac{3a^2 - c}{2}$
- (D) $b = 3a^2 - c$

TEST█QUBE Question 7 of 22 >

Annotate

8 Mark for Review

Jake is shopping at a store and plans to purchase both cookies and chips. The price of each cookie is $\$2.5$, while each chip costs $\$1.5$. Jake intends to buy 6 chips and wishes to spend a minimum of $\$26$ but no more than $\$27$ in total. How many cookies should Jake include in the purchase?

TEST█QUBE Question 8 of 22 > Back Next

Section 2, Module 2: Math Annotate ⋮

9 Mark for Review 🔖

Which of the following expressions is equivalent to $\frac{(a^4b^3c^2)(a^{-1}b^2c^5)}{(ab^2c^{-1})}$, where a, b, and c are positive?

(A) $a^{-4}b^{12}c^{-10}$

(B) $a^{-4}b^3c^{-10}$

(C) $a^4b^7c^6$

(D) $a^2b^3c^8$

Section 2, Module 2: Math Annotate ⋮

10 Mark for Review 🔖

What is the slope for the given linear function below?

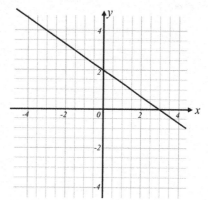

(A) $-3/2$

(B) $-2/3$

(C) $2/3$

(D) $3/2$

11 Mark for Review 🔖

The function f is defined by $f(x) = -2x + 6$ and function g is defined by $g(x) = -f(x)$. What is the value of $g(-1)$?

12 Mark for Review 🔖

Which of the following equations defines the function f as shown in the graph below?

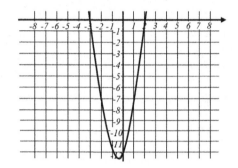

- (A) $f(x) = -2x^2 + 2x + 12$ Ⓐ
- (B) $f(x) = -2x^2 - 2x + 12$ Ⓑ
- (C) $f(x) = 2x^2 - 2x - 12$ Ⓒ
- (D) $f(x) = 2x^2 + 2x - 12$ Ⓓ

13 Mark for Review

The function $f(x)$ is illustrated below. What is the value of $f(-2)$?

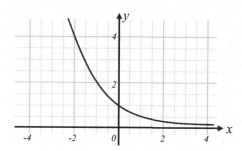

- (A) -4
- (B) -2
- (C) 2
- (D) 4

14 Mark for Review

To produce 10 grams of dough, a mixture is prepared by combining 8 grams of flour, 1.5 grams of water, and 0.5 grams of sugar. If there is a total of 65 grams of dough, how many grams of water is included in the mixture? (Ignore the gram sign.)

15 Mark for Review

Jeremy ordered a steak and wine at a restaurant. The steak costs 28 dollars and wine 12 dollars. Jeremy must pay 10 percent tax to the total amount of food he paid and an additional tip of 6 dollars above that. How much money does Jeremy have to pay at the restaurant? (ignore the dollar sign)

I

II

III

IV

V

VI

VII

Section 2, Module 2: Math Annotate ⋮

16 Mark for Review 🔖

Class A comprises 50 students, where 22 students can speak Spanish, 16 students can speak French, and 4 students can speak both languages. What is the probability that a randomly selected student from Class A speak neither Spanish nor French?

Ⓐ 16% —A—

Ⓑ 24% —B—

Ⓒ 32% —C—

Ⓓ 36% —D—

TEST◼QUBE Question 16 of 22 >

Section 2, Module 2: Math Annotate ⋮

17 Mark for Review 🔖

Anna weighs 125 pounds. Determine Anna's weight in tons. (1 pound = 0.45 kilograms and 1 kilogram = 0.001 ton)

Ⓐ 0.0056 tons —A—

Ⓑ 0.056 tons —B—

Ⓒ 0.56 tons —C—

Ⓓ 5.6 tons —D—

TEST◼QUBE Question 17 of 22 >

Section 2, Module 2: Math Annotate ⋮

18 Mark for Review 🔖

Which of the following equations best represents the line of best fit for the scatterplot below?

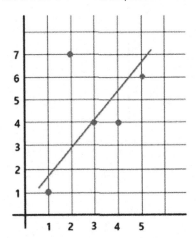

Ⓐ $y = 1.2x + 0.5$ —A—

Ⓑ $y = -1.2x + 0.5$ —B—

Ⓒ $y = 1.2x - 0.5$ —C—

Ⓓ $y = -1.2x - 0.5$ —D—

TEST◼QUBE Question 18 of 22 > Back Next

19　　　　　　　　　Mark for Review 🔖

What is the volume of a pyramid with a length of 6, a width of 4 and a height of 5?

20　　　　　　　　　Mark for Review 🔖

In the diagram below, triangle ABC is circumscribed by circle with a center O. If $\angle BAC$ is $40°$, what is $\angle BCA$?

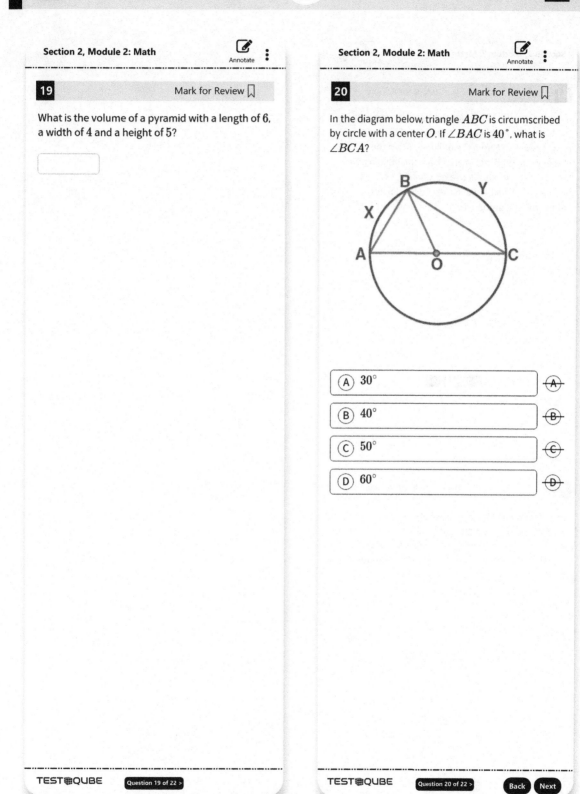

(A) $30°$

(B) $40°$

(C) $50°$

(D) $60°$

Section 2, Module 2: Math

Annotate

21 Mark for Review 🔖

A ladder, initially 15 feet long, is leaning exactly at the top of the building with the base of the ladder positioned 9 feet from the building. When the ladder is pulled 3 feet farther from the building, the top of the ladder drops to a new height. Let's denote the angle between the newly adjusted ladder and the ground as A. Find the value of $\sin(A)$.

TEST⬡QUBE   Question 21 of 22 >

Section 2, Module 2: Math

Annotate

22 Mark for Review 🔖

Consider an equilateral triangle A with a side length of $4cm$. If triangle B is similar to triangle A and has side lengths that are 50 percent longer than that of triangle A, what is the area of triangle B?

(A) $4\sqrt{3}$

(B) $6\sqrt{3}$

(C) $8\sqrt{3}$

(D) $9\sqrt{3}$

TEST⬡QUBE   Question 22 of 22 >

TESTQUBE

Digital SAT ®

Practice Test #6

Section 1, Module 1: Reading & Writing

⏱ 32:00

Annotate ✎   ⋮

The young and talented author Cassandra Wilkins took the literary world by storm with her debut novel, "Shadows of the Lost Kingdom." The novel, which follows the harrowing journey of a fiercely independent heroine, Elara, through a richly built fantasy world, was met with critical acclaim. Its complex characters and engaging plot earned widespread praise from literary critics and readers alike. The success of the book ____ her status as a promising new voice in the literary world, and readers eagerly await her next masterpiece.

1   Mark for Review 🔖

Which choice completes the text with the most logical and precise word or phrase?

Ⓐ ostracized   Ⓐ

Ⓑ cemented   Ⓑ

Ⓒ diminished   Ⓒ

Ⓓ undermined   Ⓓ

TEST❑QUBE   Question 1 of 27 >   Back Next

Section 1, Module 1: Reading & Writing

Annotate ✎   ⋮

Dr. Angela Martinez, a renowned ecologist, has dedicated her illustrious career to studying the impacts of climate change on various ecosystems. Having earned her doctorate from Stanford University, Dr. Martinez embarked on expeditions to diverse ecosystems ranging from the Amazon Rainforest to the Arctic Tundra. Her groundbreaking research has been published in prestigious journals such as Nature and Science, and it has contributed significantly to the field of ecology. Her work, which meticulously analyzes the data on the changes in flora and fauna, has ____ the understanding of how global warming affects biodiversity across the globe.

2   Mark for Review 🔖

Which choice completes the text with the most logical and precise word or phrase?

Ⓐ mystified   Ⓐ

Ⓑ trivialized

Ⓒ advanced

Ⓓ impeded

TEST❑QUBE   Question 2 of 27 >   Back Next

In the 1970s, Xerox PARC developed the Alto, a pioneering personal computer that introduced numerous innovations still used today, such as the graphical user interface, WYSIWYG text editing, and Ethernet networking. The Alto's groundbreaking design has led some to call it the ____ of modern computing.

3   Mark for Review 🔖

Which choice completes the text with the most logical and precise word or phrase?

(A) impediment   —Ⓐ—

(B) antithesis   —Ⓑ—

(C) prodigy   —Ⓒ—

(D) progenitor   —Ⓓ—

II

III

IV

Considered one of the most influential albums in music history, The Beatles' 1967 release, Sgt. Pepper's Lonely Hearts Club Band, broke new ground with its innovative recording techniques and diverse musical styles. The album's distinctive sound has been ____ as a crucial turning point in the development of rock music.

4   Mark for Review 🔖

Which choice completes the text with the most logical and precise word or phrase?

(A) deprecated   —Ⓐ—

(B) trivialized   —Ⓑ—

(C) heralded   —Ⓒ—

(D) misconstrued   —Ⓓ—

V

VI

VII

I

II

III

IV

V

VI

VII

Section 1, Module 1: Reading & Writing

Annotate ⋮

The Diablada, a traditional Bolivian dance that originated in the city of Oruro, is characterized by its elaborate costumes and masks, representing the battle between good and evil. This vibrant cultural expression has become a/an _____ symbol of Bolivia's rich heritage.

5   Mark for Review 🔖

Which choice completes the text with the most logical and precise word or phrase?

(A) devise

(B) emblematic

(C) ephemeral

(D) contradictory

Section 1, Module 1: Reading & Writing

Annotate ⋮

The 1980s saw the emergence of the genre-defying band, Talking Heads, whose fusion of punk, funk, and world music elements, along with their distinct visual style, garnered them a dedicated fan base. Their innovative approach to music has been _____ as a significant influence on the evolution of alternative rock.

6   Mark for Review 🔖

Which choice completes the text with the most logical and precise word or phrase?

(A) dismissed

(B) belittled

(C) lauded

(D) misinterpreted

Section 1, Module 1: Reading & Writing

Annotate ⋮

The following text is adapted from Emily Dickinson's 1861 poem "Hope is the thing with feathers." The poem is a metaphorical reflection on the concept of hope.

Hope is the thing with feathers
That perches in the soul,
And sings the tune without the words,
And never stops at all,

And sweetest in the gale is heard;
And sore must be the storm
That could abash the little bird
That kept so many warm.

7 Mark for Review 🔖

Which choice best states the main purpose of the text?

- (A) To emphasize the resilience of hope in the face of adversity by portraying it as a bird that continues to sing. Ⓐ
- (B) To focus on the fleeting nature of happiness and joy, suggesting that they are as fragile as a bird's song. Ⓑ
- (C) To highlight the power of song to bring people together, even in difficult times and harsh conditions. Ⓒ
- (D) To underscore the importance of appreciating the beauty of nature, particularly through the metaphor of a bird. Ⓓ

TEST🌐QUBE

Back Next

Section 1, Module 1: Reading & Writing

Annotate ⋮

The following text is adapted from W. Somerset Maugham's 1915 novel *Of Human Bondage*. Philip finds himself in a room that feels unfamiliar, despite being in his own house, after his mother's death.

Philip went downstairs slowly and found the door open. Mr. Carey had left the room. Philip walked slowly round. They had been in the house so short a time that there was little in it that had a particular interest to him. It was a stranger's room, and Philip saw nothing that struck his fancy. <u>But he knew which were his mother's things and which belonged to the landlord, and presently fixed on a little clock that he had once heard his mother say she liked.</u> With this he walked again rather disconsolately upstairs.

8 Mark for Review 🔖

Which choice best describes the function of the underlined sentence in the text as a whole?

- (A) It juxtaposes the foreign nature of the room with Philip's recognition of his mother's possessions. Ⓐ
- (B) It provides profound insights into the landlord's belongings and their significance. Ⓑ
- (C) It reveals Philip's antipathy for a particular item bearing sentimental significance to his mother. Ⓒ
- (D) It conveys Philip's sorrow over his mother's passing even after many sleepless nights of mourning in her room. Ⓓ

TEST🌐QUBE

Back Next

Section 1, Module 1: Reading & Writing

The following text is adapted from Marcus Aurelius's 180 A.D. book *Meditations*. The book is a compilation of personal reflections by the Roman Emperor, containing his thoughts on philosophy, morality, and life.

To Rusticus I am beholding, that I first entered into the conceit that my life wanted some redress and cure. And then, that I did not fall into the ambition of ordinary sophists, either to write tracts concerning the common theorems, or to exhort men unto virtue and the study of philosophy by public orations; as also that I never by way of ostentation did affect to show myself an active able man, for any kind of bodily exercises. And that I gave over the study of rhetoric and poetry, and of elegant neat language. That I did not use to walk about the house in my long robe, nor to do any such things.

9   Mark for Review 🔖

Which choice best describes the overall structure of the text?

(A) It presents a series of personal declarations made by Marcus Aurelius, tracing the path of his intellectual development and behavioral changes under the influence of Rusticus.

(B) It reveals Marcus Aurelius' confession of what he avoided doing in life, attributing these choices to his relationship with Rusticus.

(C) It commences with an acknowledgment of Rusticus' influence on Marcus Aurelius, followed by a detailed account of actions not taken due to this guidance.

(D) It first identifies the importance of Rusticus in Marcus Aurelius' life and then delves into a list of negations depicting his pursuit of particular activities.

Section 1, Module 1: Reading & Writing

Plant coloration and pigmentation play essential roles in obtaining food (such as through photosynthesis) and attracting pollinators (like flowers). However, the role of pigmentation in evading predators has not been thoroughly examined. Matthew Klooster from Harvard University, along with his team, explored whether the desiccated bracts (unique leaves) of the rare forest-dwelling Monotropsis odorata might function similarly to a tiger's stripes or a peppered moth's grey wings - to blend in. "Monotropsis odorata is a truly remarkable plant species since it depends solely on mycorrhizal fungi, which form a relationship with its roots, to provide all the necessary resources for survival," Klooster explains. "As a result, this plant isn't bound by the need for photosynthetic pigmentation (i.e., green coloration) to generate its energy, which allows it to explore a wider spectrum of coloration, much like fungi or animals."

10   Mark for Review 🔖

According to the text, why would plants' defensive mechanisms be limited?

(A) Because many plants are bound by the need for photosynthetic pigmentation.

(B) Because numerous plants are hindered by the necessity to evade predators.

(C) Because many plants do not have a wide spectrum of coloration to attract pollinators.

(D) Because numerous plants depend solely on mycorrhizal fungi for survival.

Section 1, Module 1: Reading & Writing

Annotate ⋮

The following text is adapted from Robert Louis Stevenson's 1886 novel, *The Strange Case of Dr. Jekyll and Mr. Hyde*. Here, Dr. Jekyll meditates on his inner struggle with his alter ego, Mr. Hyde.

Jekyll had more than a father's interest; Hyde had more than a son's indifference. I could have screamed aloud; I sought with tears and prayers to smother down the crowd of hideous images and sounds with which my memory swarmed against me. In the course of my life, which had been, after all, nine-tenths a life of effort, virtue and control, it had been much less exercised and much less exhausted.

11   Mark for Review 🔖

Which choice best states the main idea of the text?

(A) Jekyll's life has been mostly effortless and uncontrollable due to Hyde's indifference.

(B) Jekyll struggles to suppress Hyde, reflecting on the distress and exhaustion this internal conflict has caused him.

(C) Jekyll is apathetic towards Hyde and finds comfort in his virtuous life.

(D) Jekyll is tormented by his past actions, most of which were committed under Hyde's influence.

TEST⬛QUBE

Back   Next

Section 1, Module 1: Reading & Writing

Annotate ⋮

Much Ado About Nothing is a circa 1600 play by William Shakespeare. In the play, Beatrice's change of heart towards Benedick becomes apparent as they move from verbal sparring to genuine affection. Beatrice's emotional transformation is best illustrated when she _____

12   Mark for Review 🔖

Which choice most effectively uses a quotation from *Much Ado About Nothing* to illustrate the claim?

(A) admits to Benedick, "I love you with so much of my heart that none is left to protest."

(B) speaks to Hero, "I had rather hear my dog bark at a crow than a man swear he loves me."

(C) tells Don Pedro, "I was born to speak all mirth and no matter."

(D) addresses Benedick, "You always end with a jade's trick. I know you of old."

TEST⬛QUBE

Back   Next

Catalyst	Reaction Rate without Catalyst (s^{-1})	Reaction Rate with Catalyst (s^{-1})	Rate Enhancement Factor
Alpha	0.05	0.20	4
Beta	0.10	0.30	3
Gamma	0.05	0.10	2

The table displays the effect of three catalysts (Alpha, Beta, and Gamma) on chemical reaction rates. The reaction rate measures how quickly reactants are converted into products. The rate enhancement factor is the ratio of the reaction rate with a catalyst to the reaction rate without a catalyst. Researchers claim that Catalyst Alpha is the most effective in enhancing the reaction rate.

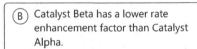

13   Mark for Review

Which choice best describes data from the table that support the researchers' claim?

- (A) Catalyst Alpha has the highest reaction rate with catalyst.
- (B) Catalyst Beta has a lower rate enhancement factor than Catalyst Alpha.
- (C) Catalyst Alpha has the highest rate enhancement factor.
- (D) All catalysts have the same rate enhancement factor.

High consumption of red meat has been associated with an increased risk of developing certain types of cancer, such as colorectal cancer. Some researchers have hypothesized that the link between red meat intake and cancer risk is due to the presence of carcinogenic compounds formed during the cooking process. However, there is no consistent evidence of a significant increase in cancer rates coinciding with the consumption of red meat prepared using different cooking methods, such as grilling, baking, or frying, suggesting that _____

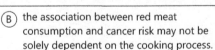

14   Mark for Review

Which choice most logically completes the text?

- (A) variations in cooking methods have no influence on the formation of carcinogenic compounds in red meat.
- (B) the association between red meat consumption and cancer risk may not be solely dependent on the cooking process.
- (C) cancer rates are higher among individuals who consume red meat prepared using certain cooking methods than among those who consume red meat prepared using other methods.
- (D) red meat consumption would not be linked to an increased cancer risk if specific cooking methods were avoided.

Section 1, Module 1: Reading & Writing

 Annotate ⋮

During the silent film era, which stretched from the late 19th century until the advent of talkies in the late 1920s, movies relied almost exclusively on visual storytelling. This period produced iconic works such as the Keystone Cops' chaotic chases, Buster Keaton's daring physical stunts, and F.W. Murnau's hauntingly atmospheric "Nosferatu". One of the most enduring examples from this era includes Charlie Chaplin's 1925 classic, "The Gold Rush." The movie, with Chaplin's inimitable combination of physical comedy and pathos, effectively communicates its narrative through gestures, facial expressions, and visual gags. Despite the passage of a century, modern audiences can still appreciate the humor, creativity, and emotional resonance of these silent films. Nevertheless, it's worth noting that certain cultural references, filming techniques, or social norms depicted may be lost on contemporary viewers who lack the historical context of the silent film era. Therefore, _____

15   Mark for Review 🔖

Which choice most logically completes the text?

(A) the appeal of silent films is primarily limited to lay audiences who are not very accustomed to watching silent films.

(B) some silent films may seem outdated or difficult to understand for contemporary viewers without the context of the era.

(C) "The Gold Rush" is the only silent film that remains popular among today's audiences.

(D) silent films are universally enjoyed by audiences regardless of their knowledge of film history.

TEST⬛QUBE   Question 15 of 27 >   Back Next

II

III

IV

Section 1, Module 1: Reading & Writing

 Annotate ⋮

When the researchers finally published their findings in 2010, it became clear that the Archimedes Palimpsest, a 10th-century Byzantine copy of works by ancient Greek mathematician Archimedes, _____ for centuries in the library's archives, hidden away from the world. The discovery and subsequent analysis of this long-lost text provided valuable insights into the history and mathematical knowledge of the ancient world.

16   Mark for Review 🔖

Which choice completes the text so that it conforms to the conventions of Standard English?

(A) had been overlooked

(B) was overlooked

(C) has been overlooked

(D) would be overlooked

V

VI

VII

TEST⬛QUBE   Question 16 of 27 >   Back Next

Section 1, Module 1: Reading & Writing

Annotate

Climate change, an issue that requires global attention, has been a growing concern for many scientists including Dr. James Hansen, former head of NASA's Goddard Institute for Space Studies. The Intergovernmental Panel on Climate Change (IPCC), led by Hoesung Lee, by the time it published its comprehensive sixth assessment report in 2021, _____ an array of scientific evidence from numerous studies to emphasize the urgent need for drastic action.

17   Mark for Review 🔖

Which choice completes the text so that it conforms to the conventions of Standard English?

- (A) had compiled
- (B) compiled
- (C) compiles
- (D) will compile

TEST QUBE

Back Next

Section 1, Module 1: Reading & Writing

Annotate

Beyond the striking facade of the historic building ___ hidden passages and rooms, waiting to be discovered by curious explorers. These secret spaces hold clues to the building's past, offering a glimpse into the lives of those who once inhabited it. Unraveling the mysteries concealed within these walls has captivated historians and enthusiasts alike.

18   Mark for Review 🔖

Which choice completes the text so that it conforms to the conventions of Standard English?

- (A) lie
- (B) lies
- (C) has lain
- (D) have lain

TEST QUBE

Back Next

Section 1, Module 1: Reading & Writing

Annotate ⋮

As Thompson's research indicates, the impact of urbanization on wildlife habitats is _____ the 185 parks and nature reserves surveyed in the study, 72 percent exhibited signs of habitat fragmentation and loss of biodiversity, revealing the alarming extent of the negative consequences inflicted upon natural environments by the relentless expansion of urban areas.

19   Mark for Review 🔖

Which choice completes the text so that it conforms to the conventions of Standard English?

(A) significant, of   (A̶)

(B) significant; of,   (B̶)

(C) significant: of   (C̶)

(D) significant of   (D̶)

TEST⬛QUBE   Question 19 of 27 >   Back   Next

Section 1, Module 1: Reading & Writing

Annotate ⋮

The Wright brothers' invention not only revolutionized _____ for military and commercial use. Their pioneering aircraft design and advancements in flight technology opened up new possibilities for aerial transportation, warfare strategies, and the growth of the aviation industry as a whole. Their contributions transformed the way people traveled and shaped the trajectory of aviation development globally.

20   Mark for Review 🔖

Which choice completes the text so that it conforms to the conventions of Standard English?

(A) transportation but also, impacted

(B) transportation, but also impacted

(C) transportation; but also, impacted

(D) transportation but also impacted

TEST⬛QUBE   Question 20 of 27 >   Back   Next

Section 1, Module 1: Reading & Writing

Annotate

Each year, numerous African elephants traverse vast distances in search of food, water, and suitable habitats, a journey that can span hundreds of kilometers and often necessitates crossing treacherous terrain, such as scorching deserts and fast-flowing rivers. The risk of predation, poaching, and habitat fragmentation is ever-present, and the African continent presents a host of challenges for these majestic _____ in their seasonal migrations, guided by their inherent instincts and strong social bonds.

21   Mark for Review 🔖

Which choice completes the text so that it conforms to the conventions of Standard English?

- (A) mammals, yet the elephants persist
- (B) mammals, yet the elephants persisting
- (C) mammals, the elephants persist
- (D) mammals; yet the elephants persist

Section 1, Module 1: Reading & Writing

Annotate

The African wild dog, a highly social and endangered species, relies on intricate communication and cooperation among pack members to successfully hunt and raise their _____ for their survival in the competitive African savannah. Their hunting strategies involve remarkable stamina and teamwork, often targeting prey much larger than themselves. The risk of confrontation with larger predators, such as lions and hyenas, is constant, and the competition for resources is fierce, yet the African wild dogs continue to thrive as a testament to their resilience and adaptability.

22   Mark for Review 🔖

Which choice completes the text so that it conforms to the conventions of Standard English?

- (A) young; which is a necessity
- (B) young; a necessity
- (C) young, a necessity
- (D) young. A necessity

V
VI
VII

Section 1, Module 1: Reading & Writing

Annotate ⋮

Even though olingos, arboreal procyonids of Central and South American rainforests, have a marked fondness for exceptionally saccharine nectar, the trees that allure them have undergone evolutionary fine-tuning to yield nectar that is merely moderately sweet. A recent study _____ sugar is energy-draining, and it is more propitious for trees to engender an ample quantity of low-sugar nectar than a small amount of high-sugar nectar. Moreover, this adaptation ensures that the nocturnal olingos, with their prehensile tails and sharp, retractile claws which facilitate adept navigation through the dense arboreal labyrinth, make recurrent nocturnal excursions amongst the flowering trees, inadvertently optimizing the likelihood of cross-pollination.

23   Mark for Review 🔖

Which choice completes the text so that it conforms to the conventions of Standard English?

- (A) explains why, fabricating
- (B) explains why: fabricating
- (C) explains, why fabricating
- (D) explains; why fabricating

TEST⬛QUBE   Question 23 of 27 >   Back   Next

Section 1, Module 1: Reading & Writing

Annotate ⋮

Despite offering unprecedented insights into the enigmatic phenomena of the cosmos, _____ capturing the first-ever image of a black hole and overcoming the limitations of terrestrial observatories.

24   Mark for Review 🔖

Which choice completes the text so that it conforms to the conventions of Standard English?

- (A) there are two significant challenges associated with the discovery of the black hole M87:
- (B) two significant challenges are associated with the discovery of the black hole M87:
- (C) the black hole M87's two associated significant challenges are that
- (D) the ground-breaking discovery of the black hole M87 faced two significant challenges:

TEST⬛QUBE   Question 24 of 27 >   Back   Next

Section 1, Module 1: Reading & Writing

While researching a topic, a student has taken the following notes:

- Paleoclimatology is the study of past climates.
- Scientists use proxies, like ice cores and tree rings, to reconstruct past climates.
- These proxies contain information about temperature, precipitation, and atmospheric gas concentrations.
- Ice cores from Greenland and Antarctica provide information dating back hundreds of thousands of years.
- Understanding past climate helps scientists predict future climate trends.

25

Mark for Review

The student wants to emphasize the methodologies used in paleoclimatology and their importance. Which choice most effectively uses relevant information from the notes to accomplish this goal?

(A) Paleoclimatology, which is the study of past climates, uses proxies like ice cores and tree rings to understand historical temperature, precipitation, and atmospheric gas concentrations.

(B) In paleoclimatology, scientists use ice cores from Greenland and Antarctica to reconstruct past climates, providing crucial data for predicting future climate trends.

(C) Through the use of proxies, such as ice cores and tree rings, paleoclimatologists can reconstruct past climates and predict future climate trends.

(D) The study of past climates, or paleoclimatology, relies on information gleaned from ice cores and tree rings to understand changes in temperature, precipitation, and atmospheric gas concentrations.

Section 1, Module 1: Reading & Writing

While researching a topic, a student has taken the following notes:

- The Tang Dynasty, lasting from 618 to 907, is often regarded as a high point in Chinese civilization.
- The dynasty was characterized by vibrant cultural and economic activities.
- Empress Wu Zetian, who reigned from 690 to 705, was the only female emperor in China's history.
- The Tang Code, a legal code enacted in 624, was a significant achievement in Chinese jurisprudence.
- Chang'an, the capital, was the most populous city in the world during the Tang Dynasty.

26

Mark for Review

The student wants to underscore the societal prosperity and unique characteristics of the Tang Dynasty. Which choice most effectively uses relevant information from the notes to accomplish this goal?

(A) The Tang Dynasty, which lasted from 618 to 907, was a period of significant cultural and economic growth in China.

(B) The Tang Dynasty, characterized by its flourishing cultural landscape and the foundational Tang Code, epitomized a golden era with unparalleled traits in Chinese history.

(C) Chang'an, as the most populous city worldwide during the Tang Dynasty, marks the culmination of Chinese civilization.

(D) Wu Zetian's reign and the enactment of the Tang Code were significant milestones in the history of the Tang Dynasty, demonstrating its unique character.

Section 1, Module 1: Reading & Writing

Annotate

While researching a topic, a student has taken the following notes:

- Social stratification refers to a society's categorization of people into socioeconomic strata.
- Stratification leads to social inequality where some groups have more resources and rights than others.
- The caste system in India is an example of social stratification.
- Karl Marx theorized that social class is determined by one's relationship to the means of production.
- Max Weber argued that social class is a multidimensional construct, encompassing wealth, status, and power.

27   Mark for Review 🔖

The student wants to clarify the concept of social stratification. Which choice most effectively uses relevant information from the notes to accomplish this goal?

(A) Social stratification, as Karl Marx posited, is dictated by an individual's relationship with the means of production, leading to distinct social classes.

(B) The caste system in India serves as a tangible manifestation of social stratification, reflecting the division of society into socioeconomic strata.

(C) Social stratification embodies a societal hierarchy, resulting in unequal distribution of resources and rights among different groups.

(D) Max Weber's multidimensional perspective on social stratification encapsulates the interplay of wealth, status, and power in determining social class.

TEST⬛QUBE

 Question 27 of 27 >

Back   Next

Move on to the Next Section

Section 1, Module 2: Reading & Writing   ⏱ 32:00   📝 Annotate   ⋮

As the planet's biodiversity continues to decline due to factors such as deforestation, pollution, and climate change, prominent conservationists like Dr. Jane Goodall and organizations like the World Wildlife Fund (WWF) tirelessly advocate for the implementation of more sustainable practices. Through documentaries, awareness campaigns, and educational programs, their work _____ the intricate web of interconnectedness that exists among all living organisms and their shared ecosystems. They emphasize the delicate balance and mutual dependencies that characterize natural habitats, urging for collective responsibility in preserving the world's biodiversity.

1   Mark for Review 🔖

Which choice completes the text with the most logical and precise word or phrase?

(A) obscures

(B) accentuates

(C) undermines

(D) trivializes

Section 1, Module 2: Reading & Writing   📝 Annotate   ⋮

The renowned physicist Dr. Akira Yoshida whose groundbreaking work on particle physics and quantum mechanics has been likened to that of Niels Bohr and Richard Feynman, _____ a new era of scientific discovery. His innovative experiments and theories, particularly concerning the behavior of subatomic particles, have been hailed as revolutionary. With a focus on understanding the fundamental forces of nature, Dr. Yoshida's work paved the way for future advancements in the field and has inspired a new generation of physicists to delve into the enigmatic world of particles and quantum phenomena.

2   Mark for Review 🔖

Which choice completes the text with the most logical and precise word or phrase?

(A) evinced

(B) inaugurated

(C) derogated

(D) mollified

Section 1, Module 2: Reading & Writing

Aria Thompson, a mountaineer and explorer, was known for her ____ demeanor and unyielding resolve in the face of adversity. Born with a physical disability, Aria never allowed it to define her limits. She scaled some of the world's most challenging peaks, including Mount Everest and K2. Her undaunted spirit, courage, and relentless pursuit of her dreams served as an inspiration to all who knew her, proving that determination and a fearless attitude can overcome even the most daunting challenges.

3   Mark for Review

Which choice completes the text with the most logical and precise word or phrase?

- (A) intrepid
- (B) irascible
- (C) sanguine
- (D) languid

Section 1, Module 2: Reading & Writing

TechTitan, a leading technology company based in Silicon Valley, recently launched a new initiative aimed at fostering a culture of ____ among its employees. The CEO, Olivia Ross, believes that openness and honest communication are integral to innovation. The initiative encourages employees to share their ideas, concerns, and suggestions without the fear of judgment or retribution. Through workshops, open forums, and idea-sharing platforms, TechTitan seeks to engage in open dialogue to promote creativity and innovation, ensuring that it remains at the forefront of technological advancement.

4   Mark for Review

Which choice completes the text with the most logical and precise word or phrase?

- (A) insularity
- (B) candor
- (C) reticence
- (D) dogmatism

Section 1, Module 2: Reading & Writing

Annotate ⋮

The following text is adapted from Herman Melville's 1853 short story *Bartleby, the Scrivener*. The narrator, a lawyer, is describing his new employee, Bartleby.

At the period just preceding the advent of Bartleby, I had two persons as copyists in my employment, and a promising lad as an office-boy. First, Turkey; second, Nippers; third, Ginger Nut. These may seem names, the like of which are not usually found in the Directory. In truth they were nicknames, mutually <u>conferred</u> upon each other by my three clerks, and were deemed expressive of their respective persons or characters.

5   Mark for Review 🔖

As used in the text, what does the word "conferred" most nearly mean?

(A) Granted   Ⓐ

(B) Whispered   Ⓑ

(C) Confiscated   Ⓒ

(D) Debated   Ⓓ

TEST❖QUBE   Question 5 of 27 >   Back   Next

Section 1, Module 2: Reading & Writing

Annotate ⋮

The following text is adapted from Robert Frost's 1928 poem "Acquainted with the Night."

I have been one acquainted with the night.
I have walked out in rain—and back in rain.
I have outwalked the furthest city light.

I have looked down the saddest city lane.
<u>I have passed by the watchman on his beat</u>
<u>And dropped my eyes, unwilling to explain.</u>

I have stood still and stopped the sound of feet
When far away an interrupted cry
Came over houses from another street,

But not to call me back or say good-bye;
And further still at an unearthly height,
One luminary clock against the sky

6   Mark for Review 🔖

Which choice best describes the function of the underlined portion in the text as a whole?

(A) It portrays the speaker's desire for anonymity and avoidance of interaction during his nocturnal wanderings.

(B) It characterizes the night as a time of patrol and surveillance, indicating societal norms.

(C) It signifies the speaker's guilt or regret which he does not wish to acknowledge or explain.

(D) It demonstrates the solace and silence the speaker seeks in the night away from human contact.

TEST❖QUBE   Question 6 of 27 >   Back   Next

Section 1, Module 2: Reading & Writing

The process of natural selection, first conceptualized by Charles Darwin in the 19th century, drives the evolution of species by favoring traits that increase an organism's chances of survival and reproduction in a given environment. A related concept, sexual selection, is a specific form of natural selection that Darwin also described in his work, "The Descent of Man, and Selection in Relation to Sex". According to an acclaimed modern-day biologist, Dr. Emma Richardson, sexual selection has played a significant role in shaping the diverse and often extravagant traits seen in many animal species. She suggests that sexual selection occurs when individuals within a population differ in their ability to attract mates or compete for reproductive opportunities. Through this process, certain traits that may not necessarily provide survival advantages can become more common in a population because they confer a reproductive advantage. Dr. Richardson argues that this can lead to the evolution of elaborate physical or behavioral traits, especially in males of many species, who typically invest heavily in competing for mates.

7   Mark for Review 🔖

Which finding, if true, would most directly support Dr. Emma Richardson's claim?

(A) Sexual selection can be driven by mate choice or competition among individuals of the same sex, resulting in the evolution of traits that increase an individual's reproductive success.

(B) Many animal species exhibit sexual dimorphism, where males and females differ in size, coloration, or other physical traits, which can be a result of sexual selection acting differently on the two sexes.

(C) In some species, males possess elaborate ornaments or engage in complex displays that have evolved specifically to attract females, even if these traits might be costly in terms of survival.

(D) The peacock's elaborate and colorful tail feathers, which have been shown to play a role in attracting mates, are an example of a trait that has evolved through sexual selection.

TEST⬚QUBE   Question 7 of 27 >   Back   Next

Section 1, Module 2: Reading & Writing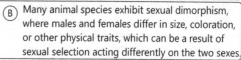

Consider the European honeybee and the Asian honeybee—two distinct species of bees that play a vital role in pollination across the globe. Both species of bees collect nectar and pollen from flowers, which they bring back to their respective hives to create honey and feed their young. These bees have evolved unique communication systems, including the famous waggle dance, to share the location of rich sources of nectar with their fellow hive members. However, they face different challenges in their native habitats. The European honeybee has been widely introduced to different continents, where it has faced competition and threats from local bee species, diseases, and pests. In contrast, the Asian honeybee has remained more localized to Asia, where it faces challenges from habitat loss and the infamous Asian giant hornet, a predator that can wipe out entire colonies.

8   Mark for Review 🔖

According to the text what is one similarity between the European honeybee and the Asian honeybee?

(A) They both have been widely introduced to different continents.

(B) They both collect nectar and pollen from flowers to create honey and feed their young.

(C) They both face the same challenges from diseases and pests in their native habitats.

(D) They both are heavily impacted by competition from local bee species.

TEST⬚QUBE   Question 8 of 27 >   Back   Next

Section 1, Module 2: Reading & Writing

Labor union laws in the United States have undergone significant changes since the late 19th century. Initially, there was little protection for workers seeking to unionize, which often led to conflict between laborers and employers. However, with the passing of the Wagner Act in 1935, also known as the National Labor Relations Act, workers were granted the right to form unions and engage in collective bargaining. While this represented a major step forward, it was not without its critics. Many employers felt that the Wagner Act gave too much power to unions, leading to the enactment of the Taft-Hartley Act in 1947. This act placed restrictions on union activities and balanced the playing field for employers. In recent years, there has been a shift towards "right-to-work" laws, which seek to give individuals more choice in whether or not to join a union. Critics of these laws argue that they undermine the power of unions and hurt collective bargaining efforts.

9 Mark for Review

Which choice best describes the overall structure of the text?

(A) It chronologically outlines the evolution of labor union laws, and then discusses the ongoing debate between the rights of workers and employers.

(B) It introduces the concept of labor unions, then compares the different labor union laws in various countries.

(C) It describes the historical challenges faced by labor unions, and then explains how recent laws have addressed these challenges.

(D) It provides a historical account of a single labor union, and then analyzes how its actions have influenced labor union laws.

TEST QUBE Back Next

Section 1, Module 2: Reading & Writing

Text 1
Embedded in the heart of societal structures, law plays a critical role in mediating social relationships and maintaining order. Legal scholar Dr. Elaine Matthews posits in her monograph "The Tapestry of Law," a perspective highlighting the dynamic interplay between codified laws and evolving societal norms. This perspective de-emphasizes the top-down nature of law, arguing instead for a reflexive process in which laws are both shaped by and shape society.

Text 2
In "Social Order and the Implicit Code," sociologist Professor Michael Dawson articulates a theory suggesting that informal, implicit social norms bear an outsized influence on societal regulation. Dawson's research seeks to unearth these tacit guidelines, which he contends shape behaviors and interactions to a degree even greater than formalized legal systems.

10 Mark for Review

Considering both texts, how might Professor Dawson react to Dr. Matthews' thesis?

(A) Dawson would likely argue that Matthews' thesis, while valid, may underrepresent the role of implicit social norms.

(B) Dawson might appreciate Matthews' view, but stress the difficulty in measuring the influence of codified laws against implicit social norms.

(C) Dawson would probably dismiss Matthews' argument, stating that societal norms evolve independently of formal laws.

(D) Dawson might endorse Matthews' idea, emphasizing the two-way influence between law and society.

TEST QUBE Back Next

Section 1, Module 2: Reading & Writing

Annotate ⋮

Arms and the Man is an 1898 play by George Bernard Shaw. The character Raina experiences a wide range of emotions upon hearing about her fiancé Sergius's victory in the battle. Her admiration for Sergius and her patriotic ideals make her question whether such heroism could be real or merely influenced by literature and theatre, as is evident when she says, _____

11   Mark for Review 🔖

Which quotation from Arms and the Man most effectively illustrates the claim?

(A) "I sent her away. I wanted to be alone. The stars are so beautiful! What is the matter?"

(B) "What will he care for my poor little worship after the acclamations of a whole army of heroes?"

(C) "Our ideas of what Sergius would do—our patriotism—our heroic ideals. Oh, what faithless little creatures girls are!—I sometimes used to doubt whether they were anything but dreams."

(D) "Oh, to think that it was all true—that Sergius is just as splendid and noble as he looks—that the world is really a glorious world for women who can see its glory and men who can act its romance!"

II

Section 1, Module 2: Reading & Writing

Annotate ⋮

Transport Method in Different Communities

■ Cars ▨ Public Transport ▥ Bikes ▦ Walking

Urban planners are analyzing the distribution of various transportation modes used by residents in three different cities. They believe that certain factors, such as population density and availability of public transit, may influence the choice of transportation. The planners have collected data on the percentage of residents using private cars, bicycles, public transit, and walking in each neighborhood. The planners assert the standard of living in each city plays a large role in determining the utilization of different kinds of transportation. In cities where the standard of living is higher, individuals are more prone to utilizing cars and walking.

12   Mark for Review 🔖

Which statement best describes data from the graph that supports the urban planners' claim?

(A) City C is likely to foster a high standard of living with public transportation being a commonly used method of transportation.

(B) City C is likely to foster a high standard of living with its high usage of private car transportation and walking.

(C) City A is likely to foster a high standard of living with its high usage of private car transportation and walking.

(D) It is difficult to posit what city has a higher standard of living with the data above.

V

VI

VII

Section 1, Module 2: Reading & Writing

Annotate ⋮

Economist Alex Rodriguez conducted a comprehensive study examining the relationship between increases in the minimum wage and small business growth across multiple regions. Rodriguez postulated that a higher minimum wage would inexorably lead to a decline in the number of small businesses, as elevated labor costs would render it more challenging for small businesses to thrive. The study also considered the effects of regional economic disparities, industry-specific variations, and the adaptability of small businesses in the face of rising labor costs.

13 Mark for Review 🔖

Which finding, if true, would most directly undermine Rodriguez's hypothesis?

(A) In some metropolises where the minimum wage was recently augmented, the number of large businesses has remained impervious to the change.

(B) In several locations not included in the study, an increase in the minimum wage engendered a commensurate rise in the number of small businesses.

(C) In various areas, small businesses have devised creative stratagems to counterbalance increased labor costs, such as employing cost-saving technologies.

(D) Within certain industries, businesses have reacted to minimum wage increases by curtailing employee hours and benefits.

TEST❖QUBE

Back Next

Section 1, Module 2: Reading & Writing

Annotate ⋮

Zebras are well known for their distinct black-and-white striped pattern. For many years, the purpose of these stripes has been a subject of scientific debate. One hypothesis is that the stripes serve to deter biting flies, which can spread diseases and drain the zebras of blood. In a study conducted by Tim Caro and colleagues, it was discovered that fewer biting flies landed on striped surfaces compared to uniformly colored surfaces. This finding suggests that _____

14 Mark for Review 🔖

Which choice most logically completes the text?

(A) biting flies are more attracted to uniformly colored surfaces, regardless of the animal species.

(B) the black-and-white pattern of zebra stripes has no significant effect on the behavior of biting flies.

(C) the stripes on zebras could be an adaptation to repel biting flies and reduce the impact of disease and blood loss.

(D) zebras' stripes serve primarily as a means of camouflage rather than as a deterrent for biting flies.

TEST❖QUBE

Back Next

Section 1, Module 2: Reading & Writing

Annotate

Although Brazilian Jiu-Jitsu (BJJ) practitioners make up a specific subset of mixed martial arts (MMA) fighters, they have achieved a disproportionately high number of winning streaks in prominent MMA competitions, such as the UFC. One possible explanation for this successful performance is that Brazilian Jiu-Jitsu training emphasizes ground fighting techniques and submission holds, which are highly effective in MMA bouts. This specialized focus on grappling and submissions thus ____

15   Mark for Review 🔖

Which choice most logically completes the text?

(A) makes BJJ practitioners particularly well-suited to excel in MMA competitions.

(B) discourages MMA fighters with other martial arts backgrounds from competing against BJJ practitioners.

(C) leads to an overemphasis on ground fighting techniques in MMA matches, detracting from other aspects of the sport.

(D) increases the likelihood of MMA competitions implementing rule changes to favor striking-based martial arts.

Section 1, Module 2: Reading & Writing

Annotate

In a study of the effects of social media usage on self-esteem in teenagers, researchers neglected to control for the amount of time participants spent on various platforms. The self-esteem of teenagers who primarily used platforms known for positive interactions, such as supportive hobby groups, was evaluated using the same criteria as those who primarily used platforms with higher rates of negative interactions, such as anonymous forums. The results of the study, therefore, ____

16   Mark for Review 🔖

Which choice most logically completes the text?

(A) reveal more about the teenagers' self-esteem when exposed to controlled environments than when interacting in real-life social settings.

(B) are useful for identifying the relationship between social media and self-esteem but not for identifying the impact of individual platforms.

(C) should not be taken as indicative of the effects of social media on selfesteem for any age group other than teenagers.

(D) could suggest that there are differences in self-esteem among teenagers based on social media usage, even though such differences might be due to the specific platforms they use.

Section 1, Module 2: Reading & Writing

Annotate ⋮

In the coastal regions of Japan, a traditional fishing technique called "ama" has been practiced for centuries, involving female free-divers who descend to depths of up to 82 feet to collect pearls, shellfish, and seaweed. Ama divers rely on their exceptional breath-holding abilities and a simple loincloth for protection against the elements. The tradition's survival, despite modern technological advancements, is a testament to the ama _____ and the cultural significance of their craft.

17 Mark for Review 🔖

Which choice completes the text so that it conforms to the conventions of Standard English?

(A) divers dedication

(B) diver's dedication

(C) divers's dedication

(D) divers' dedication

TEST🌐QUBE Question 17 of 27 > Back Next

Section 1, Module 2: Reading & Writing

Annotate ⋮

The Galápagos Islands, an archipelago located in the Pacific Ocean, are renowned for their unique and diverse wildlife, which played a crucial role in shaping Charles Darwin's theory of natural selection. The islands' isolation has allowed many species, such as the famous Galápagos tortoises and marine iguanas, to evolve in ways distinct from their mainland counterparts. _____ of these fascinating creatures continue to provide valuable insights into the processes of evolution and adaptation, highlighting the importance of preserving the archipelago's delicate ecosystems for future generations.

18 Mark for Review 🔖

Which choice completes the text so that it conforms to the conventions of Standard English?

(A) Researchers' ongoing studies'

(B) Researchers' ongoing studies

(C) Researcher's ongoing studies

(D) Researchers's ongoing studies

TEST🌐QUBE Question 18 of 27 > Back Next

I

Annotate

Despite their reputation for having poor eyesight, _____ are quite capable of detecting movement and changes in light intensity. This ability greatly aids them in their nocturnal hunting. Their keen hearing also plays a vital role in locating prey.

19   Mark for Review

Which choice completes the text so that it conforms to the conventions of Standard English?

- (A) ornithologists track the nighttime hunting of owls
- (B) it is owls that, when hunting at night,
- (C) owls, known for hunting at night,
- (D) when owls hunt at night, they

II

III

TEST◉QUBE   Question 19 of 27 >   Back   Next

IV

Annotate

As reported in a political science article by The Economist, "Electoral systems can have a significant impact on the outcome of an election. Proportional representation systems tend to give smaller parties a better chance of winning seats, while majoritarian systems usually benefit larger parties. However, no single system is perfect, as each has ____ own advantages and disadvantages."

20   Mark for Review

Which choice completes the text so that it conforms to the conventions of Standard English?

- (A) its
- (B) their
- (C) one's
- (D) it

V

VI

VII

TEST◉QUBE   Question 20 of 27 >   Back   Next

I

II

III

IV

Section 1, Module 2: Reading & Writing   ✎ Annotate   ⋮

_____ Stephanie realized that many successful entrepreneurs also faced numerous setbacks before achieving their goals. In a recent documentary, the story of a prominent businesswoman highlighted her resilience and determination despite the odds.

21   Mark for Review 🔖

Which choice completes the text so that it conforms to the conventions of Standard English?

- (A) She finished watching a documentary on successful entrepreneurs
- (B) After she watched a documentary on successful entrepreneurs;
- (C) Upon watching a documentary on successful entrepreneurs,
- (D) Having watched a documentary on successful entrepreneurs—

TEST◉QUBE   Question 21 of 27 >   Back   Next

V

VI

VII

Section 1, Module 2: Reading & Writing   ✎ Annotate   ⋮

Throughout history, people have found innovative ways to communicate _____ the well-known inventions like the printing press, lesser-known methods have also played crucial roles. One such example is the use of pigeons as messengers in ancient civilizations. Pigeon post, as it was called, was employed by the Romans, Greeks, and Persians, using specially trained homing pigeons to carry messages across great distances. These birds could travel up to 600 miles in a single day, with an impressive 95% success rate in reaching their intended destination.

22   Mark for Review 🔖

Which choice completes the text so that it confirms to the conventions of Standard English?

- (A) , and share information, besides
- (B) and share information; besides
- (C) and share information; besides,
- (D) and share information besides

TEST◉QUBE   Question 22 of 27 >   Back   Next

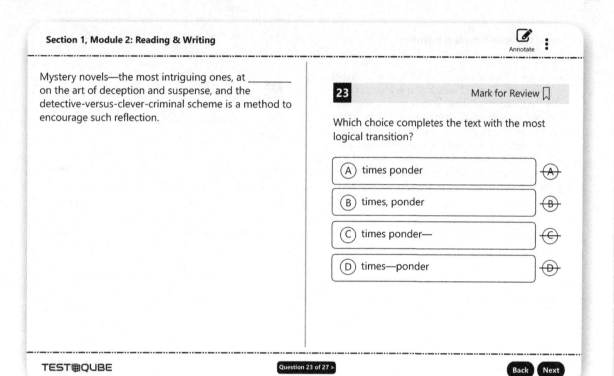

Section 1, Module 2: Reading & Writing

Mystery novels—the most intriguing ones, at _____ on the art of deception and suspense, and the detective-versus-clever-criminal scheme is a method to encourage such reflection.

23   Mark for Review

Which choice completes the text with the most logical transition?

- (A) times ponder
- (B) times, ponder
- (C) times ponder—
- (D) times—ponder

TEST⬛QUBE

Back   Next

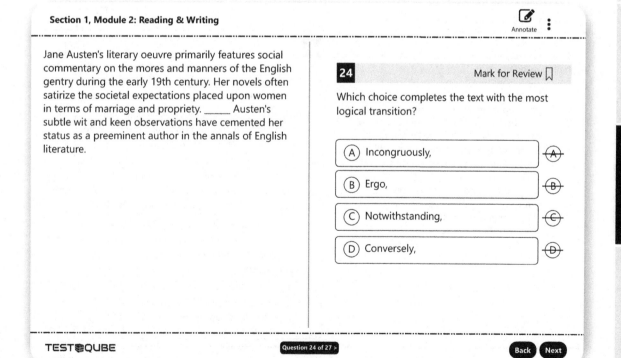

Section 1, Module 2: Reading & Writing

Jane Austen's literary oeuvre primarily features social commentary on the mores and manners of the English gentry during the early 19th century. Her novels often satirize the societal expectations placed upon women in terms of marriage and propriety. _____ Austen's subtle wit and keen observations have cemented her status as a preeminent author in the annals of English literature.

24   Mark for Review

Which choice completes the text with the most logical transition?

- (A) Incongruously,
- (B) Ergo,
- (C) Notwithstanding,
- (D) Conversely,

TEST⬛QUBE

Back   Next

I

II

III

IV

V

VI

VII

Section 1, Module 2: Reading & Writing

Annotate

⋮

Quantum mechanics, a fundamental theory in physics, describes the behavior of matter and energy at the atomic and subatomic scales. Although its predictions have been experimentally confirmed with remarkable precision, the theory presents a vastly different and counterintuitive view of reality compared to classical physics. _____ the interpretation of quantum mechanics remains a subject of ongoing debate among physicists.

25   Mark for Review 🔖

Which choice completes the text with the most logical transition?

(A) In spite of this,   Ⓐ

(B) Consequently,   Ⓑ

(C) Simultaneously,   Ⓒ

(D) Moreover,   Ⓓ

Section 1, Module 2: Reading & Writing

Annotate

⋮

While researching a topic, a student has taken the following notes:

- Thomas Hobbes was an influential political philosopher in the 17th century.
- He is best known for his book "Leviathan," where he discusses the social contract.
- According to Hobbes, in the state of nature, life would be "nasty, brutish, and short."
- To avoid this state, individuals give up some rights to a strong central authority.
- This exchange of rights for protection is known as the social contract.

26   Mark for Review 🔖

The student wants to encapsulate Hobbes's view of the social contract. Which choice most effectively uses relevant information from the notes to accomplish this goal?

(A) Hobbes's "Leviathan" outlines his view of the social contract where individuals sacrifice some rights to a central authority to escape a harsh state of nature.   Ⓐ

(B) Hobbes, in his seminal work "Leviathan," portrays a bleak picture of life in the state of nature as being "nasty, brutish, and short."   Ⓑ

(C) The concept of the social contract, as put forth by Hobbes, involves a trade-off between individual rights and societal protection.   Ⓒ

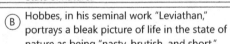

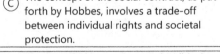

(D) Thomas Hobbes, a renowned political philosopher, is widely recognized for his contributions to the understanding of the social contract.   Ⓓ

Section 1, Module 2: Reading & Writing

Annotate ⋮

While researching a topic, a student has taken the following notes:

- Gravitational lensing occurs when a massive object bends the path of light from a distant source.
- This phenomenon was predicted by Einstein's general theory of relativity.
- Gravitational lensing can be used to study dark matter, which does not emit or absorb light.
- The effect enables astronomers to observe objects that would otherwise be too faint or too far away.
- The discovery of the first gravitational lens, known as the "Twin Quasar," confirmed Einstein's predictions.

27 Mark for Review 🔖

The student wants to explain the significance of gravitational lensingin astrophysics. Which choice most effectively uses relevant information from the notes to accomplish this goal?

(A) Gravitational lensing, a phenomenon resulting from the curvature of spacetime, has proven invaluable in the investigation of elusive dark matter.

(B) The discovery of the "Twin Quasar," the first observed instance of gravitational lensing, provided empirical evidence supporting Einstein's general theory of relativity.

(C) Einstein's general theory of relativity, which predicted the occurrence of gravitational lensing, has been substantiated by the observation of the "Twin Quasar."

(D) Gravitational lensing serves as a tool for astronomers to study otherwise inaccessible celestial objects, shedding light on the composition of the cosmos.

TEST◾QUBE | **End of Test 6 Reading/Writing Section** | Back Next

---

Upcoming Math Section: Reference Formula Sheet

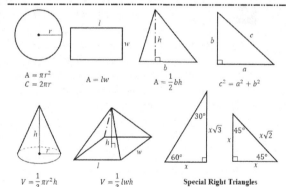

$A = \pi r^2$
$C = 2\pi r$

$A = lw$

$A = \frac{1}{2}bh$

$c^2 = a^2 + b^2$

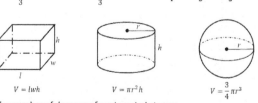

$V = \frac{1}{3}\pi r^2 h$

$V = \frac{1}{3}lwh$

Special Right Triangles

$V = lwh$

$V = \pi r^2 h$

$V = \frac{3}{4}\pi r^3$

The number of degrees of arc in a circle is 360.
The number of radians of arc in a circle is 2π.
The sum of the measures in degrees of the angles of a triangle is 180.

Directions for Student-Produced Response

- **TEST QUBE** recommends students to use decimals for most answers but suggests using fractions only in cases where the answers involve repeating decimals (e.g., 0.333 = 1/3).
- For cases with more than one answer, enter **just one of the answers.**
- You can enter up to 5 characters for your answer. (For negative answers, the **negative sign** does not count as one character)
- For **fractions** that don't fit the answer box, enter the decimal equivalent (Unless advised to do otherwise)
- For **decimals** that exceed the answer box, round to the fourth digit. (Unless advised to do otherwise)
- For mixed number (such as $4\frac{1}{4}$), enter it as an improper fraction $(17/4)$ or its decimal equivalent (4.25)
- For all answers, you may omit the symbols and units such as $,%, cm^3, m^2, etc.

Acceptable vs Non-Acceptable Answers

Answer	Acceptable ways to receive credit	Ways you**WON'T** receive credit
4.25	4.25 , 17/4	41/4 , 4 1/4
4/6	2/3 .6666 , .6667 0.666 , 0.667	0.66 , .66 0.67 , .67
-1/6	-1/6 -0.166 , -0.167 -.1666 , -.1667	-0.16 , -.16 -0.17 , -.167

Move on to the Next Section ≫

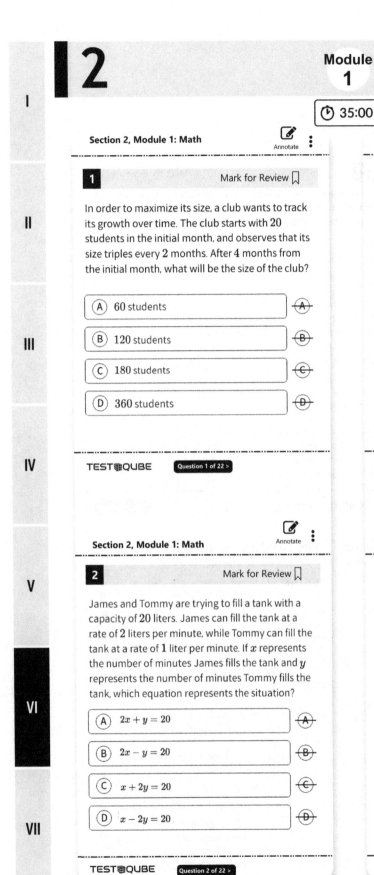

Section 2, Module 1: Math   ✎ Annotate   ⋮

1   Mark for Review 🔖

In order to maximize its size, a club wants to track its growth over time. The club starts with 20 students in the initial month, and observes that its size triples every 2 months. After 4 months from the initial month, what will be the size of the club?

- (A) 60 students
- (B) 120 students
- (C) 180 students
- (D) 360 students

TEST◉QUBE   Question 1 of 22 >

Section 2, Module 1: Math   ✎ Annotate   ⋮

2   Mark for Review 🔖

James and Tommy are trying to fill a tank with a capacity of 20 liters. James can fill the tank at a rate of 2 liters per minute, while Tommy can fill the tank at a rate of 1 liter per minute. If x represents the number of minutes James fills the tank and y represents the number of minutes Tommy fills the tank, which equation represents the situation?

- (A) $2x + y = 20$
- (B) $2x - y = 20$
- (C) $x + 2y = 20$
- (D) $x - 2y = 20$

TEST◉QUBE   Question 2 of 22 >

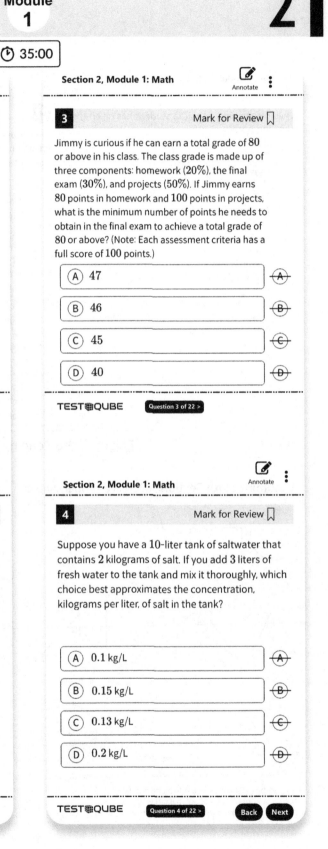

Section 2, Module 1: Math   ✎ Annotate   ⋮

3   Mark for Review 🔖

Jimmy is curious if he can earn a total grade of 80 or above in his class. The class grade is made up of three components: homework (20%), the final exam (30%), and projects (50%). If Jimmy earns 80 points in homework and 100 points in projects, what is the minimum number of points he needs to obtain in the final exam to achieve a total grade of 80 or above? (Note: Each assessment criteria has a full score of 100 points.)

- (A) 47
- (B) 46
- (C) 45
- (D) 40

TEST◉QUBE   Question 3 of 22 >

Section 2, Module 1: Math   ✎ Annotate   ⋮

4   Mark for Review 🔖

Suppose you have a 10-liter tank of saltwater that contains 2 kilograms of salt. If you add 3 liters of fresh water to the tank and mix it thoroughly, which choice best approximates the concentration, kilograms per liter, of salt in the tank?

- (A) 0.1 kg/L
- (B) 0.15 kg/L
- (C) 0.13 kg/L
- (D) 0.2 kg/L

TEST◉QUBE   Question 4 of 22 >   Back   Next

Section 2, Module 1: Math Annotate ⋮

---

5 Mark for Review 🔖

In the figure below, lines k and g are parallel and lines f and h are parallel. If the measure of $\angle 2$ is $30°$, what is the measure of $\angle 1$, in degrees?

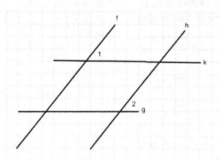

Section 2, Module 1: Math Annotate ⋮

---

6 Mark for Review 🔖

Consider the equation $y = x^2 - 26x + 169$ in the xy-plane. If the equation intersects the line $y = 0$ at exactly one point, what is the coordinate of that point?

- (A) $(13, 0)$
- (B) $(0, 13)$
- (C) $(26, 0)$
- (D) $(0, 26)$

I

II

III

IV

V

VI

VII

7   Mark for Review 🔖

If $5x + 6y = 30$ and $x + 4 = 4$, what is the value of y?

TEST⬚QUBE   Question 7 of 22 >

8   Mark for Review 🔖

James rolls a fair six-sided dice two times. What is the probability that the second number he rolls is 6?

(A) $1/36$

(B) $1/18$

(C) $1/12$

(D) $1/6$

TEST⬚QUBE   Question 8 of 22 >

9   Mark for Review 🔖

Jenny wants to put a gift inside a box with a length of 10 inches, a width of 8 inches, and a height of 6 inches. However, she realizes that the gift is slightly larger than the box and decides to increase the length of the box by 10% to make it fit. What is the volume of the new box?

(A) 480 cubic inches

(B) 528 cubic inches

(C) 5280 cubic inches

(D) 40 cubic inches

TEST⬚QUBE   Question 9 of 22 >

10   Mark for Review 🔖

For the function g defined below, a is a constant and $g(2) = 24$. What is the value of a?

$$g(x) = ax^3 + 8$$

TEST⬚QUBE   Question 10 of 22 >   Back   Next

11   Mark for Review 🔖

What is the volume, in cubic centimeters, of a cone with three times the radius and half the height of a cone whose volume is 30 cubic centimeters?

(A) 15 cubic centimeters   A̶

(B) 45 cubic centimeters   B̶

(C) 90 cubic centimeters   C̶

(D) 135 cubic centimeters   D̶

TEST⬤QUBE   Question 11 of 22 >

---

12   Mark for Review 🔖

Alice works a total of 12 hours per week, x hours as an engineer and y hours as a tutor. She earns $\$12$ per hour as an engineer and $\$20$ per hour as a tutor. Alice wants to earn at least $\$300$ per week. Which of the following systems of inequalities represents this situation?

(A) $x + y \geq 12, 12x + 20y = 300$ A̶

(B) $x + y \geq 12, 12x + 20y \geq 300$ B̶

(C) $x + y = 12, 12x + 20y \leq 300$ C̶

(D) $x + y = 12, 12x + 20y \geq 300$ D̶

TEST⬤QUBE   Question 12 of 22 >

---

13   Mark for Review 🔖

Find one value of x where the equation $|x^2 - 2x + 1| - 1$ equal to 0.

TEST⬤QUBE   Question 13 of 22 >

---

14   Mark for Review 🔖

If $2x - y = 4$, what is the value of $4^x \div 2^y$?

(A) 16   A̶

(B) 8   B̶

(C) 4   C̶

(D) 2   D̶

TEST⬤QUBE   Question 14 of 22 >   Back   Next

15   Mark for Review 🔖

Eve wants to rent an apartment. The monthly rental cost is $1600, and she needs to pay a $300 deposit. Eve wants to keep her rental expenses under $12,000, and the apartment rental must be for a whole number of months. What is the maximum number of months she can rent the apartment for?

(A) 6 months

(B) 7 months

(C) 8 months

(D) 9 months

TEST⬤QUBE   Question 15 of 22 >

16   Mark for Review 🔖

James runs at a constant speed of 2 kilometers per hour. How many hours will it take for him to travel 52 kilometers?

TEST⬤QUBE   Question 16 of 22 >

17   Mark for Review 🔖

In the given system of equations, a is a constant. If the system has no solution, what is the value of a?

$$6x + 8y = 15$$
$$3x - 6 = ay$$

(A) 4

(B) −4

(C) 8

(D) −8

TEST⬤QUBE   Question 17 of 22 >   Back Next

18 Mark for Review 🔖

The given graph shows three distinct functions. From the graph, how many solutions are there that satisfy all three functions?

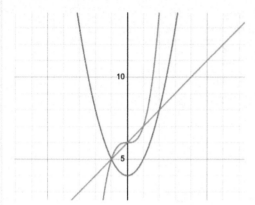

(A) 1

(B) 2

(C) 3

(D) 4

19 Mark for Review 🔖

The given equation relates the numbers c, b, and a. Which of the equations correctly expresses c in terms of a and b?
$$2c^2 - 6b = 8a$$

(A) $c = (4a + 3b)$

(B) $c = (4a + 3b)^2$

(C) $c = (4a + 3b)^{1/2}$

(D) $c = (4a + 3b)^{\sqrt{2}}$

I
II
III
IV
V
VI
VII

Section 2, Module 1: Math Annotate ⋮

20   Mark for Review 🔖

What is the y-intercept of the graph shown?

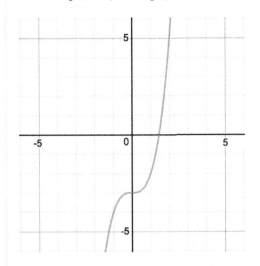

(A) -1 (A)

(B) -4 (B)

(C) 1.5 (C)

(D) None of the above   (D)

Section 2, Module 1: Math Annotate ⋮

21   Mark for Review 🔖

Which of the following is equivalent to $8^{2/3}$?

(A) 16 (A)

(B) 4 (B)

(C) 8 (C)

(D) 32 (D)

Section 2, Module 1: Math ⋮

22   Mark for Review 🔖

The line graph illustrates the percentage of students who failed a class over the years. Which interval on the graph represents the greatest percentage change?

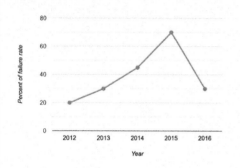

(A) 2012 – 2013   ⊘A⊘

(B) 2013 – 2014   ⊘B⊘

(C) 2014 – 2015   ⊘C⊘

(D) 2015 – 2016   ⊘D⊘

Move on to the
Next Section ≫

⏱ 35:00

---

1 Mark for Review 🔖

The function f is defined by the equation $f(x) = 6x - 3$. What is the value of x when $f(x) = -9$?

- (A) 3
- (B) 1
- (C) -1
- (D) -3

---

2 Mark for Review 🔖

The total cost, in dollars, it takes for James to rent a room consists of a monthly fixed $1250 rent fee and $0.5 per hour fee for electricity. This April, he used electricity for 180 hours. What is the total cost James must pay for this month?

- (A) $1250
- (B) $1340
- (C) $1430
- (D) $1520

---

3 Mark for Review 🔖

What is the value of y that satisfies the two systems of equations given below?

$$-2x + 3y = 11$$
$$y = 2x + 1$$

---

4 Mark for Review 🔖

m is a constant and x and y are variables given in the system of equations below. For which value of m does the system of equations have infinitely many solutions?

$$4x - y = -6$$
$$-10x + my = 15$$

Annotate ⋮

5 Mark for Review 🔖

From the given graph below, find the y-intercept.

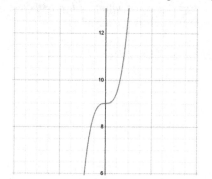

(A) 12	(A)
(B) 10	(B)
(C) 9	(C)
(D) 6	(D)

 Annotate ⋮

6 Mark for Review 🔖

The graph below shows the relationship between the time a candle burns, x (in hours), and the height of a candle, y (in centimeters). Which equation represents this relationship?

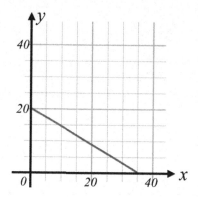

(A) $y = -4/7x + 20$	(A)
(B) $y = -7/4x + 20$	(B)
(C) $y = 4/7x + 20$	(C)
(D) $y = 7/4x + 20$	(D)

I

II

III

IV

V

VI

VII

Annotate

7   Mark for Review 🔖

Which of the following equations is perpendicular to $2x - y = 4$?

(A) $2x - y = 4$ (A)

(B) $-2x - y = 4$ (B)

(C) $\frac{1}{2}x - y = 4$ (C)

(D) $-\frac{1}{2}x - y = 4$ (D)

TEST⬛QUBE   Question 7 of 22 >

Annotate

8   Mark for Review 🔖

What is the maximum number of boxes that Sarah can bring with her in an elevator with a maximum load capacity of 210 pounds, if she weighs 110 pounds and each box weighs 15 pounds?

(A) 4   (A)

(B) 5   (B)

(C) 6   (C)

(D) 7   (D)

TEST⬛QUBE   Question 8 of 22 >

Annotate

9   Mark for Review 🔖

If the expression below is rewritten in the form $ax^3 + bx^2 + cx + d$, where $a, b, c,$ and d are constants, what is the value of c?

$$3x(2x^2 - x + 5) - x(6x - 2) + 3$$

TEST⬛QUBE   Question 9 of 22 >

Annotate

10   Mark for Review 🔖

Find the sum of two solutions for the given equation below.

$$2x^2 + 9x - 5 = 0$$

(A) $9/2$ (A)

(B) $-9/2$ (B)

(C) $2/9$ (C)

(D) $-2/9$ (D)

TEST⬛QUBE   Question 10 of 22 >   Back   Next

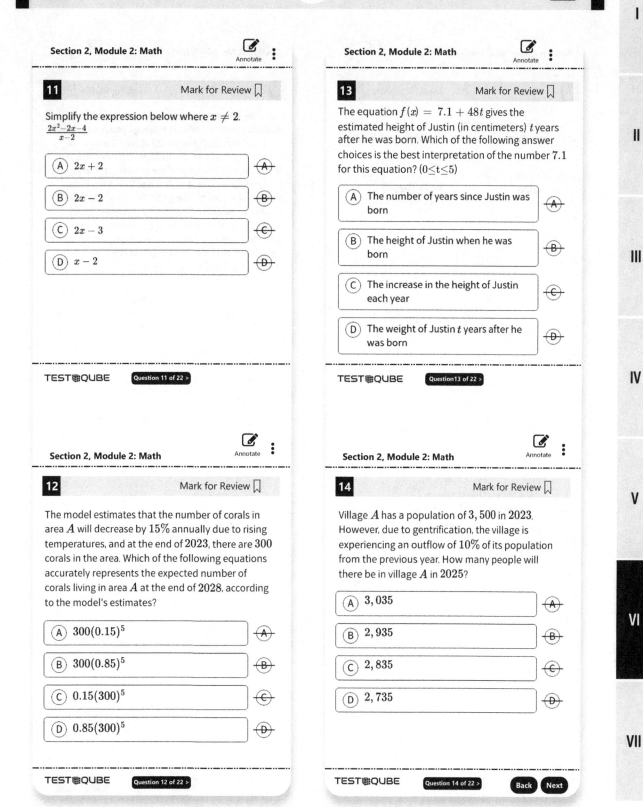

11   Mark for Review 🔖

Simplify the expression below where $x \neq 2$.

$$\frac{2x^2 - 2x - 4}{x - 2}$$

(A) $2x + 2$ Ⓐ

(B) $2x - 2$ Ⓑ

(C) $2x - 3$ Ⓒ

(D) $x - 2$ Ⓓ

12   Mark for Review 🔖

The model estimates that the number of corals in area A will decrease by 15% annually due to rising temperatures, and at the end of 2023, there are 300 corals in the area. Which of the following equations accurately represents the expected number of corals living in area A at the end of 2028, according to the model's estimates?

(A) $300(0.15)^5$ Ⓐ

(B) $300(0.85)^5$ Ⓑ

(C) $0.15(300)^5$ Ⓒ

(D) $0.85(300)^5$ Ⓓ

13   Mark for Review 🔖

The equation $f(x) = 7.1 + 48t$ gives the estimated height of Justin (in centimeters) t years after he was born. Which of the following answer choices is the best interpretation of the number 7.1 for this equation? $(0 \leq t \leq 5)$

(A) The number of years since Justin was born   Ⓐ

(B) The height of Justin when he was born   Ⓑ

(C) The increase in the height of Justin each year   Ⓒ

(D) The weight of Justin t years after he was born   Ⓓ

14   Mark for Review 🔖

Village A has a population of $3,500$ in 2023. However, due to gentrification, the village is experiencing an outflow of 10% of its population from the previous year. How many people will there be in village A in 2025?

(A) $3,035$ Ⓐ

(B) $2,935$ Ⓑ

(C) $2,835$ Ⓒ

(D) $2,735$ Ⓓ

I

II

III

IV

V

VI

VII

Section 2, Module 2: Math   Annotate ⋮

15   Mark for Review 🔖

The table below summarizes the 30 data values in a set of data. Which of the following sentences are true?

Value	Frequency
0	1
1	3
2	2
3	5
4	4
5	7
6	4
7	1
8	3

$i.$)   The mean is larger than the mode of this data set.

$ii.$)   The mode of this data set is 8.

$iii.$)   The range of this data set is 8.

(A) i only

(B) iii only

(C) i and iii

(D) ii and iii

Section 2, Module 2: Math   Annotate ⋮

16   Mark for Review 🔖

The table below summarizes the number of students who took different college entrance exams in class A and B. There are 29 students who took SAT in class A and there are 58 students who took SAT in class B. The ratio of the number of students who took IB in class A to B is 3 to 2, and the total number of students taking CSAT is half of the total number of students who took IB. There are a total of 40 students who took IB. If one student is chosen at random from a total pool of students, what is the probability that he or she took IB at class B? (Round to the nearest hundredth)

Class	Test		
	SAT	IB	CSAT
A	29	?	?
B	58	?	?
Total	87	40	?

I

17   Mark for Review 🔖

In triangle ABC, the following information is given: Angle B measures 90 degrees, and Angle C measures 45 degrees. If the length of side BC is 10, find the length of the hypotenuse for triangle ABC.

- (A) $10\sqrt{3}$ A̶
- (B) $10\sqrt{2}$ B̶
- (C)   20   C̶
- (D)   40   D̶

18   Mark for Review 🔖

There is an equilateral triangle inscribed in a circle as shown below. If the radius of this circle is 4, what is the area of this equilateral triangle?

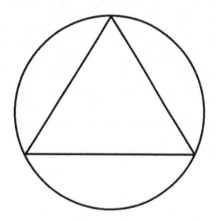

- (A) $4\sqrt{3}$ A̶
- (B) $8\sqrt{3}$ B̶
- (C) $12\sqrt{3}$ C̶
- (D) $16\sqrt{3}$ D̶

II

III

IV

V

VI

VII

I

II

III

IV

V

VI

VII

19   Mark for Review 🔖

Tim is driving a car between his home and work. The distance between the two places is d and it takes h hours to travel from home to work. Which expression represents the average speed of this trip?

(A) $d + h$ ─A─

(B) $d - h$ ─B─

(C) $d \times h$ ─C─

(D) d/h ─D─

20   Mark for Review 🔖

In the triangle below, triangle ABC is an isosceles triangle in which $AB = AC$. If $BD = BE$, $CE = CF$, and angle $\angle A = 72°$, what is the measure of angle $\angle DEF$?

Note: Figure Not Drawn to Scale

(A) $36°$ ─A─

(B) $54°$ ─B─

(C) $63°$ ─C─

(D) $72°$ ─D─

Annotate ⋮

21   Mark for Review 🔖

The function f is defined by
$f(x) = -2x^2 + 9x - 4$ and function g is defined
by $g(x) = -f(x)$. Find one x-intercept of the
function $g(x)$.

Section 2, Module 2: Math

Annotate ⋮

22   Mark for Review 🔖

In the figure below, the two horizontal lines run
parallel to each other. What is the value of x?

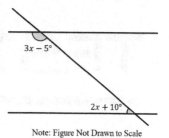

$3x - 5°$

$2x + 10°$

Note: Figure Not Drawn to Scale

(A) 35   Ⓐ

(B) 45   Ⓑ

(C) 55   Ⓒ

(D) 65   Ⓓ

I
II
III
IV
V
VI
VII

TESTQUBE

Digital SAT ®

Practice Test #7

Section 1, Module 1: Reading & Writing

🕐 32:00

Annotate ⋮

The economic turmoil caused by the recent global pandemic, which many compare to the Great Depression in terms of its devastating effects, has cast doubt on an economic analyst's prediction of a quick recovery for the tourism sector. Thomas McAllister, a leading analyst at Goldman Sachs, had initially predicted a rapid resurgence in travel and tourism post-pandemic. However, the persisting travel restrictions due to new virus variants, and health concerns among travelers, may not ____ his forecast completely, but are likely to delay its realization.

1   Mark for Review 🔖

Which choice completes the text with the most logical and precise word or phrase?

- (A) endorse   Ⓐ
- (B) retract   Ⓑ
- (C) underline   Ⓒ
- (D) invalidate   Ⓓ

TEST❖QUBE

Question 1 of 27 >

Back   Next

Section 1, Module 1: Reading & Writing

Annotate ⋮

After analyzing a series of unexplained phenomena, renowned paranormal investigator Dr. Robert Holmes was able to ____ that the occurrences were not random but followed a specific pattern. His work has been acclaimed for its meticulous attention to detail and his ability to draw conclusions from seemingly unrelated events.

2   Mark for Review 🔖

Which choice completes the text with the most logical and precise word or phrase?

- (A) obstruct
- (B) surmise
- (C) dispute
- (D) eradicate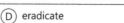

TEST❖QUBE

Question 2 of 27 >

Back   Next

Section 1, Module 1: Reading & Writing

Annotate ⋮

In the literary world, Alice Munro's latest novel has caused quite a stir. Despite her previous success, her newest work has seen mixed reviews and was even _____ by the critics. They felt the narrative was overly complicated and lacked the emotional depth present in her earlier works.

3   Mark for Review 🔖

Which choice completes the text with the most logical and precise word or phrase?

(A) disparaged   ⒶÌ¶

(B) overlooked   Ⓑ̶

(C) complemented   Ⓒ̶

(D) disregarded   Ⓓ̶

TEST◉QUBE   Question 3 of 27 >   Back   Next

Section 1, Module 1: Reading & Writing

Annotate ⋮

In a quaint coastal town in North Carolina, named Edgewater, anticipation of the incoming storm, Hurricane Athena, gripped the community. Meteorologists predicted Hurricane Athena to be of unprecedented severity, and even drew comparisons with Hurricane Katrina. The town's residents, who had a long history of resilience and community bonding, worked together to _____ their homes and businesses. They placed sandbags around their properties, boarded up vulnerable windows, and gathered emergency supplies.

4   Mark for Review 🔖

Which choice completes the text with the most logical and precise word or phrase?

(A) jeer   Ⓐ̶

(B) fortify   Ⓑ̶

(C) exacerbate   Ⓒ̶

(D) compliment   Ⓓ̶

TEST◉QUBE   Question 4 of 27 >   Back   Next

Section 1, Module 1: Reading & Writing

Annotate ⋮

In the modern tragic novel "Faded Quill," written by the award-winning author Isabelle Harding, the protagonist, William Hargrave, was a once-renowned poet during the early 20th century, celebrated for his lyrical mastery and evocative imagery. However, as the story unfolds, William is seen leading a _____ lifestyle after a series of personal tragedies. His days were spent in smoky taverns and bustling gambling dens of London, his nights in the questionable company of drifters and opportunists.

5   Mark for Review 🔖

Which choice completes the text with the most logical and precise word or phrase?

(A) regimented   Ⓐ

(B) ascetic   Ⓑ

(C) dissolute   Ⓒ

(D) prosperous   Ⓓ

TEST🧊QUBE   Question 5 of 27 >   Back Next

Section 1, Module 1: Reading & Writing

Annotate ⋮

The following text is adapted from George Eliot's 1887 poem "Count That Day Lost."

    If you sit down at set of sun
    And count the acts that you have done,
    And, counting, find
    One self-denying deed, one word
    That eased the heart of him who heard,
    One glance most kind
    That fell like sunshine where it went—
    Then you may count that day well spent.

    But if, through all the livelong day,
    You've cheered no heart, by yea or nay—
    If, through it all
    You've nothing done that you can trace
    That brought the sunshine to one face—
    No act most small
    That helped some soul and nothing cost—
    Then count that day as worse than lost.

6   Mark for Review 🔖

Which choice best states the main idea of the text?

(A) The speaker is advising that reflecting on one's actions at the end of the day is an essential routine to understand personal growth.   Ⓐ

(B) The speaker is emphasizing that a day is truly meaningful if even the smallest kind gestures or words have positively impacted someone's life.   Ⓑ

(C) The speaker is urging individuals to adopt a goal-oriented approach to ensure productivity and make each day count.   Ⓒ

(D) The speaker is pointing out the importance of sunlight and how it symbolizes positivity, encouraging people to spend more time outside.   Ⓓ

TEST🧊QUBE   Question 6 of 27 >   Back Next

Section 1, Module 1: Reading & Writing

Annotate

The following text is adapted from E.M. Forster's 1908 novel *A Room with a View*. Lucy Honeychurch is a young Englishwoman touring Italy, where she experiences personal growth and self-discovery.

Mr. Beebe was right. Lucy never knew her desires so clearly as after music. She had not really appreciated the clergyman's wit, nor the suggestive twitterings of Miss Alan. Conversation was tedious; she wanted something big, and she believed that it would have come to her on the wind-swept platform of an electric tram. This she might not attempt. It was unladylike. Why? Why were most big things unladylike? Charlotte had once explained to her why. It was not that ladies were inferior to men; it was that they were different. Their mission was to inspire others to achievement rather than to achieve themselves. Indirectly, by means of tact and a spotless name, a lady could accomplish much.

7   Mark for Review

According to the text, what is true about Lucy?

(A) Lucy enjoys witty talks with people like Mr. Beebe and Miss Alan.

(B) Lucy wants to fit into society and inspire others through tact.

(C) Lucy feels held back by society and longs for an experience of great magnitude.

(D) Lucy thinks women are more capable than men and should have grand ambitions.

Section 1, Module 1: Reading & Writing

Annotate

In a 2013 study led by Dr. Jeffrey Gordon at Washington University in St. Louis, researchers found a link between the gut microbiome and obesity. They transplanted gut bacteria from human twins, where one was obese and the other lean, into germ-free mice. The mice receiving the gut bacteria from the obese twin gained more weight and accumulated more fat than those receiving bacteria from the lean twin, despite having the same diet. The researchers also observed that the mice with bacteria from the lean twin had a greater variety of bacterial species in their gut. The study suggests that the composition of the gut microbiome might play a role in weight management.

8   Mark for Review

According to the text, what is true about the mice that received gut bacteria from the lean human twin?

(A) They gained more weight and accumulated more fat than mice with bacteria from the obese twin.

(B) They had a reduced variety of bacterial species in their gut.

(C) They gained less weight and accumulated less fat than mice with bacteria from the obese twin.

(D) They experienced no difference in weight gain compared to mice with bacteria from the obese twin.

Section 1, Module 1: Reading & Writing

Annotate

The western corn rootworm is a type of beetle that poses a significant threat to corn crops in the United States. Adult beetles prefer to lay their eggs in cornfields, ensuring that their subterranean offspring emerge into a bountiful supply of corn roots. This life cycle relies on a consistent annual availability of corn. To counteract this dependency, farmers alternate between planting corn and soybeans each year. This strategy causes rootworms to lay their eggs in cornfields, but their larvae are born amid soybeans and ultimately perish. Nonetheless, some rootworms have evolved to overcome this approach by diminishing their innate preference for egg-laying in cornfields. These rotation-adaptable female rootworms might deposit their eggs in soybean fields, allowing their larvae to hatch in the presence of corn.

9   Mark for Review 🔖

According to the text, what is a shared characteristic between rotation-adaptable rootworms and conventional rootworms?

(A) They both negatively impact agricultural productivity by depleting soil nutrients.

(B) They both give rise to offspring that consume the root systems of crops.

(C) They both respond to crop rotation practices by sustaining elevated enzyme levels in their digestive systems.

(D) They both possess identical amounts and varieties of gut bacteria.

TEST❖QUBE

Back Next

Section 1, Module 1: Reading & Writing

Annotate

"Charles Dickens" is a 1906 biography by G.K. Chesterton, an English writer, philosopher, and critic, originally written in English. In the book, Chesterton explores the vividness of Charles Dickens' personality, arguing that a writer's personal eccentricities are often reflected in their literary style and characters: _____

10   Mark for Review 🔖

"Which quotation from "Charles Dickens" most effectively illustrates the claim?"

(A) "Many modern people, chiefly women, have been heard to object to the Bacchic element in the books of Dickens, that celebration of social drinking as a supreme symbol of social living."

(B) "His face had a peculiar tint or quality which is hard to describe even after one has contrived to imagine it. It was the quality which Mrs. Carlyle felt to be, as it were metallic, and compared to clear steel."

(C) "He had no objection to being stared at, if he were also admired. He did not exactly pose in the oriental manner of Disraeli; his instincts were too clean for that; but he did pose somewhat in the French manner, of some leaders like Mirabeau and Gambetta."

(D) "His whole life was full of such unexpected energies, precisely like those of the pantomime clown. In his lectures, in later years, he could turn his strange face into any of the innumerable mad masks that were the faces of his grotesque characters."

TEST❖QUBE

Back Next

Section 1, Module 1: Reading & Writing

The Minoan civilization, the earliest advanced society in Europe, arose around 2600 B.C.E. on the island of Crete in the Mediterranean Sea and suddenly declined around 1450 B.C.E., leaving behind elaborate palaces and artifacts indicative of their sophisticated culture. Recent analysis of pottery shards found at Akrotiri, a well-preserved Minoan settlement on the nearby island of Santorini, and samples from contemporary pottery at Knossos, the largest Minoan palace on Crete, revealed that both sites shared a distinct style and composition of ceramics, with this connection appearing most prominently between 1600 and 1450 B.C.E. Consequently, researchers concluded that during this period, _____

11   Mark for Review

Which choice most logically completes the text?

(A) Minoan pottery production reached its peak, leading to widespread distribution of their distinct ceramics.

(B) the Minoan civilization expanded its influence to neighboring islands, spreading their cultural practices and artistic techniques.

(C) a trade route was established between Akrotiri and Knossos, facilitating the exchange of goods and ideas.

(D) a shared pottery workshop was in operation, serving both the Minoan settlements on Crete and Santorini.

Section 1, Module 1: Reading & Writing

One challenge when researching the impact of therapy on mental health is the problem of ensuring that the experiment has an appropriate control group. To determine the effectiveness of a therapeutic intervention, researchers must compare individuals who receive therapy with those who do not receive therapy but who are otherwise similar to the treatment group. Given the ethical considerations surrounding the withholding of therapy from individuals who require it, researchers therefore _____

12   Mark for Review

Which choice most logically completes the text?

(A) may opt for alternative research methods that don't require strict control groups.

(B) often struggle to establish a suitable control group for their investigations.

(C) must seek approval from ethics committees before proceeding with their studies.

(D) need to prioritize the well-being of their participants over the validity of their findings.

Annotate

The following text is from Gerard Manley Hopkins's 1881 poem "Inversnaid."

Degged with dew, dappled with dew,
Are the groins of the braes that the brook treads through,
Wiry heathpacks, flitches of fern,
And the beadbonny ash that sits over the burn.

What would the world be, once bereft
Of wet and of wildness? Let them be left,
O let them be left, wildness and wet;
Long live the weeds and the wilderness yet.

13   Mark for Review 🔖

Which choice best describes the function of the underlined portion in the text as a whole?

(A) It suggests that the speaker is overwhelmed by the untamed beauty of the wilderness.

(B) It suggests a world without nature would be a wild and unpredictable place.

(C) It introduces a debate on the merits and drawbacks of unchecked environmental conservation.

(D) It poses a rhetorical question to advocate for the preservation of untouched, wild nature

TEST QUBE

Question 13 of 27 >

Back   Next

Annotate

In the world of literature, Jane Austen is celebrated for her witty and insightful novels that provide social commentary on the British gentry of the early 19th century. Among her most well-known works, "Pride and Prejudice" _____ as a timeless classic, offering readers a glimpse into the societal norms and expectations of that era.

14   Mark for Review 🔖

Which choice completes the text so that it conforms to the conventions of Standard English?

(A) endures

(B) endured

(C) enduring

(D) will endure

TEST QUBE

Question 14 of 27 >

Back   Next

I

II

III

IV

V

VI

VII

Section 1, Module 1: Reading & Writing

Annotate ⋮

Owing to the interconnected consequences of habitat loss and climate change on wildlife _____ need to evaluate both factors when determining an ecosystem's overall resilience. This does not imply that current habitat preservation efforts are inadequate; conserving natural spaces is still crucial for maintaining biodiversity, but addressing climate change impacts is equally essential.

15   Mark for Review 🔖

Which choice completes the text with the most logical and precise word or phrase?

(A) populations, researchers

(B) populations; researchers

(C) populations, and researchers

(D) populations. Researchers

Section 1, Module 1: Reading & Writing

Annotate ⋮

A 2019 analysis by the Green Integrity Organization discovered that 45 percent of the respondents were convinced that companies occasionally exaggerated their environmental efforts for _____ felt that businesses engaged in such practices regularly.

16   Mark for Review 🔖

Which choice completes the text so that it conforms to the conventions of Standard English?

(A) publicity, another 20 percent

(B) publicity, while another 20 percent

(C) publicity; while another 20 percent

(D) publicity. While another 20 percent

Section 1, Module 1: Reading & Writing

Annotate

In the dense tropical rainforests of South America ___ a remarkable array of plant and animal species that have evolved unique adaptations to thrive in their environment. These species form complex interdependent relationships, contributing to the overall biodiversity of the ecosystem. Scientists continue to study the rainforest to better understand the delicate balance that exists within this rich habitat.

17 Mark for Review

Which choice completes the text so that it conforms to the conventions of Standard English?

(A) lives ⊝Ⓐ

(B) live ⊝Ⓑ

(C) has lived ⊝Ⓒ

(D) have lived ⊝Ⓓ

TEST◼QUBE

Back Next

Section 1, Module 1: Reading & Writing

Annotate

In the illustrious Johnson City Library exists a quaint and intimately curated section that pays homage to the local authors of Johnsonville. Adorning the shelves of this distinguished space, the assemblage of various genres encapsulates the veritable essence of Johnsonville through the written word. The pinnacle of this literary endeavor manifests itself in the form of an annual festival, aptly named "The Johnsonville Literary Soirée," wherein the ____ are brought into the limelight through an engaging blend of stimulating book readings, insightful author panels, and spirited community discussions. This gala not only showcases and celebrates the literary wealth of Johnsonville but also serves as an instrumental platform to foster an environment of support and encouragement for the inexhaustible talent in the community.

18 Mark for Review

Which choice completes the text so that it conforms to the conventions of Standard English?

(A) authors' works ⊝Ⓐ

(B) author's works ⊝Ⓑ

(C) author's works' ⊝Ⓒ

(D) authors works ⊝Ⓓ

TEST◼QUBE

Back Next

Section 1, Module 1: Reading & Writing

✏️ Annotate ⋮

For years, it was assumed that birds descended from a group of two-legged dinosaurs known as theropods. However, after reevaluating fossil structures and performing detailed analysis, _____ now proposes that the origin of birds is more complex.

19   Mark for Review 🔖

Which choice completes the text so that it conforms to the conventions of Standard English?

(A) paleontologist John Ostrom's theory Ⓐ

(B) paleontologist John Ostrom Ⓑ

(C) the theory of paleontologist John Ostrom Ⓒ

(D) it is now theorized by paleontologist John Ostrom who Ⓓ

Section 1, Module 1: Reading & Writing

✏️ Annotate ⋮

Environmentalist Ingrid Johansson serves on the committee responsible for reviewing the European Union's climate policies, which include emissions reduction targets and renewable energy investments. Johansson doesn't make such decisions _____ all policy recommendations must be approved by a group of nine other experts from the fields of energy, conservation, economics, and climate science.

20   Mark for Review 🔖

Which choice completes the text so that it conforms to the conventions of Standard English?

(A) unilaterally, however;

(B) unilaterally; however,

(C) unilaterally, however,

(D) unilaterally however

Annotate

Polaris, also known as the North Star, is not a single star, but rather a multiple star system. The main component, Polaris A, is a yellow supergiant, while its smaller companions are part of a binary system orbiting around _____.

21   Mark for Review 🔖

Which choice completes the text so that it conforms to the conventions of Standard English?

- (A) them
- (B) it
- (C) one
- (D) themselves

Annotate

The Montreal Protocol, an international treaty signed in 1987, aimed to protect the Earth's ozone layer by phasing out the production and use of ozone-depleting substances, such as chlorofluorocarbons (CFCs). It is considered one of the most successful environmental agreements in history. _____ the production and consumption of ozone-depleting substances have been drastically reduced, leading to a significant recovery of the ozone layer.

22   Mark for Review 🔖

Which choice completes the text with the most logical transition?

- (A) In consequence,
- (B) Conversely,
- (C) Nonetheless,
- (D) Meanwhile,

Section 1, Module 1: Reading & Writing

Annotate

The Northern Renaissance, a cultural and intellectual movement in Northern Europe during the 15th and 16th centuries, paralleled the Italian Renaissance yet exhibited distinct characteristics. While the Italian Renaissance focused on reviving the classical art and literature of ancient Rome and Greece, the Northern Renaissance emphasized religious themes and the development of new artistic techniques. _____ the invention of the printing press in Northern Europe facilitated the spread of humanist ideas and contributed to the Protestant Reformation.

23 Mark for Review

Which choice completes the text with the most logical transition?

(A) In addition,

(B) On the contrary,

(C) However,

(D) In comparison,

Section 1, Module 1: Reading & Writing

Annotate

The Silk Road, a network of trade routes connecting the East and the West, played a pivotal role in the cultural, economic, and political interactions between civilizations throughout history. It facilitated the exchange of goods, ideas, and technologies, significantly influencing the development of societies along its path. _____ the Silk Road enabled the spread of major world religions, such as Buddhism, Christianity, and Islam.

24 Mark for Review

Which choice completes the text with the most logical transition?

(A) In summation,

(B) Consequently,

(C) Similarly,

(D) Nevertheless,

Section 1, Module 1: Reading & Writing

Annotate ⋮

While researching a topic, a student has taken the following notes:

- Machine learning is a subset of artificial intelligence that involves the development of algorithms that can learn from and make predictions based on data.
- Supervised learning, unsupervised learning, and reinforcement learning are the main types of machine learning.
- Supervised learning uses labeled data to train algorithms, while unsupervised learning relies on unlabeled data.
- Reinforcement learning focuses on training algorithms to make decisions based on rewards and penalties.
- Machine learning has applications in various fields, such as computer vision, natural language processing, and recommendation systems.

25   Mark for Review 🔖

The student wants to explain the primary distinction between supervised and unsupervised learning. Which choice most effectively uses relevant information from the notes to accomplish this goal?

(A) Supervised learning is a type of machine learning that uses labeled data to train algorithms, whereas unsupervised learning relies on unlabeled data to discover patterns and relationships in the data.

(B) Supervised and unsupervised learning are both subsets of machine learning, focusing on the development of algorithms that can learn from and make predictions based on different types of data.

(C) Machine learning, including supervised and unsupervised learning, has applications in various fields, such as computer vision, natural language processing, and recommendation systems.

(D) The main types of machine learning—supervised learning, unsupervised learning, and reinforcement learning—differ in their approach to training algorithms and making predictions based on data.

TEST QUBE   Question 25 of 27 >   Back   Next

Section 1, Module 1: Reading & Writing

Annotate ⋮

While researching a topic, a student has taken the following notes:

- Cultural anthropology is the study of human cultures, beliefs, practices, and social structures.
- Ethnography is a primary research method in cultural anthropology, involving the in-depth study of a specific cultural group.
- Participant observation, interviews, and the collection of artifacts are common techniques used in ethnographic research.
- Cultural relativism is the belief that cultural practices and beliefs should be understood within the context of the culture in which they occur.
- Ethnocentrism is the belief that one's own culture is superior to others and should be used as the standard for evaluating other cultures.

26   Mark for Review 🔖

The student wants to discuss the main research method used in cultural anthropology. Which choice most effectively uses relevant information from the notes to accomplish this goal?

(A) Cultural anthropology, focused on the study of human cultures and social structures, primarily utilizes ethnography as a research method, which involves the in-depth study of a specific cultural group.

(B) While ethnographic research in cultural anthropology employs techniques such as participant observation, interviews, and artifact collection, it's important to note that cultural relativism plays a significant role in interpreting the findings from these methods.

(C) Cultural relativism, a belief central to cultural anthropology, supports the idea that cultural practices and beliefs should be studied and understood within the context of their own culture.

(D) The concept of ethnocentrism, which is often criticized in cultural anthropology, argues that one's own culture should be the standard for evaluating other cultures and their practices.

TEST QUBE   Question 26 of 27 >   Back   Next

Section 1, Module 1: Reading & Writing

Annotate

While researching a topic, a student has taken the following notes:

- The Paris Commune was a radical socialist government that ruled Paris from March 18 to May 28, 1871.
- Karl Marx (1818-1883) was a philosopher, economist, and socialist revolutionary.
- Marx's book "The Civil War in France" (1871) provides an analysis of the Paris Commune.
- He argued that the Paris Commune was an example of the dictatorship of the proletariat.
- Marx believed the Commune demonstrated how workers could seize political power.

27   Mark for Review 🔖

The student wants to emphasize Marx's interpretation of the Paris Commune. Which choice most effectively uses relevant information from the notes to accomplish this goal?

(A) The Paris Commune, which ruled Paris in 1871, was the subject of Karl Marx's book "The Civil War in France."

(B) Karl Marx, in his book "The Civil War in France," saw the Paris Commune as an example of how workers could seize political power.

(C) Karl Marx, a philosopher and economist, wrote about the Paris Commune in his book "The Civil War in France."

(D) The Paris Commune, according to Karl Marx, demonstrated the potential of the proletariat.

TEST❖QUBE   Question 27 of 27 >   Back Next

Move on to the Next Section ≫

⏱ 32:00

Annotate ⋮

Traditional paper-making methods are often criticized as being _____ due to the deforestation they cause and the high energy consumption involved. However, environmental scientist Dr. John Green has been instrumental in developing a new method of recycling waste paper that reduces the environmental impact significantly.

1

Mark for Review 🔖

Which choice completes the text with the most logical and precise word or phrase?

(A) sustainable

(B) viable

(C) ephermeral

(D) pernicious

TEST🧊QUBE

Question 1 of 27 >

Back   Next

Annotate ⋮

During the power vacuum in the medieval Kingdom of England, the ambitious Baron Gilbert de Clare attempted to _____ the throne. His actions led to a series of conflicts that would last for several years, contributing to the tumultuous period known as The Anarchy, which saw various nobles vying for control. The chaos of this period has been depicted in numerous historical novels and films, highlighting the ruthlessness and cunning required in the struggle for power.

2

Mark for Review 🔖

Which choice completes the text with the most logical and precise word or phrase?

(A) rectify

(B) usurp

(C) validate

(D) relinquish

TEST🧊QUBE

Question 2 of 27 >

Back   Next

Section 1, Module 2: Reading & Writing

Annotate

The claims made by the tabloid "National Enquirer" about the celebrity Tom Cruise's private life were completely ____, as they were based on rumors and speculation rather than hard evidence. As a result, the tabloid faced considerable backlash and was even threatened with legal action by Cruise's representatives. The incident raised questions about the ethics and credibility of tabloid journalism, with many calling for stricter regulation of such publications.

3 Mark for Review

Which choice completes the text with the most logical and precise word or phrase?

(A) unfounded — Ⓐ

(B) impassioned — Ⓑ

(C) dispassionate — Ⓒ

(D) unintelligible — Ⓓ

TEST✦QUBE

Back Next

Section 1, Module 2: Reading & Writing

Annotate

The idea that the tiny startup "Pebble Technology" could compete with the multinational corporation Apple in the smartwatch market was considered ____ by industry analysts. The vast differences in resources and market presence made the notion seem absurd. However, Pebble gained a cult following, though it eventually succumbed to market pressures.

4 Mark for Review

Which choice completes the text with the most logical and precise word or phrase?

(A) preposterous — Ⓐ

(B) plausible — Ⓑ

(C) feasible — Ⓒ

(D) probable — Ⓓ

TEST✦QUBE

Back Next

Section 1, Module 2: Reading & Writing

Annotate ⋮

When confronted with the serious nature of the topic of climate change, Senator John Doe's _____ response during a congressional hearing was considered inappropriate by many. His lack of sensitivity was criticized by environmental advocates, including well-known figures such as Greta Thunberg and Leonardo DiCaprio, reflecting poorly on his judgment and highlighting the need for informed leadership on critical issues like rising sea levels and extreme weather patterns.

5 Mark for Review 🔖

Which choice completes the text with the most logical and precise word or phrase?

(A) flippant ⊝Ⓐ

(B) sober ⊝Ⓑ

(C) meticulous ⊝Ⓒ

(D) penitent ⊝Ⓓ

TEST✦QUBE Question 5 of 27 > Back Next

Section 1, Module 2: Reading & Writing

Annotate ⋮

The following text is adapted from Susan Glaspell's 1917 short story "A Jury of Her Peers." Martha Hale is about to leave her house in a hurry on an unusually important errand.

When Martha Hale opened the storm-door and got a cut of the north wind, she ran back for her big woolen scarf. As she hurriedly wound that round her head her eye made a scandalized sweep of her kitchen. It was no ordinary thing that called her away—it was probably farther from ordinary than anything that had ever happened in Dickson County. But what her eye took in was that her kitchen was in no shape for leaving: her bread all ready for mixing, half the flour sifted and half unsifted.

6 Mark for Review 🔖

Which choice best states the main purpose of the text?

(A) To reveal the chilling environment of the north by illustrating how the north wind's harshness compelled Martha Hale to retrieve her scarf.

(B) To provide a glimpse into Martha Hale's domestic life, focusing particularly on her involvement and meticulousness in the bread-making process.

(C) To build a sense of mystery and intrigue around the event that necessitates Martha Hale's departure, emphasizing its abnormality in the context of Dickson County.

(D) To portray Martha Hale's internal conflict between her sense of domestic responsibility and the urgency of the extraordinary event that calls her away.

TEST✦QUBE Question 6 of 27 > Back Next

Section 1, Module 2: Reading & Writing

Annotate

The following text is adapted from Gilbert Keith Chesterton's 1909 essay "The Fallacy of Success." The author criticizes books glorifying financial success for promoting snobbishness and materialism.

At least, let us hope that we shall all live to see these absurd books about Success covered with a proper derision and neglect. They do not teach people to be successful, but they do teach people to be snobbish; they do spread a sort of evil poetry of worldliness. The Puritans are always denouncing books that inflame lust; <u>what shall we say of books that inflame the viler passions of avarice and pride?</u> A hundred years ago we had the ideal of the Industrious Apprentice; boys were told that by thrift and work they would all become Lord Mayors. This was fallacious, but it was manly, and had a minimum of moral truth. In our society, temperance will not help a poor man to enrich himself, but it may help him to respect himself.

7   Mark for Review

Which choice best describes the function of the underlined portion in the text as a whole?

- (A) It serves to reinforce the author's critique of books promoting materialism.
- (B) It questions the universal perspective on the values of pride and avarice promoted in literature.
- (C) It denounces the notion that modern society rewards hard work with financial success.
- (D) It mentions the Puritans to illustrate the author's support for religious objections to certain books.

TEST QUBE

Back   Next

Section 1, Module 2: Reading & Writing

Annotate

The following text is adapted from W.B. Yeats' 1939 poem "An Acre of Grass."

PICTURE and book remain,
An acre of green grass
For air and exercise,
<u>Now strength of body goes;</u>
<u>Midnight, an old house</u>
<u>Where nothing stirs but a mouse.</u>

My temptation is quiet.
Here at life's end
Neither loose imagination,
Nor the mill of the mind
Consuming its rag and bone,
Can make the truth known.

8   Mark for Review

Which choice best describes the function of the underlined portion in the text as a whole?

- (A) It suggests that the speaker is finding consolation in literature and visual art.
- (B) It indicates the speaker's preference for solitude and tranquility during the night.
- (C) It serves to underscore the yearning for physical strength and idyllic life with a companion.
- (D) It illustrates an absence of youthful vigor and the ensuing silence of the surroundings.

TEST QUBE

Back   Next

Section 1, Module 2: Reading & Writing

Annotate ⋮

Text 1

In his sweeping narrative "The Symphony of Life," acclaimed biologist Dr. Adrian Clarke presents an in-depth exploration of the complex interrelationships within ecosystems. Dr. Clarke posits that all organisms, no matter how small or seemingly insignificant, have a role to play in maintaining the balance of their ecosystems. This delicate balance, he suggests, is akin to a symphony, where each species, like individual instruments, contributes to the overall harmony. Understanding these intricate relationships, Clarke asserts, is fundamental to biodiversity conservation efforts and our response to environmental challenges.

Text 2

Dr. Vanessa Hamilton, a leading ecologist with a focus on urban ecosystems, appreciates the intricate web of interactions that define natural ecosystems in her work. In her research, "Nature in Concrete Jungles," Hamilton explores the often overlooked ecosystems within urban landscapes. While she acknowledges the significance of understanding traditional ecosystems, she argues that the study of urban ecology is equally important. Urban ecosystems, she asserts, are not only significant habitats for diverse species but also crucial for human well-being and sustainable cities. Hamilton emphasizes the need to balance the understanding of both traditional and urban ecosystems to address contemporary ecological challenges.

9   Mark for Review 🔖

Based on the texts, how would Dr. Hamilton (Text 2) most likely characterize Dr. Clarke's "Symphony of Life" proposition in Text 1?

- (A) As valid yet narrow, because while it is a sound proposition, it doesn't thoroughly consider the significance of urban ecosystems in ecological balance.

- (B) As inapplicable, because in her perspective, the urban ecosystems, central to her studies, may not align with Clarke's "Symphony of Life."

- (C) As comprehensive, because it captures the essence of intricate ecological relationships which she can incorporate into her research on urban ecosystems.

- (D) As over-simplified, because it uses a symphony as a metaphor to describe complex ecological relationships, which she might find reductionist.

TEST🌐QUBE   Question 9 of 27 >   Back   Next

Section 1, Module 2: Reading & Writing

Annotate ⋮

Earthquake Magnitudes and Depths for Four Regions

Region	Magnitude Range	Average Depth (km)	Tectonic Setting
A	4.0-6.5	15	Continental Rift
B	6.0-9.0	20	Subduction Zone
C	3.0-5.0	8	Intraplate
D	5.0-7.5	12	Transform Fault

The table above presents data on earthquake magnitudes, average depths, and tectonic settings for four different regions, A, B, C, and D. Seismologists study earthquake patterns and their relationship with tectonic settings to better understand the dynamics of Earth's crust. A recent study found that regions with deeper earthquakes are associated with higher magnitude earthquakes. However, there was a certain region in the study that strongly contradicted the study, specifically _____.

10   Mark for Review 🔖

Which choice most effectively uses data from the table to complete the statement?

- (A) Region A, as it has a relatively shallow average depth and moderate earthquake magnitudes.

- (B) Region B, since it has a relatively deeper average depth and higher earthquake magnitudes.

- (C) Region C, because it has the shallowest average depth and the lowest range of earthquake magnitudes.

- (D) Region D, as its average depth is shallower than Region A, yet it has a higher range of earthquake magnitudes.

TEST🌐QUBE   Question 10 of 27 >   Back   Next

V

VI

VII

Section 1, Module 2: Reading & Writing

 Annotate

In coastal regions near Nova Scotia in Canada, sea urchins consume vast amounts of kelp, their primary food source, causing damage to the kelp forests. However, in a specific area near Nova Scotia, the kelp forests are more robust than those found in other parts of Canada's coast. Marine biologist Noah Thompson and colleagues compared this specific kelp forest to others where sea urchins are absent or were reintroduced only recently. Discovering that the healthier kelp forest has a more diverse gene pool than the others, Thompson hypothesized that increased consumption by sea urchins prompts the kelp to undergo more sexual reproduction, which in turn enhances genetic diversity, benefiting the kelp forest's overall health.

11　　　　　　　　　Mark for Review 🔖

Which finding, if true, would most directly undermine Thompson's hypothesis?

(A) In some regions within the study, kelp forests are found near sea urchin populations that are small and have only recently been reintroduced.

(B) At several sites not included in the study, there are large, well-established sea urchin populations but no kelp forests.

(C) At several sites not included in the study, kelp forests' health correlates negatively with the length of residence and size of sea urchin populations.

(D) At some sites in the study, the health of plants unrelated to kelp correlates negatively with the length of residence and size of sea urchin populations.

TEST🧊QUBE

Back　Next

Section 1, Module 2: Reading & Writing

Annotate

The Merchant of Venice is a circa 1600 play by William Shakespeare. In the play, Antonio had sealed a bond with Shylock, stipulating that should he default on his loan, Shylock was entitled to a pound of Antonio's flesh. The character of Portia demonstrates wisdom and cunning when she helps Antonio escape his bond with Shylock. Her resourcefulness is evident when she _____

12　　　　　　　　　Mark for Review 🔖

Which choice most effectively uses a quotation from *The Merchant of Venice* to illustrate the claim?

(A) disguised as Dr. Balthazar, declares to Shylock, "A pound of that same merchant's flesh is thine; The court awards it, and the law doth give it."

(B) disguised as Dr. Balthazar, instructs Shylock, "Tarry a little; there is something else. This bond doth give thee here no jot of blood. The words expressly are 'a pound of flesh:'"

(C) disguised as Dr. Balthazar, advises Shylock, "Have by some surgeon, Shylock, on your charge, To stop his wounds, lest he do bleed to death."

(D) disguised as Dr. Balthazar, dictates to Sylock, "For the intent and purpose of the law, Hath full relation to the penalty, Which here appeareth due upon the bond;—"

TEST🧊QUBE

Back　Next

Section 1, Module 2: Reading & Writing

Annotate ⋮

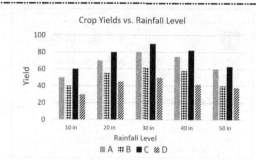

Crop Yields vs. Rainfall Level

Agricultural economists at a national research institute are studying the impact of varying levels of rainfall on crop yield for four different types of crops: wheat (Crop A), corn (Crop B), soybeans (Crop C), and rice (Crop D). These crops were chosen because they represent a significant portion of the country's total agricultural production. The economists hypothesize that even considerable amounts of rainfall will result in similar relative yield outcomes among certain crops. This study aims to help farmers plan their planting and irrigation strategies more efficiently, potentially leading to increased productivity and sustainability.

13   Mark for Review 🔖

Which statement best describes data from the graph that supports the economists' claim?

(A) Crop A has the highest yield at all levels of rainfall.

(B) Crop D is most sensitive to changes in rainfall.

(C) Rice (Crop D) has the lowest yield at all levels of rainfall and Soybeans (Crop C) has the highest yield at all levels of rainfall.

(D) Each crop has different optimal ranges of rainfall for maximum yield.

TEST⬡QUBE   Question 13 of 27 >   Back Next

Section 1, Module 2: Reading & Writing

Annotate ⋮

Anthropologist Javier Ruiz-Martínez and his team have been studying two distinct subcultures within the same geographic region in Ecuador. One subculture has a nomadic lifestyle, constantly moving, while the other is sedentary, living in permanent villages. They found that the nomadic group uses a more varied range of tonal inflections when speaking their common language. The researchers suggest that these tonal differences might allow each subculture to identify members of their own group, promoting social cohesion and driving further cultural divergence over time.

14   Mark for Review 🔖

Which finding, if true, would most directly support Ruiz-Martínez and his team's hypothesis?

(A) The nomadic group travels over a wider geographic area, which might require a more varied range of tonal inflections to communicate effectively in different environments.

(B) Over several generations, the tonal range used by the nomadic group has grown progressively more varied compared to the sedentary group.

(C) Different meanings are assigned to the same words in their common language depending on the tonal inflection used.

(D) The lifestyle habits of the nomadic and sedentary groups have remained generally the same over several generations.

TEST⬡QUBE   Question 14 of 27 >   Back Next

Section 1, Module 2: Reading & Writing

Annotate ⋮

Planetary Data for Four Exoplanets

Exoplanet	Distance from Star (AU)	Surface Temperature (°C)	Atmospheric Composition
A	0.5	150	Mainly Carbon Dioxide
B	1.0	25	Nitrogen, Oxygen, Carbon Dioxide
C	2.0	-50	Mostly Hydrogen and Helium
D	0.7	100	Nitrogen, Methane, Water Vapor

The table above displays data on the distance from the star, surface temperature, and atmospheric composition for four exoplanets, A, B, C, and D. Astrobiologists often study the relationship between the distance from a star and the surface temperature of a planet to assess the likelihood of habitable conditions for life. It is generally believed that planets with surface temperatures between -50°C and 50°C and a reasonable proximity from the star have a higher potential for life. Therefore, in reviewing the data, astrobiologists concluded that of the four exoplanets studied, the planet that most likely has life is _____.

15   Mark for Review 🔖

Which choice most effectively uses data from the table to complete the statement?

(A) Exoplanet A, as it has a close distance from the star and a high surface temperature.   Ⓐ

(B) Exoplanet B, because it has a moderate distance from the star and a surface temperature within the habitable range.   Ⓑ

(C) Exoplanet C, since it has a far distance from the star and a surface temperature below the habitable range.   Ⓒ

(D) Exoplanet D, as it has a close distance from the star and a surface temperature above the habitable range.   Ⓓ

Section 1, Module 2: Reading & Writing

Annotate ⋮

The following text is adapted from Herman Melville's 1924 novella, *Billy Budd*. The story revolves around Billy Budd, a seaman impressed into service aboard HMS Indomitable in the year 1797. The Lieutenant mentioned in this excerpt is a higher-ranking officer onboard the same ship.

To be sure, Billy's action was a terrible breach of naval decorum. But in that decorum he had never been instructed; in consideration of which the Lieutenant would hardly have been so energetic in reproof but for the concluding farewell to the ship. This he rather took as meant to convey a covert sally on the new recruit's part, a sly slur at impressment in general, and that of himself in especial. And yet, more likely, if satire it was in effect, it was hardly so by intention, for Billy, though happily endowed with the gayety of high health, youth, and a free heart, was yet by no means of a satirical turn. The will to it and the sinister dexterity were alike wanting. To deal in double meanings and insinuations of any sort was quite foreign to his nature.

16   Mark for Review 🔖

According to the text, what is true about Billy?

(A) Billy Budd often utilizes satire and double meanings in his speech.   Ⓐ

(B) Billy Budd has a deep understanding and respect for naval decorum.   Ⓑ

(C) Billy Budd is known for his clear and direct communication, without resorting to insinuations.   Ⓒ

(D) Billy Budd is cheerful and healthy, but does not have the inclination or skill for subversive humor.   Ⓓ

Section 1, Module 2: Reading & Writing

Annotate ⋮

The introduction of renewable energy sources, such as solar and wind power, has provided an environmentally sustainable alternative to traditional fossil fuels. However, the intermittent nature of these energy sources presents challenges in terms of grid stability and energy storage. To ensure a reliable and consistent supply of electricity from renewable sources, it is crucial to _____

17 Mark for Review 🔖

Which choice most logically completes the text?

(A) invest in research and development of innovative energy storage solutions.

(B) rely solely on hydropower as the primary source of renewable energy.

(C) continue to utilize fossil fuels as the backbone of global energy systems.

(D) discard the pursuit of renewable energy in favor of nuclear power.

TEST🧩QUBE

Back Next

Section 1, Module 2: Reading & Writing

Annotate ⋮

While numerous filmmakers aim to create movies with the most advanced visual effects and _____ others are drawn to classic cinema, producing films that evoke the style and atmosphere of the 1940s and 1950s film noir era. (The term "film noir" refers to a genre characterized by its dark, moody visuals, and complex, morally ambiguous characters.)

18 Mark for Review 🔖

Which choice completes the text so that it conforms to the conventions of Standard English?

(A) cutting-edge technology but

(B) cutting-edge technology, but

(C) cutting-edge technology,

(D) cutting-edge technology

TEST🧩QUBE

Back Next

Section 1, Module 2: Reading & Writing

Annotate ⋮

Frida Kahlo is best known for her self-portraits and deeply personal paintings, such as The Two Fridas (1939), but she was also an avid collector of indigenous Mexican _____ a collection of more than 200 pieces that greatly influenced her artistic style and contributing to the preservation and appreciation of Mexico's cultural heritage.

19 Mark for Review 🔖

Which choice completes the text so that it conforms to the conventions of Standard English?

(A) art; amassing

(B) art, amassing

(C) art amassing

(D) art. Amassing

Section 1, Module 2: Reading & Writing

Annotate ⋮

Marine biology, the study of ocean-dwelling organisms and their ecosystems, offers a wealth of fascinating trivia. One particularly intriguing fact, for example, is that the _____ an incredible array of biodiversity: it is estimated that over 200,000 species inhabit the depths of the ocean, many of which are yet to be discovered. This vast variety of life - from the microscopic plankton to the colossal blue whale - underlines the importance of marine ecosystems in maintaining global biodiversity.

20 Mark for Review 🔖

Which choice completes the text so that it conforms to the conventions of Standard English?

(A) ocean, covering more than 70% of the Earth's surface, supports

(B) ocean, covering more than 70% of the Earth's surface supports

(C) ocean covering more than 70% of the Earth's surface, supports

(D) ocean — covering more than 70% of the Earth's surface, supports

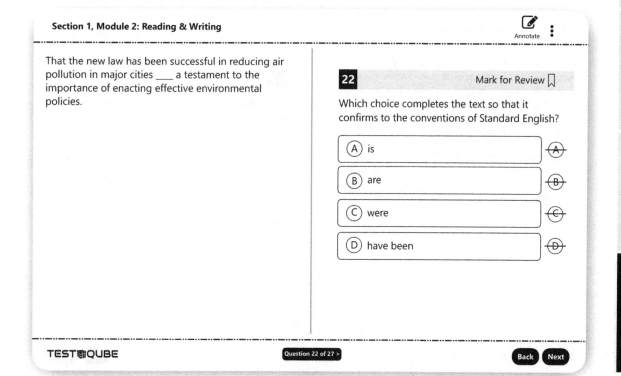

In March 1955, nine months prior to Rosa Parks' historic protest, 15-year-old Claudette Colvin _____ a similar act of defiance by refusing to give up her seat to a white passenger on a segregated bus in Montgomery, Alabama. Although her act of resistance preceded Parks', it was Parks' refusal that became a pivotal moment in the American Civil Rights Movement.

21   Mark for Review

Which choice completes the text so that it conforms to the conventions of Standard English?

(A) had performed

(B) performs

(C) has performed

(D) would perform

TEST QUBE   Question 21 of 27 >   Back Next

That the new law has been successful in reducing air pollution in major cities ____ a testament to the importance of enacting effective environmental policies.

22   Mark for Review

Which choice completes the text so that it confirms to the conventions of Standard English?

(A) is

(B) are

(C) were

(D) have been

TEST QUBE   Question 22 of 27 >   Back Next

Section 1, Module 2: Reading & Writing

Annotate

The Treaty of Tordesillas, signed in 1494 by Spain and Portugal, aimed to resolve territorial disputes arising from the exploration of the New World. This agreement established a meridian line, with lands to the west allocated to Spain and those to the east given to Portugal. _____ the treaty had significant ramifications on the colonization and future geopolitical landscape of the Americas.

23 Mark for Review

Which choice completes the text with the most logical transition?

(A) In essence,

(B) Nonetheless,

(C) Correspondingly,

(D) Incidentally,

Section 1, Module 2: Reading & Writing

Annotate

In the field of astronomy, the discovery of exoplanets—planets that orbit stars outside our solar system—has revolutionized our understanding of the universe and the potential for life beyond Earth. Scientists' meticulous observations and data analysis have revealed thousands of these celestial bodies, with new discoveries being made regularly. The diversity of ____ sizes, compositions, and orbits offers a tantalizing glimpse into the vast array of planetary systems that exist within our galaxy, fueling the ongoing search for Earth-like worlds and extraterrestrial life.

24 Mark for Review

Which choice completes the text with the most logical transition?

(A) exoplanet's

(B) exoplanets

(C) exoplanets's

(D) exoplanets'

Annotate

While researching a topic, a student has taken the following notes:

- "Pride and Prejudice" is a novel by Jane Austen, published in 1813.
- The story is set in rural England during the early 19th century.
- The novel follows the protagonist, Elizabeth Bennet, and her four sisters as they navigate societal expectations and pursue romantic relationships.
- The story explores themes of love, social class, and the importance of first impressions.
- The relationship between Elizabeth Bennet and the wealthy, reserved Mr. Darcy is central to the novel's plot.

25 Mark for Review

The student wants to emphasize the themes of "Pride and Prejudice." Which choice most effectively uses relevant information from the notes to accomplish this goal?

(A) "Pride and Prejudice" is a classic novel by Jane Austen that takes place in rural England, where Elizabeth Bennet and her sisters navigate the complex world of societal expectations and romance. — Ⓐ

(B) Jane Austen's "Pride and Prejudice" tells the story of Elizabeth Bennet and her four sisters as they experience love and relationships in early 19th-century England. — Ⓑ

(C) The novel "Pride and Prejudice" explores themes of love, social class, and the importance of first impressions, as exemplified by the relationship between Elizabeth Bennet and Mr. Darcy. — Ⓒ

(D) Set in the early 19th century, "Pride and Prejudice" follows the protagonist, Elizabeth Bennet, as she encounters the wealthy and reserved Mr. Darcy in a story filled with romance and societal expectations. — Ⓓ

TEST QUBE Question 25 of 27 > Back Next

Annotate

While researching a topic, a student has taken the following notes:

- Cognitive dissonance is a psychological phenomenon where an individual experiences discomfort due to conflicting beliefs or attitudes.
- The theory was developed by psychologist Leon Festinger.
- To resolve cognitive dissonance, individuals may change their beliefs, attitudes, or behaviors.
- Cognitive dissonance can occur in various situations, including decision-making, moral dilemmas, and social interactions.
- The concept is an essential component of many theories of attitude change and persuasion.

26 Mark for Review

The student wants to explain the primary goal of individuals experiencing cognitive dissonance. Which choice most effectively uses relevant information from the notes to accomplish this goal?

(A) Cognitive dissonance, a psychological phenomenon resulting from conflicting beliefs or attitudes, often leads individuals to change their beliefs, attitudes, or behaviors in order to reduce the discomfort. — Ⓐ

(B) The theory of cognitive dissonance, developed by psychologist Leon Festinger, focuses on the discomfort people experience when faced with conflicting beliefs or attitudes in various situations. — Ⓑ

(C) Cognitive dissonance plays a significant role in decision-making, moral dilemmas, and social interactions, as individuals attempt to resolve the discomfort caused by conflicting beliefs or attitudes. — Ⓒ

(D) As an essential component of many theories of attitude change and persuasion, cognitive dissonance explores the psychological impact of conflicting beliefs or attitudes on individuals. — Ⓓ

TEST QUBE Question 26 of 27 > Back Next

I
II
III
IV
V
VI
VII

Section 1, Module 2: Reading & Writing

Annotate

While researching a topic, a student has taken the following notes:

- The Chicago Pile-1 was the world's first artificial nuclear reactor.
- It was built under the bleachers of Stagg Field, a sports stadium at the University of Chicago.
- The project, led by Enrico Fermi, initiated the first controlled nuclear chain reaction on December 2, 1942.
- This event marked the beginning of the Atomic Age and opened the way for the development of nuclear power and atomic weapons.
- The site is now a National Historic Landmark, commemorated by the Henry Moore sculpture, "Nuclear Energy".

27   Mark for Review 🔖

The student wants to emphasize the historical significance and the outcome of the Chicago Pile-1 project. Which choice most effectively uses relevant information from the notes to accomplish this goal?

(A) The Chicago Pile-1, the world's first artificial nuclear reactor, was built at the University of Chicago under Enrico Fermi's leadership.

(B) On December 2, 1942, Enrico Fermi initiated the first controlled nuclear chain reaction at the Chicago Pile-1, marking the beginning of the Atomic Age.

(C) The Chicago Pile-1, built under the bleachers of Stagg Field, is now a National Historic Landmark commemorated by the "Nuclear Energy" sculpture.

(D) The creation of the Chicago Pile-1 led to the development of nuclear power and atomic weapons, marking a significant turn in world history.

TEST❖QUBE   <u>**End of Test 7 Reading/Writing Section**</u>   Back   Next

---

Upcoming Math Section: Reference Formula Sheet

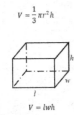

$A = \pi r^2$
$C = 2\pi r$

$A = lw$

$A = \frac{1}{2}bh$

$c^2 = a^2 + b^2$

$V = \frac{1}{3}\pi r^2 h$

$V = \frac{1}{3}lwh$

Special Right Triangles

$V = lwh$

$V = \pi r^2 h$

$V = \frac{3}{4}\pi r^3$

The number of degrees of arc in a circle is 360.
The number of radians of arc in a circle is 2π.
The sum of the measures in degrees of the angles of a triangle is 180.

Directions for Student-Produced Response

- **TEST QUBE** recommends students to use decimals for most answers but suggests using fractions only in cases where the answers involve repeating decimals (e.g., 0.333 ≈ 1/3)
- For cases with more than one answer, enter **just one of the answers.**
- You can enter up to 5 characters for your answer. (For negative answers, the **negative sign** does not count as one character)
- For **fractions** that don't fit the answer box, enter the decimal equivalent (Unless advised to do otherwise)
- For **decimals** that exceed the answer box, round to the fourth digit. (Unless advised to do otherwise)
- For mixed number (such as $4\frac{1}{4}$), enter it as an improper fraction ($17/4$) or its decimal equivalent (4.25)
- For all answers, you may omit the symbols and units such as \$.%, cm^3, m^2, etc.

Acceptable vs Non-Acceptable Answers

Answer	Acceptable ways to receive credit	Ways you **WON'T** receive credit
4.25	4.25 , 17/4	41/4 , 4 1/4
4/6	2/3 .6666 , .6667 0.666 , 0.667	0.66 , .66 0.67 , .67
-1/6	-1/6 -0.166 , -0.167 -.1666 , -.1667	-0.16 , -.16 -0.17 , -.167

Move on to the Next Section ≫

1 Mark for Review ◻

$\frac{36}{x} = 4$. What is the value of x?

- (A) 4
- (B) 6
- (C) 8
- (D) 9

2 Mark for Review ◻

What is 120% of 80?

- (A) 64
- (B) 72
- (C) 96
- (D) 176

3 Mark for Review ◻

The function f is defined by $f(x) = 4x^2 + 2$. What is the value when $f(\frac{1}{2})$?

- (A) 1
- (B) 3
- (C) 5
- (D) 6

4 Mark for Review ◻

$y > 3x + 5$

If the value of x is -2, which value of y satisfies the inequality above?

- (A) -5
- (B) -3
- (C) -1
- (D) 2

I

II

III

IV

V

VI

VII

5 Mark for Review

Jason works at a car dealership where his monthly wage fluctuates depending on the number of cars he sells each month. His wage is calculated using the formula $y = 30x + 110$, where 30 represents the commission he receives for selling one car. What does the value 110 represent in this formula?

- (A) The number of times he sold a car to his customers
- (B) The minimum wage he receives every month
- (C) The hours he spends per month working at the dealership
- (D) The amount of money it takes to sell one car

TEST⬢QUBE   Question 5 of 22 >

6 Mark for Review

If a car travels 60 miles in 1 hour, what is its average speed in feet per second? (1 mile $= 5280$ feet)

- (A) 12
- (B) 44
- (C) 88
- (D) 5280

TEST⬢QUBE   Question 6 of 22 >

7 Mark for Review

$x^2 + 4xy + 4y^2 = 16$. What is one possible value for $x + 2y$?

- (A) 4
- (B) 8
- (C) 64
- (D) 256

TEST⬢QUBE   Question 7 of 22 >

8 Mark for Review

If the first integer is 3 more than twice the second integer, and the sum of the two integers is 24, what is the value of the second integer?

- (A) 3
- (B) 5
- (C) 7
- (D) 11

TEST⬢QUBE   Question 8 of 22 >   Back Next

9 Mark for Review 🔖

Astra, a company renowned for specializing in space travel technology, experienced a tumultuous week with various news events impacting its stock price. The stock began the week at $12. However, on the second day, the price dipped by 7 percent due to negative news. Fortunately, on the third day, positive forecasts led to a 12 percent increase in the stock price. Which answer is closest to the stock's final price at the end of the third day?

Stock Price: ASTRA

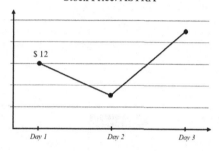

A) $11.50

B) $12.50

C) $14.50

D) $17.00

10 Mark for Review 🔖

$$\frac{1-\frac{3}{x}}{x-\frac{9}{x}}$$

Which of the following equation is equivalent to the expression shown above?

A) $\frac{1}{x-3}$

B) $\frac{x-3}{x+3}$

C) $\frac{1}{x+3}$

D) $\frac{x+3}{x^2-9}$

11 Mark for Review 🔖

What is the equation of a circle with center $(2, 3)$ and radius of 5?

A) $(x+2)^2 + (y+3)^2 = 5$

B) $(x+2)^2 + (y+3)^2 = 25$

C) $(x-2)^2 + (y-3)^2 = 5$

D) $(x-2)^2 + (y-3)^2 = 25$

I
II
III
IV
V
VI
VII

12 Mark for Review 🔖

There are 6 different types of marbles inside a bag. Dylan chooses one marble at random from the bag. What is the probability that Dylan grabs either a rough green marble or a blue marble?

	Red	Blue	Green
Smooth	4	2	3
Rough	2	7	6
Total	6	9	9

(A) 15/18

(B) 5/24

(C) 1/2

(D) 5/8

13 Mark for Review 🔖

The expression $\sqrt[3]{\frac{a^{37}b^{40}c^{25}}{(abc)^{10}}}$ is equivalent to $a^x b^y c^z$, where x,y,z are positive constants. What is the value of $x+y+z$?

14 Mark for Review 🔖

$$\begin{cases} y = 2x + 8 \\ y = 3px + 4 \end{cases}$$

The set of equations is given above. Find the value of p so that there are no solutions to the given system of equations.

(A) 1/2

(B) 4/5

(C) 2/3

(D) 1

15   Mark for Review 🔖

A study is being conducted to assess the physical fitness of 100 high school seniors. One of the categories being quantitatively measured is the number of consecutive push-ups students can perform within a 2-minute time frame. The data is organized in a table with increments of 10. What is the median number of push-ups performed by the group, according to the table?

Number of Push-ups	10	20	30	40	50
Number of People	27	32	22	15	4

- (A) 10
- (B) 20
- (C) 22
- (D) 32

16   Mark for Review 🔖

What value satisfies the inequality below?
$$|x + 1| < 3$$

- (A) -4
- (B) 0
- (C) 2
- (D) 3

I
II
III
IV
V
VI
VII

Annotate ⋮

17   Mark for Review 🔖

The rational function f is defined by an equation in the form of $f(x) = \frac{x+3}{x^2-4}$. How many values of x is not defined for $f(x)$?

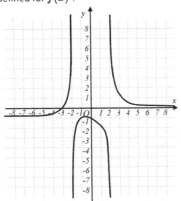

(A) 0   (A)

(B) 1   (B)

(C) 2   (C)

(D) 3   (D)

 Annotate ⋮

18   Mark for Review 🔖

For a right triangle with side lengths 6 and 8, what is a possible side length of the third side?

 (A) 3   (A)

 (B) $3\sqrt{5}$ (B)

(C) $2\sqrt{7}$ (C)

(D) 12   (D)

 Annotate ⋮

19   Mark for Review 🔖

$$y = 3x^2 - 5x - 12$$

The given equations above is a polynomial function with two roots. If the values of the two roots are denoted as a and b, what is the value of ab?

 (A) -4 (A)

 (B) -3 (B)

 (C) 3   (C)

 (D) 4   (D)

Section 2, Module 1: Math ⋮

20   Mark for Review 🔖

In Physics, there is a widely used formula in understanding the movement of a fluid. The equation, adapted from the founder himself, is called the Bernoulli's Equation. This equation is used to gain insight in the motion of a fluid, specifically related to the pressure, speed and height. Assuming that there is no static pressure, the formula can be expressed as follows. Which equation correctly expresses p in terms of $h, v, c,$ and g?

$$\frac{p}{2}v^2 + pgh = c$$

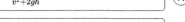

- (A) $p = \frac{2c}{v^2+2gh}$ (A)
- (B) $p = \frac{c}{gvh}$ (B)
- (C) $p = \frac{2c}{vgh+2}$ (C)
- (D) $p = \frac{gc}{v^2+2vh}$ (D)

Section 2, Module 1: Math ⋮

21   Mark for Review 🔖

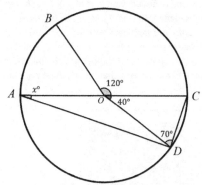

Note: Figure Not Drawn to Scale

In the shown figure, the segment AC is the diameter of the circle with the center O. Also, $\angle BOC = 120°$, $\angle COD = 40°$, and $\angle CDO = 70°$. Find the angle of $x°$.

- (A) $70°$ (A)
- (B) $45°$ (B)
- (C) $30°$ (C)
- (D) $20°$ (D)

TEST QUBE   Question 20 of 22 >
TEST QUBE   Question 21 of 22 >   Back   Next
305

I

II

III

IV

V

VI

VII

Section 2, Module 1: Math

Annotate

---

22   Mark for Review 🔖

John is trying to decide what kind of fence he should use for his garden. The dimension of the garden is $10m \times 20m$ and John decides $10m^2$ to be the overall area of the fence. If the fence goes around the garden and is uniform in thickness, and the thickness is denoted as t in meters, what is the closest value of t?

t

(A) $1.54m$ (A)

(B) $0.85m$ (B)

(C) $0.53m$ (C)

(D) $0.17m$ (D)

Move on to the
Next Section ≫

⏱ 35:00

Annotate ⋮

1 Mark for Review 🔖

If a rectangle has a length of 8 units and a width of 5 units, what is its area?

Ⓐ 13 square units   Ⓐ

Ⓑ 25 square units   Ⓑ

Ⓒ 30 square units   Ⓒ

Ⓓ 40 square units   Ⓓ

TEST⬛QUBE   Question 1 of 22 >

Annotate ⋮

2 Mark for Review 🔖

Jenna owns a thrift store that sells second-hand goods at a fixed price of $20 each. During a clearance sale, the store reduces the price of these items by 30%. What is the final price of the goods during the clearance sale?

Ⓐ $6   Ⓐ

Ⓑ $14   Ⓑ

Ⓒ $18   Ⓒ

Ⓓ $30   Ⓓ

TEST⬛QUBE   Question 2 of 22 >

Annotate ⋮

3 Mark for Review 🔖

A car is traveling at a constant speed, and after 2 hours it has covered a distance of 350km. What is the car's speed in km/hour?

Ⓐ 100 km/hour   Ⓐ

Ⓑ 120 km/hour   Ⓑ

Ⓒ 150 km/hour   Ⓒ

Ⓓ 175 km/hour   Ⓓ

TEST⬛QUBE   Question 3 of 22 >

Annotate ⋮

4 Mark for Review 🔖

A factory is responsible for producing shoes for its district. For every 200 shoes that the factory produces, 8 of them have a defect. If a shoe is randomly selected from the factory's production, what is the probability of selecting a shoe that has a defect?

Ⓐ 8/100   Ⓐ

Ⓑ 8/1000   Ⓑ

Ⓒ 4/100   Ⓒ

Ⓓ 4/10   Ⓓ

TEST⬛QUBE   Question 4 of 22 >   Back Next

I   II   III   IV   V   VI   VII

Section 2, Module 2: Math

5   Mark for Review 🔖

The graph of $f(x) = 3x - 4$ is shown. What would be the y-intercept of the line for the function $f(x+3)$?

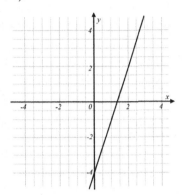

 A -1 Ⓐ

B 5 Ⓑ

C 11 Ⓒ

D 13 Ⓓ

Section 2, Module 2: Math

6   Mark for Review 🔖

In a right triangle, if the measure of one acute angle is $\angle 45°$ and the length of the side opposite to it is 8 units, what is the length of the hypotenuse?

Ⓐ $6\sqrt{2}$ units   Ⓐ

Ⓑ 8 units   Ⓑ

Ⓒ $8\sqrt{2}$ units   Ⓒ

Ⓓ 12 units   Ⓓ

Section 2, Module 2: Math   Annotate

7   Mark for Review 🔖

Consider the system of equations:

$$2x - y = 5$$
$$(3x + y)^2 = 25$$

Which ordered pair (x, y) is a possible solution to the given system of equations?

Ⓐ $(2, -1)$

Ⓑ $(2, -5)$

Ⓒ $(0, -1)$

Ⓓ $(0, 2)$

8   Mark for Review 🔖

What value of x is the solution to the given equation?

$3x + 7 = 28$

(A) 15

(B) 12

(C) 9

(D) 7

9   Mark for Review 🔖

$f(x) = x^2 + 4x + 3.$

The given equation defines the function f. For the ordered pair of (x, y) where $f(x)$ is at its minimum, what is the sum of $x + y$?

(A) -4

(B) -3

(C) 1

(D) 3

10   Mark for Review 🔖

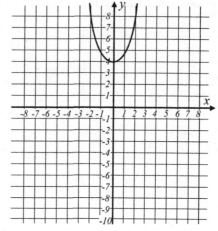

The graph of $y = x^2 + 4$ is shown. What is the value of x at $(x, 4)$?

(A) -2

(B) 0

(C) 2

(D) 4

Annotate

11   Mark for Review 🔖

Which expression is equivalent to
$(x^3 + y^2) - (3y^2 - x^3)$?

(A) $2y^2$ Ⓐ

(B) $-2y^2$ Ⓑ

(C) $2y^2 + 2x^3$ Ⓒ

(D) $-2y^2 + 2x^3$ Ⓓ

TEST🍎QUBE   Question 8 of 22 >

Annotate

13   Mark for Review 🔖

A company produces and sells widgets at a rate of $10 per widget. However, the company needs to rent out a warehouse to make the product which has a fixed cost of $200. Let P represent the profit in dollars and w represent the number of widgets sold. Which equation correctly models the relationship between P and w?

(A) $P = 10w - 200$ Ⓐ

(B) $P = 10w + 200$ Ⓑ

(C) $P = 200w - 10$ Ⓒ

(D) $P = 200w + 10$ Ⓓ

TEST🍎QUBE   Question 13 of 22 >

Annotate

12   Mark for Review 🔖

Jonathan keeps track of his record for how many times he scores during each football practice. The record for the latest 10 games are,

$7, 2, 0, 3, 2, 1, 0, 2, 3, 2$

By analyzing the mean, mode, and median, which of the value is the highest?

(A) Mean   Ⓐ

(B) Mode   Ⓑ

(C) Median   Ⓒ

(D) All values are the same   Ⓓ

TEST🍎QUBE   Question 12 of 22 >

Annotate

14   Mark for Review 🔖

In the figure $ABCD$, find the value of x. (Ignore the degree sign)

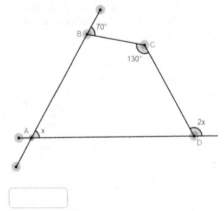

TEST🍎QUBE   Question 14 of 22 >   Back   Next

Annotate

15 — Mark for Review

John is a plumber who is in charge of maintaining a water tank that supplies water to multiple villas. There is an annual checkup of the tank during which John drains all the water and then refills it. However, due to the high demand for water, the drainage pipe is left open while the tank is being filled. The pipe used for filling the tank can fill it in 4 hours, while the drainage pipe would take 6 hours to drain it completely. Assuming the tank starts off empty and both pipes are opened at the same time, how long, rounded to the nearest hour, will it take to fill the tank to its full capacity?

- (A) 8 hours
- (B) 10 hours
- (C) 12 hours
- (D) 24 hours

Annotate

16 — Mark for Review

The formula to calculate the compound interest on an investment is given by $A = P(1 + r/n)^{nt}$ where A represents the final amount, P is the principal amount, r is the annual interest rate, n is the number of times interest is compounded per year, and t is the number of years. Rearrange the formula to express the annual interest rate, r, in terms of A, P, n, t.

- (A) $r = n[(A/P)^{1/nt} - 1]$
- (B) $r = n[(P/A)^{nt} - 1]$
- (C) $r = n[(P/A)^{1/nt} - 1]$
- (D) $r = n[(A/P)^{nt} + 1]$

Annotate

17 — Mark for Review

A circle with center $(3, -2)$ and radius of 5 is represented by the equation $(x - 3)^2 + (y + 2)^2 = 25$. Which point lies on the circle?

- (A) $(7, -2)$
- (B) $(3, -8)$
- (C) $(-2, 3)$
- (D) $(8, -2)$

I

II

III

IV

V

VI

VII

18
Mark for Review 🔖

A company conducted a survey to collect data on customer preferences regarding various products. The results are displayed in the table below. If a male customer is selected at random, what is the probability that his preferred product category is "Electronics"? Round your answer to the **nearest hundredth**.

Preferred Category	Male	Female	Total
Electronics	150	80	230
Clothing	120	90	210
Home Goods	70	60	130
Sports & Outdoor	50	70	120
Total	390	300	690

19
Mark for Review 🔖

The population of a town is modeled by the function $P(t) = 5000(1.03)^t$, where P represents the population and t represents the number of years since the start of the model. If the population is expected to reach $10,000$, which of the following answer choice is the closest to the year this occurs?

(A) 15 years

(B) 20 years

(C) 25 years

(D) 30 years

20
Mark for Review 🔖

A bookstore sells books at a 20% discount from the original price. During Thanksgiving, there is another 25% discount applied to the already discounted price. If a book's original price is $100, what is the difference in price between buying the book during the regular discount and after the Thanksgiving sale?

(A) $10

(B) $15

(C) $20

(D) $60

Annotate

21 Mark for Review

The figure below depicts a circle with center O. If chord AB is parallel to diameter CD, where AB measures 6 cm and CD measures 10 cm, what is the shortest distance between point O and chord AB?

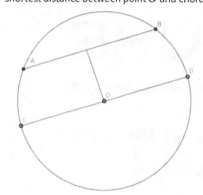

(A) $3cm$ A

(B) $4cm$ B

(C) $5cm$ C

(D) $6cm$ D

Annotate

22 Mark for Review

A rectangular prism has a volume of 990 cubic units. If the length, width, and height of the prism are consecutive positive integers, what is the sum of the length, width, and height?

(A) 29 units   A

(B) 30 units   B

(C) 31 units   C

(D) 32 units   D

I

II

III

IV

V

VI

VII

TEST█QUBE

Digital SAT ®

Answer
Keys

Reading and Writing: Module 1

QUESTION NUMBER	CORRECT ANSWER	DOMAIN	SKILL
1	C	Craft & Structure	Words In Context
2	D	Craft & Structure	Words In Context
3	B	Craft & Structure	Text Structure & Purpose
4	D	Craft & Structure	Text Structure & Purpose
5	A	Craft & Structure	Cross-Text Connections
6	C	Information & Ideas	Command of Evidence: Textual
7	A	Craft & Structure	Text Structure & Purpose
8	B	Craft & Structure	Text Structure & Purpose
9	B	Information & Ideas	Command of Evidence: Textual
10	C	Information & Ideas	Command of Evidence: Quantitative
11	C	Information & Ideas	Command of Evidence: Quantitative
12	C	Information & Ideas	Command of Evidence: Quantitative
13	A	Information & Ideas	Command of Evidence: Quantitative
14	B	Information & Ideas	Inferences
15	A	Standard English Conventions	Boundaries
16	B	Standard English Conventions	Form, Structure, and Sense
17	B	Standard English Conventions	Boundaries
18	B	Standard English Conventions	Form, Structure, and Sense
19	C	Standard English Conventions	Boundaries
20	A	Standard English Conventions	Form, Structure, and Sense
21	D	Standard English Conventions	Boundaries
22	C	Expression of Ideas	Transitions
23	B	Expression of Ideas	Transitions
24	B	Expression of Ideas	Transitions
25	A	Expression of Ideas	Transitions
26	B	Expression of Ideas	Rhetorical Synthesis
27	B	Expression of Ideas	Rhetorical Synthesis

Reading and Writing: Module 2

QUESTION NUMBER	CORRECT ANSWER	DOMAIN	SKILL
1	C	Craft & Structure	Words In Context
2	C	Craft & Structure	Words In Context
3	D	Craft & Structure	Words In Context

4	D	Craft & Structure	Words In Context
5	C	Craft & Structure	Words In Context
6	D	Craft & Structure	Words In Context
7	B	Craft & Structure	Words In Context
8	C	Craft & Structure	Words In Context
9	B	Information & Ideas	Central Ideas and Details
10	C	Information & Ideas	Command of Evidence: Textual
11	C	Information & Ideas	Command of Evidence: Textual
12	A	Information & Ideas	Command of Evidence: Textual
13	B	Craft & Structure	Text Structure & Purpose
14	D	Information & Ideas	Inferences
15	A	Information & Ideas	Inferences
16	D	Information & Ideas	Inferences
17	A	Standard English Conventions	Boundaries
18	A	Standard English Conventions	Form, Structure, and Sense
19	B	Standard English Conventions	Boundaries
20	A	Standard English Conventions	Boundaries
21	A	Standard English Conventions	Form, Structure, and Sense
22	A	Standard English Conventions	Boundaries
23	D	Expression of Ideas	Transitions
24	B	Expression of Ideas	Transitions
25	B	Expression of Ideas	Transitions
26	B	Expression of Ideas	Rhetorical Synthesis
27	B	Expression of Ideas	Rhetorical Synthesis

Math: Module 1

QUESTION NUMBER	CORRECT ANSWER	CATEGORY	SUB-CATEGORY
1	D	Heart of Algebra	Algebra
2	C	Problem Solving and Data Analysis	Probability
3	A	Problem Solving and Data Analysis	Percentages
4	D	Heart of Algebra	Linear Equations
5	C	Problem Solving and Data Analysis	Ratio
6	D	Problem Solving and Data Analysis	Plots and Diagrams
7	A	Problem Solving and Data Analysis	Plots and Diagrams
8	B	Heart of Algebra	Mathematical Modelling, Inequality
9	5, 0.5, .5, 1/2	Heart of Algebra	Linear Equations
10	D	Problem Solving and Data Analysis	Probability

11	C	Heart of Algebra	Mathematical Modelling, Exponential
12	13	Problem Solving and Data Analysis	Statistics
13	D	Heart of Algebra	Linear Equations
14	C	Additional Topics in Math	Circles
15	51	Additional Topics in Math	Trigonometry
16	A	Passport to Advanced Math	Polynomial
17	C	Additional Topics in Math	Angles and Radians
18	A	Passport to Advanced Math	Quadratic Equations
19	C	Passport to Advanced Math	Translation Transformation
20	46	Passport to Advanced Math	Rational Functions
21	12000	Problem Solving and Data Analysis	Percentages
22	A	Problem Solving and Data Analysis	Probability

Math: Module 2

QUESTION NUMBER	CORRECT ANSWER	CATEGORY	SUB-CATEGORY
1	C	Problem Solving and Data Analysis	Percentages
2	D	Heart of Algebra	Mathematical Modelling
3	C	Heart of Algebra	Linear Equations
4	B	Heart of Algebra	Mathematical Modelling
5	A	Heart of Algebra	Linear Equations
6	A	Heart of Algebra	Mathematical Modelling
7	C	Problem Solving and Data Analysis	Percentages
8	2.5, 5/2	Passport to Advanced Math	Rational Functions
9	A	Problem Solving and Data Analysis	Plots and Diagram
10	B	Additional Topics in Math	Trigonometry
11	C	Problem Solving and Data Analysis	Statistics
12	81	Passport to Advanced Math	Irrational Functions
13	B	Problem Solving and Data Analysis	Exponential Functions
14	A	Additional Topics in Math	Trigonometry
15	A	Passport to Advanced Math	Quadratic Equations
16	117	Additional Topics in Math	Trigonometry
17	20	Heart of Algebra	Linear Equations
18	A	Problem Solving and Data Analysis	Plots and Diagrams
19	10	Passport to Advanced Math	Quadratic Equations
20	A	Additional Topics in Math	Geometry
21	D	Problem Solving and Data Analysis	Plots and Diagrams
22	D	Problem Solving and Data Analysis	Ratio

Reading and Writing: Module 1

QUESTION NUMBER	CORRECT ANSWER	DOMAIN	SKILL
1	C	Craft & Structure	Words In Context
2	C	Craft & Structure	Words In Context
3	B	Craft & Structure	Words In Context
4	B	Craft & Structure	Words In Context
5	A	Craft & Structure	Text Structure & Purpose
6	A	Craft & Structure	Text Structure & Purpose
7	D	Craft & Structure	Text Structure & Purpose
8	D	Information & Ideas	Command of Evidence: Textual
9	B	Information & Ideas	Central Ideas and Details
10	B	Information & Ideas	Central Ideas and Details
11	B	Information & Ideas	Command of Evidence: Textual
12	C	Information & Ideas	Command of Evidence: Quantitative
13	D	Information & Ideas	Command of Evidence: Quantitative
14	A	Information & Ideas	Inferences
15	D	Standard English Conventions	Boundaries
16	B	Standard English Conventions	Boundaries
17	C	Standard English Conventions	Boundaries
18	C	Standard English Conventions	Form, Structure, and Sense
19	B	Standard English Conventions	Boundaries
20	C	Standard English Conventions	Boundaries
21	A	Expression of Ideas	Transitions
22	B	Expression of Ideas	Rhetorical Synthesis
23	B	Expression of Ideas	Rhetorical Synthesis
24	C	Expression of Ideas	Rhetorical Synthesis
25	A	Expression of Ideas	Rhetorical Synthesis
26	A	Expression of Ideas	Rhetorical Synthesis
27	B	Expression of Ideas	Rhetorical Synthesis

Reading and Writing: Module 2

QUESTION NUMBER	CORRECT ANSWER	DOMAIN	SKILL
1	B	Craft & Structure	Words In Context
2	B	Craft & Structure	Words In Context
3	A	Craft & Structure	Words In Context

4	D	Craft & Structure	Words In Context
5	B	Craft & Structure	Cross-Text Connections
6	A	Craft & Structure	Main Purpose
7	B	Information & Ideas	Central Ideas and Details
8	D	Information & Ideas	Central Ideas and Details
9	D	Information & Ideas	Command of Evidence: Textual
10	C	Information & Ideas	Command of Evidence: Quantitative
11	A	Information & Ideas	Command of Evidence: Textual
12	B	Information & Ideas	Command of Evidence: Textual
13	B	Information & Ideas	Inferences
14	C	Information & Ideas	Inferences
15	C	Information & Ideas	Inferences
16	B	Standard English Conventions	Boundaries
17	A	Standard English Conventions	Boundaries
18	B	Standard English Conventions	Form, Structure, and Sense
19	B	Standard English Conventions	Boundaries
20	A	Standard English Conventions	Form, Structure, and Sense
21	A	Standard English Conventions	Form, Structure, and Sense
22	B	Standard English Conventions	Boundaries
23	D	Expression of Ideas	Transitions
24	C	Expression of Ideas	Transitions
25	C	Expression of Ideas	Transitions
26	A	Expression of Ideas	Rhetorical Synthesis
27	A	Expression of Ideas	Rhetorical Synthesis

Math: Module 1

QUESTION NUMBER	CORRECT ANSWER	CATEGORY	SUB-CATEGORY
1	C	Heart of Algebra	Algebra
2	A	Heart of Algebra	Inequality
3	B	Heart of Algebra	Graphs
4	90	Additional Topics in Math	Trigonometry
5	C	Passport to Advanced Math	Translation Transformation
6	B	Heart of Algebra	Linear Equations
7	B	Additional Topics in Math	Trigonometry
8	D	Problem Solving and Data Analysis	Probability
9	D	Passport to Advanced Math	Quadratic Equations
10	C	Heart of Algebra	Mathematical Modelling

11	A	Passport to Advanced Math	Absolute Value
12	B	Problem Solving and Data Analysis	Exponential Functions
13	C	Additional Topics in Math	Trigonometry
14	6	Heart of Algebra	Linear Equations
15	A	Passport to Advanced Math	Polynomial
16	A	Passport to Advanced Math	Plots and Diagrams
17	B	Passport to Advanced Math	Polynomial
18	D	Problem Solving and Data Analysis	Percentages
19	C	Problem Solving and Data Analysis	Exponential Functions
20	109	Problem Solving and Data Analysis	Statistics
21	B	Additional Topics in Math	Geometry
22	D	Passport to Advanced Math	Translation Transformation

Math: Module 2

QUESTION NUMBER	CORRECT ANSWER	CATEGORY	SUB-CATEGORY
1	72	Problem Solving and Data Analysis	Percentages
2	A	Heart of Algebra	Mathematical Modelling
3	D	Heart of Algebra	Linear Equations
4	D	Heart of Algebra	Graphs
5	B	Heart of Algebra	Mathematical Modelling
6	A	Passport to Advanced Math	Polynomial
7	D	Heart of Algebra	Mathematical Modelling
8	B	Additional Topics in Math	Geometry
9	C	Problem Solving and Data Analysis	Probability
10	B	Problem Solving and Data Analysis	Exponential Functions
11	B	Problem Solving and Data Analysis	Percentages
12	11	Heart of Algebra	Algebra
13	C	Problem Solving and Data Analysis	Plots and Diagrams
14	B	Heart of Algebra	Graphs
15	C	Heart of Algebra	Mathematical Modelling
16	D	Problem Solving and Data Analysis	Unit Conversion
17	D	Additional Topics in Math	Trigonometry
18	A	Passport to Advanced Math	Quadratic Equations
19	19	Problem Solving and Data Analysis	Statistics
20	5	Passport to Advanced Math	Irrational Functions
21	B	Heart of Algebra	Mathematical Modelling
22	D	Heart of Algebra	Linear Equations

Reading and Writing: Module 1

QUESTION NUMBER	CORRECT ANSWER	DOMAIN	SKILL
1	A	Craft & Structure	Words In Context
2	A	Craft & Structure	Words In Context
3	A	Craft & Structure	Words In Context
4	B	Craft & Structure	Words In Context
5	A	Craft & Structure	Words In Context
6	A	Craft & Structure	Words In Context
7	B	Information & Ideas	Command of Evidence: Textual
8	A	Craft & Structure	Text Structure & Purpose
9	B	Craft & Structure	Text Structure & Purpose
10	D	Information & Ideas	Command of Evidence: Textual
11	D	Information & Ideas	Command of Evidence: Quantitative
12	A	Information & Ideas	Inferences
13	A	Information & Ideas	Inferences
14	B	Standard English Conventions	Boundaries
15	A	Standard English Conventions	Boundaries
16	D	Standard English Conventions	Forms, Structure, and Sense
17	C	Standard English Conventions	Boundaries
18	B	Standard English Conventions	Forms, Structure, and Sense
19	C	Standard English Conventions	Boundaries
20	C	Standard English Conventions	Forms, Structure, and Sense
21	B	Expression of Ideas	Transitions
22	A	Expression of Ideas	Rhetorical Synthesis
23	A	Expression of Ideas	Rhetorical Synthesis
24	B	Expression of Ideas	Rhetorical Synthesis
25	B	Expression of Ideas	Rhetorical Synthesis
26	A	Expression of Ideas	Rhetorical Synthesis
27	A	Expression of Ideas	Rhetorical Synthesis

Reading and Writing: Module 2

QUESTION NUMBER	CORRECT ANSWER	DOMAIN	SKILL
1	A	Craft & Structure	Words In Context
2	C	Craft & Structure	Words In Context
3	B	Craft & Structure	Words In Context

Reading and Writing: Module 2

QUESTION NUMBER	CORRECT ANSWER	DOMAIN	SKILL
4	C	Craft & Structure	Words In Context
5	B	Craft & Structure	Text Structure & Purpose
6	D	Craft & Structure	Text Structure & Purpose
7	C	Craft & Structure	Text Structure & Purpose
8	D	Craft & Structure	Text Structure & Purpose
9	A	Craft & Structure	Cross-Text Connections
10	C	Information & Ideas	Command of Evidence: Quantitative
11	B	Information & Ideas	Command of Evidence: Textual
12	C	Information & Ideas	Command of Evidence: Quantitative
13	B	Information & Ideas	Command of Evidence: Textual
14	A	Information & Ideas	Command of Evidence: Textual
15	B	Information & Ideas	Inferences
16	A	Information & Ideas	Inferences
17	A	Standard English Conventions	Boundaries
18	A	Standard English Conventions	Forms, Structure, and Sense
19	B	Standard English Conventions	Boundaries
20	C	Standard English Conventions	Forms, Structure, and Sense
21	A	Standard English Conventions	Boundaries
22	D	Standard English Conventions	Boundaries
23	B	Standard English Conventions	Boundaries
24	B	Expression of Ideas	Transitions
25	C	Expression of Ideas	Transitions
26	B	Expression of Ideas	Transitions
27	B	Expression of Ideas	Rhetorical Synthesis

Math: Module 1

QUESTION NUMBER	CORRECT ANSWER	CATEGORY	SUB-CATEGORY
1	D	Heart of Algebra	Linear Equations
2	D	Heart of Algebra	Mathematical Modelling
3	C	Passport to Advanced Math	Polynomial
4	147	Additional Topics in Math	Geometry
5	6	Passport to Advanced Math	Quadratic Equation
6	B	Additional Topics in Math	Geometry

7	B	Heart of Algebra	Mathematical Modelling
8	D	Heart of Algebra	Linear Equations
9	11	Problem Solving and Data Analysis	Statistics
10	B	Passport to Advanced Math	Irrational Functions
11	D	Passport to Advanced Math	Polynomial
12	162	Heart of Algebra	Mathematical Modelling
13	C	Problem Solving and Data Analysis	Unit Conversion
14	A	Additional Topics in Math	Trigonometry
15	36	Heart of Algebra	Linear Equations
16	B	Problem Solving and Data Analysis	Exponential Functions
17	C	Passport to Advanced Math	Absolute Value
18	-7	Passport to Advanced Math	Quadratic Equation
19	4	Problem Solving and Data Analysis	Exponential Functions
20	C	Heart of Algebra	Algebra
21	C	Problem Solving and Data Analysis	Statistics
22	B	Additional Topics in Math	Geometry

Math: Module 2

QUESTION NUMBER	CORRECT ANSWER	CATEGORY	SUB-CATEGORY
1	D	Problem Solving and Data Analysis	Plots and Diagrams
2	C	Heart of Algebra	Linear Equations
3	C	Passport to Advanced Math	Polynomial
4	A	Additional Topics in Math	Geometry
5	12	Heart of Algebra	Mathematical Modelling
6	D	Problem Solving and Data Analysis	Irrational Function
7	4	Additional Topics in Math	Geometry
8	B	Additional Topics in Math	Circles
9	B	Problem Solving and Data Analysis	Statistics
10	D	Problem Solving and Data Analysis	Percentages
11	2,4	Passport to Advanced Math	Quadratic Equation
12	B	Heart of Algebra	Mathematical Modelling
13	C	Heart of Algebra	Algebra
14	A	Heart of Algebra	Mathematical Modelling
15	B	Passport to Advanced Math	Rational Functions
16	C	Heart of Algebra	Linear Equations
17	1	Heart of Algebra	Algebra
18	B	Additional Topics in Math	Geometry
19	A	Additional Topics in Math	Geometry

20	D	Problem Solving and Data Analysis	Probability
21	C	Problem Solving and Data Analysis	Statistics
22	3	Additional Topics in Math	Angles and Radians

Reading and Writing: Module 1

QUESTION NUMBER	CORRECT ANSWER	DOMAIN	SKILL
1	C	Craft & Structure	Words In Context
2	A	Craft & Structure	Words In Context
3	B	Craft & Structure	Words In Context
4	D	Craft & Structure	Words In Context
5	B	Craft & Structure	Words In Context
6	D	Craft & Structure	Text Structure & Purpose
7	D	Information & Ideas	Central Ideas and Details
8	B	Information & Ideas	Central Ideas and Details
9	D	Information & Ideas	Central Ideas and Details
10	B	Information & Ideas	Command of Evidence: Textual
11	C	Information & Ideas	Inferences
12	A	Information & Ideas	Inferences
13	B	Information & Ideas	Inferences
14	D	Standard English Conventions	Form, Structure, and Sense
15	A	Standard English Conventions	Form, Structure, and Sense
16	D	Standard English Conventions	Boundaries
17	A	Standard English Conventions	Form, Structure, and Sense
18	A	Standard English Conventions	Boundaries
19	A	Standard English Conventions	Form, Structure, and Sense
20	A	Standard English Conventions	Boundaries
21	B	Expression of Ideas	Transitions
22	B	Expression of Ideas	Transitions
23	B	Expression of Ideas	Transitions
24	A	Expression of Ideas	Rhetorical Synthesis
25	B	Expression of Ideas	Rhetorical Synthesis
26	B	Expression of Ideas	Rhetorical Synthesis
27	B	Expression of Ideas	Rhetorical Synthesis

Reading and Writing: Module 2

QUESTION NUMBER	CORRECT ANSWER	DOMAIN	SKILL
1	C	Craft & Structure	Words In Context
2	A	Craft & Structure	Words In Context
3	C	Craft & Structure	Words In Context
4	B	Craft & Structure	Words In Context

5	B	Craft & Structure	Words In Context
6	B	Craft & Structure	Text Structure & Purpose
7	A	Information & Ideas	Text Structure & Purpose
8	A	Information & Ideas	Text Structure & Purpose
9	A	Craft & Structure	Cross-Text Connections
10	D	Information & Ideas	Command of Evidence: Quantitative
11	B	Information & Ideas	Command of Evidence: Textual
12	D	Information & Ideas	Command of Evidence: Textual
13	C	Information & Ideas	Command of Evidence: Quantitative
14	C	Information & Ideas	Command of Evidence: Textual
15	B	Information & Ideas	Command of Evidence: Quantitative
16	D	Information & Ideas	Command of Evidence: Textual
17	A	Information & Ideas	Inferences
18	A	Standard English Conventions	Boundaries
19	A	Standard English Conventions	Boundaries
20	D	Standard English Conventions	Boundaries
21	C	Standard English Conventions	Form, Structure, and Sense
22	C	Standard English Conventions	Boundaries
23	C	Expression of Ideas	Transitions
24	D	Expression of Ideas	Rhetorical Synthesis
25	A	Expression of Ideas	Rhetorical Synthesis
26	B	Expression of Ideas	Rhetorical Synthesis
27	A	Expression of Ideas	Rhetorical Synthesis

Math: Module 1

QUESTION NUMBER	CORRECT ANSWER	CATEGORY	SUB-CATEGORY
1	A	Problem Solving and Data Analysis	Statistics
2	C	Heart of Algebra	Graphs
3	C	Problem Solving and Data Analysis	Statistics
4	D	Heart of Algebra	Linear Equations
5	B	Passport to Advanced Math	Polynomial
6	C	Heart of Algebra	Mathematical Modelling
7	A	Problem Solving and Data Analysis	Probability
8	C	Additional Topics in Math	Trigonometry
9	D	Problem Solving and Data Analysis	Exponential Functions
10	A	Heart of Algebra	Linear Equations

11	C	Heart of Algebra	Mathematical Modelling
12	480	Additional Topics in Math	Geometry
13	D	Passport to Advanced Math	Quadratic Equation
14	C	Heart of Algebra	Linear Equations
15	C	Problem Solving and Data Analysis	Percentages
16	600	Heart of Algebra	Mathematical Modelling
17	60	Problem Solving and Data Analysis	Plots and Diagrams
18	A	Problem Solving and Data Analysis	Probability
19	B	Problem Solving and Data Analysis	Probability
20	D	Additional Topics in Math	Geometry
21	6	Additional Topics in Math	Circles
22	B	Heart of Algebra	Mathematical Modelling

Math: Module 2

QUESTION NUMBER	CORRECT ANSWER	CATEGORY	SUB-CATEGORY
1	D	Passport to Advanced Math	Quadratic Equation
2	B	Heart of Algebra	Mathematical Modelling
3	10	Heart of Algebra	Algebra
4	A	Additional Topics in Math	Geometry
5	C	Heart of Algebra	Mathematical Modelling
6	6	Passport to Advanced Math	Quadratic Equation
7	D	Passport to Advanced Math	Polynomial
8	B	Passport to Advanced Math	Polynomial
9	14	Additional Topics in Math	Geometry
10	A	Heart of Algebra	Graphs
11	B	Passport to Advanced Math	Translation Transformation
12	D	Heart of Algebra	Graphs
13	B	Heart of Algebra	Graphs
14	24	Passport to Advanced Math	Quadratic Equation
15	210	Heart of Algebra	Mathematical Modelling
16	B	Problem Solving and Data Analysis	Exponential Functions
17	B	Problem Solving and Data Analysis	Plots and Diagrams
18	D	Problem Solving and Data Analysis	Probability
19	92	Additional Topics in Math	Angles and Radians
20	B	Additional Topics in Math	Circles
21	C	Additional Topics in Math	Circles
22	41.6	Additional Topics in Math	Geometry

Reading and Writing: Module 1

QUESTION NUMBER	CORRECT ANSWER	DOMAIN	SKILL
1	C	Craft & Structure	Words In Context
2	A	Craft & Structure	Words In Context
3	C	Craft & Structure	Words In Context
4	C	Craft & Structure	Words In Context
5	A	Craft & Structure	Words In Context
6	B	Craft & Structure	Text Structure & Purpose
7	C	Information & Ideas	Central Ideas and Details
8	B	Information & Ideas	Central Ideas and Details
9	C	Information & Ideas	Central Ideas and Details
10	D	Information & Ideas	Command of Evidence: Textual
11	A	Information & Ideas	Central Ideas and Details
12	D	Information & Ideas	Inferences
13	B	Information & Ideas	Inferences
14	A	Standard English Conventions	Boundaries
15	D	Standard English Conventions	Forms, Structure, and Sense
16	A	Standard English Conventions	Forms, Structure, and Sense
17	C	Standard English Conventions	Boundaries
18	A	Standard English Conventions	Boundaries
19	D	Standard English Conventions	Boundaries
20	C	Standard English Conventions	Boundaries
21	B	Standard English Conventions	Forms, Structure, and Sense
22	B	Standard English Conventions	Forms, Structure, and Sense
23	D	Standard English Conventions	Boundaries
24	A	Standard English Conventions	Forms, Structure, and Sense
25	B	Expression of Ideas	Transitions
26	A	Expression of Ideas	Rhetorical Synthesis
27	A	Expression of Ideas	Rhetorical Synthesis

Reading and Writing: Module 2

QUESTION NUMBER	CORRECT ANSWER	DOMAIN	SKILL
1	A	Craft & Structure	Words In Context
2	C	Craft & Structure	Words In Context
3	B	Craft & Structure	Words In Context

4	B	Craft & Structure	Words In Context
5	A	Craft & Structure	Words In Context
6	D	Information & Ideas	Central Ideas and Details
7	C	Craft & Structure	Text Structure & Purpose
8	A	Craft & Structure	Text Structure & Purpose
9	C	Information & Ideas	Central Ideas and Details
10	A	Craft & Structure	Cross-Text Connections
11	C	Information & Ideas	Command of Evidence: Quantitative
12	C	Information & Ideas	Command of Evidence: Quantitative
13	A	Information & Ideas	Command of Evidence: Textual
14	A	Information & Ideas	Command of Evidence: Textual
15	C	Information & Ideas	Inferences
16	A	Standard English Conventions	Forms, Structure, and Sense
17	A	Standard English Conventions	Forms, Structure, and Sense
18	B	Standard English Conventions	Forms, Structure, and Sense
19	C	Standard English Conventions	Boundaries
20	A	Standard English Conventions	Boundaries
21	D	Standard English Conventions	Forms, Structure, and Sense
22	A	Standard English Conventions	Boundaries
23	D	Expression of Ideas	Transitions
24	C	Expression of Ideas	Transitions
25	C	Expression of Ideas	Rhetorical Synthesis
26	A	Expression of Ideas	Rhetorical Synthesis
27	B	Expression of Ideas	Rhetorical Synthesis

Math: Module 1

QUESTION NUMBER	CORRECT ANSWER	CATEGORY	SUB-CATEGORY
1	C	Passport to Advanced Math	Quadratic Equation
2	B	Heart of Algebra	Mathematical Modelling
3	C	Additional Topics in Math	Geometry
4	B	Problem Solving and Data Analysis	Probability
5	A	Problem Solving and Data Analysis	Probability
6	B	Additional Topics in Math	Trigonometry
7	C	Passport to Advanced Math	Quadratic Equation
8	D	Problem Solving and Data Analysis	Statistics
9	A	Passport to Advanced Math	Translation Transformation
10	13	Heart of Algebra	Algebra

11	A	Heart of Algebra	Linear Equations
12	C	Heart of Algebra	Graphs
13	16.7	Heart of Algebra	Mathematical Modelling
14	D	Heart of Algebra	Mathematical Modelling
15	D	Problem Solving and Data Analysis	Percentages
16	B	Heart of Algebra	Linear Equations
17	A	Passport to Advanced Math	Quadratic Equation
18	D	Additional Topics in Math	Geometry
19	50/7, 7.142, 7.143	Heart of Algebra	Linear Equations
20	D	Problem Solving and Data Analysis	Probability
21	8	Heart of Algebra	Linear Equations
22	B	Heart of Algebra	Mathematical Modelling

Math: Module 2

QUESTION NUMBER	CORRECT ANSWER	CATEGORY	SUB-CATEGORY
1	30	Heart of Algebra	Algebra
2	D	Heart of Algebra	Linear Equations
3	D	Heart of Algebra	Mathematical Modelling
4	A	Heart of Algebra	Linear Equations
5	B	Passport to Advanced Math	Quadratic Equation
6	A	Passport to Advanced Math	Quadratic Equation
7	C	Passport to Advanced Math	Polynomial
8	7	Heart of Algebra	Mathematical Modelling
9	D	Passport to Advanced Math	Polynomial
10	B	Heart of Algebra	Linear Equations
11	-8	Heart of Algebra	Linear Equations
12	D	Heart of Algebra	Graphs
13	D	Heart of Algebra	Graphs
14	9.75, 39/4	Problem Solving and Data Analysis	Ratio
15	50	Problem Solving and Data Analysis	Percentages
16	C	Problem Solving and Data Analysis	Probability
17	B	Problem Solving and Data Analysis	Unit Conversion
18	A	Heart of Algebra	Linear Equations
19	40	Additional Topics in Math	Geometry
20	C	Additional Topics in Math	Circles
21	3/5, 0.6, .6	Additional Topics in Math	Trigonometry
22	D	Additional Topics in Math	Geometry

Reading and Writing: Module 1

QUESTION NUMBER	CORRECT ANSWER	DOMAIN	SKILL
1	B	Craft & Structure	Words In Context
2	C	Craft & Structure	Words In Context
3	D	Craft & Structure	Words In Context
4	C	Craft & Structure	Words In Context
5	B	Craft & Structure	Words In Context
6	C	Craft & Structure	Words In Context
7	A	Craft & Structure	Text Structure & Purpose
8	A	Craft & Structure	Text Structure & Purpose
9	C	Craft & Structure	Text Structure & Purpose
10	A	Information & Ideas	Central Ideas and Details
11	B	Information & Ideas	Central Ideas and Details
12	A	Information & Ideas	Command of Evidence: Textual
13	C	Information & Ideas	Command of Evidence: Quantitative
14	B	Information & Ideas	Inferences
15	B	Information & Ideas	Inferences
16	A	Standard English Conventions	Form, Structure, and Sense
17	A	Standard English Conventions	Form, Structure, and Sense
18	A	Standard English Conventions	Form, Structure, and Sense
19	C	Standard English Conventions	Boundaries
20	D	Standard English Conventions	Boundaries
21	A	Standard English Conventions	Boundaries
22	C	Standard English Conventions	Boundaries
23	B	Standard English Conventions	Boundaries
24	D	Standard English Conventions	Form, Structure, and Sense
25	C	Expression of Ideas	Rhetorical Synthesis
26	B	Expression of Ideas	Rhetorical Synthesis
27	C	Expression of Ideas	Rhetorical Synthesis

Reading and Writing: Module 2

QUESTION NUMBER	CORRECT ANSWER	DOMAIN	SKILL
1	B	Craft & Structure	Words In Context
2	B	Craft & Structure	Words In Context
3	A	Craft & Structure	Words In Context

4	B	Craft & Structure	Words In Context
5	A	Craft & Structure	Words In Context
6	A	Craft & Structure	Text Structure & Purpose
7	C	Information & Ideas	Command of Evidence: Textual
8	B	Information & Ideas	Central Ideas and Details
9	A	Craft & Structure	Text Structure & Purpose
10	A	Information & Ideas	Cross-Text Connections
11	C	Information & Ideas	Command of Evidence: Textual
12	C	Information & Ideas	Command of Evidence: Quantitative
13	B	Information & Ideas	Command of Evidence: Textual
14	C	Information & Ideas	Inferences
15	A	Information & Ideas	Inferences
16	D	Information & Ideas	Inferences
17	D	Standard English Conventions	Boundaries
18	B	Standard English Conventions	Boundaries
19	C	Standard English Conventions	Form, Structure, and Sense
20	A	Standard English Conventions	Form, Structure, and Sense
21	C	Standard English Conventions	Boundaries
22	B	Standard English Conventions	Boundaries
23	D	Standard English Conventions	Boundaries
24	B	Expression of Ideas	Transitions
25	B	Expression of Ideas	Transitions
26	A	Expression of Ideas	Rhetorical Synthesis
27	A	Expression of Ideas	Rhetorical Synthesis

Math: Module 1

QUESTION NUMBER	CORRECT ANSWER	CATEGORY	SUB-CATEGORY
1	C	Problem Solving and Data Analysis	Exponential Functions
2	A	Heart of Algebra	Mathematical Modelling
3	A	Problem Solving and Data Analysis	Percentages
4	B	Heart of Algebra	Mathematical Modelling
5	30	Additional Topics in Math	Geometry
6	A	Passport to Advanced Math	Quadratic Equation
7	5	Heart of Algebra	Linear Equations
8	D	Problem Solving and Data Analysis	Probability
9	B	Additional Topics in Math	Geometry
10	2	Heart of Algebra	Algebra

11	D	Additional Topics in Math	Geometry
12	D	Heart of Algebra	Mathematical Modelling
13	2,0	Passport to Advanced Math	Absolute Value
14	A	Heart of Algebra	Algebra
15	B	Heart of Algebra	Mathematical Modelling
16	26	Problem Solving and Data Analysis	Unit Conversion
17	B	Heart of Algebra	Linear Equations
18	A	Heart of Algebra	Graphs
19	C	Passport to Advanced Math	Polynomials
20	D	Heart of Algebra	Graphs
21	B	Heart of Algebra	Algebra
22	D	Problem Solving and Data Analysis	Plots and Diagrams

Math: Module 2

QUESTION NUMBER	CORRECT ANSWER	CATEGORY	SUB-CATEGORY
1	C	Heart of Algebra	Linear Equations
2	B	Heart of Algebra	Mathematical Modelling
3	5	Heart of Algebra	Linear Equations
4	2.5,5/2	Heart of Algebra	Linear Equations
5	C	Heart of Algebra	Graphs
6	A	Heart of Algebra	Graphs
7	D	Heart of Algebra	Linear Equations
8	C	Heart of Algebra	Mathematical Modelling
9	17	Passport to Advanced Math	Polynomials
10	B	Passport to Advanced Math	Quadratic Equation
11	A	Passport to Advanced Math	Rational Functions
12	B	Problem Solving and Data Analysis	Exponential Functions
13	B	Heart of Algebra	Mathematical Modelling
14	C	Problem Solving and Data Analysis	Exponential Functions
15	B	Problem Solving and Data Analysis	Statistics
16	0.11, .11	Problem Solving and Data Analysis	Probability
17	B	Additional Topics in Math	Geometry
18	C	Additional Topics in Math	Geometry
19	D	Heart of Algebra	Mathematical Modelling
20	B	Additional Topics in Math	Geometry
21	½, 0.5, .5, 4	Passport to Advanced Math	Quadratic Equation
22	A	Additional Topics in Math	Geometry

Reading and Writing: Module 1

QUESTION NUMBER	CORRECT ANSWER	DOMAIN	SKILL
1	D	Craft & Structure	Words In Context
2	B	Craft & Structure	Words In Context
3	A	Craft & Structure	Words In Context
4	B	Craft & Structure	Words In Context
5	C	Craft & Structure	Words In Context
6	B	Information & Ideas	Central Ideas and Details
7	C	Information & Ideas	Central Ideas and Details
8	C	Information & Ideas	Central Ideas and Details
9	B	Information & Ideas	Central Ideas and Details
10	D	Information & Ideas	Command of Evidence: Textual
11	B	Information & Ideas	Inferences
12	B	Information & Ideas	Inferences
13	D	Craft & Structure	Text Structure & Purpose
14	A	Standard English Conventions	Form, Structure, and Sense
15	A	Standard English Conventions	Boundaries
16	B	Standard English Conventions	Boundaries
17	A	Standard English Conventions	Form, Structure, and Sense
18	A	Standard English Conventions	Boundaries
19	B	Standard English Conventions	Form, Structure, and Sense
20	A	Standard English Conventions	Boundaries
21	B	Standard English Conventions	Form, Structure, and Sense
22	A	Expression of Ideas	Transitions
23	A	Expression of Ideas	Transitions
24	C	Expression of Ideas	Transitions
25	A	Expression of Ideas	Rhetorical Synthesis
26	A	Expression of Ideas	Rhetorical Synthesis
27	B	Expression of Ideas	Rhetorical Synthesis

Reading and Writing: Module 2

QUESTION NUMBER	CORRECT ANSWER	DOMAIN	SKILL
1	D	Craft & Structure	Words In Context
2	B	Craft & Structure	Words In Context
3	A	Craft & Structure	Words In Context

4	A	Craft & Structure	Words In Context
5	A	Craft & Structure	Words In Context
6	D	Craft & Structure	Text Structure & Purpose
7	A	Information & Ideas	Text Structure & Purpose
8	D	Information & Ideas	Text Structure & Purpose
9	A	Craft & Structure	Cross-Text Connections
10	D	Information & Ideas	Command of Evidence: Quantitative
11	C	Information & Ideas	Command of Evidence: Textual
12	B	Information & Ideas	Command of Evidence: Textual
13	C	Information & Ideas	Command of Evidence: Quantitative
14	B	Information & Ideas	Command of Evidence: Textual
15	B	Information & Ideas	Command of Evidence: Quantitative
16	D	Information & Ideas	Central Ideas and Details
17	A	Information & Ideas	Inferences
18	C	Standard English Conventions	Boundaries
19	B	Standard English Conventions	Boundaries
20	A	Standard English Conventions	Boundaries
21	A	Standard English Conventions	Form, Structure, and Sense
22	A	Standard English Conventions	Form, Structure, and Sense
23	C	Expression of Ideas	Transitions
24	D	Standard English Conventions	Boundaries
25	C	Expression of Ideas	Rhetorical Synthesis
26	A	Expression of Ideas	Rhetorical Synthesis
27	D	Expression of Ideas	Rhetorical Synthesis

Math: Module 1

QUESTION NUMBER	CORRECT ANSWER	CATEGORY	SUB-CATEGORY
1	D	Heart of Algebra	Algebra
2	C	Problem Solving and Data Analysis	Percentages
3	B	Passport to Advanced Math	Quadratic Equation
4	D	Heart of Algebra	Inequality
5	B	Heart of Algebra	Mathematical Modelling
6	C	Problem Solving and Data Analysis	Unit Conversion
7	A	Heart of Algebra	Algebra
8	C	Heart of Algebra	Mathematical Modelling
9	B	Problem Solving and Data Analysis	Percentages
10	C	Passport to Advanced Math	Rational Functions

11	D	Additional Topics in Math	Circles
12	D	Problem Solving and Data Analysis	Probability
13	24	Passport to Advanced Math	Polynomial
14	C	Heart of Algebra	Linear Equations
15	B	Problem Solving and Data Analysis	Statistics
16	B	Passport to Advanced Math	Absolute Value
17	C	Passport to Advanced Math	Rational Functions
18	C	Additional Topics in Math	Geometry
19	A	Passport to Advanced Math	Quadratic Equation
20	A	Passport to Advanced Math	Polynomials
21	D	Additional Topics in Math	Circles
22	D	Heart of Algebra	Mathematical Modelling

Math: Module 2

QUESTION NUMBER	CORRECT ANSWER	CATEGORY	SUB-CATEGORY
1	D	Additional Topics in Math	Geometry
2	B	Problem Solving and Data Analysis	Percentages
3	D	Problem Solving and Data Analysis	Unit Conversion
4	C	Problem Solving and Data Analysis	Probability
5	B	Heart of Algebra	Linear Equations
6	C	Additional Topics in Math	Geometry
7	A	Passport to Advanced Math	Quadratic Equation
8	D	Heart of Algebra	Algebra
9	B	Passport to Advanced Math	Quadratic Equation
10	B	Heart of Algebra	Graphs
11	D	Passport to Advanced Math	Polynomials
12	A	Problem Solving and Data Analysis	Statistics
13	A	Heart of Algebra	Mathematical Modelling
14	60	Additional Topics in Math	Geometry
15	C	Heart of Algebra	Mathematical Modelling
16	A	Passport to Advanced Math	Polynomials
17	D	Additional Topics in Math	Circles
18	0.38, .38, 5/13	Problem Solving and Data Analysis	Probability
19	C	Passport to Advanced Math	Exponential Functions
20	C	Problem Solving and Data Analysis	Percentages
21	B	Additional Topics in Math	Geometry
22	B	Additional Topics in Math	Geometry

TEST QUBE

Digital SAT ®

Scoring Conversion Tables

TEST 1: Raw Score Conversion Table

Raw Score	Reading and Writing	Math	Raw Score	Reading and Writing	Math
1	200	200	28	540	590
2	200	200	29	550	610
3	200	200	30	560	620
4	200	220	31	570	640
5	200	240	32	590	650
6	220	260	33	610	660
7	230	270	34	620	670
8	240	290	35	630	680
9	250	300	36	640	690
10	270	310	37	650	710
11	280	330	38	660	730
12	300	350	39	670	740
13	310	360	40	670	760
14	330	380	41	680	770
15	350	390	42	690	780
16	360	400	43	680	790
17	370	420	44	690	800
18	380	440	45	700	
19	400	450	46	700	
20	420	470	47	710	
21	430	490	48	730	
22	450	500	49	740	
23	470	510	50	750	
24	490	530	51	770	
25	500	540	52	780	
26	510	560	53	790	
27	530	580	54	800	

TEST 2: Raw Score Conversion Table

Raw Score	Reading and Writing	Math	Raw Score	Reading and Writing	Math
1	200	200	28	540	590
2	200	200	29	550	600
3	200	200	30	560	620
4	200	220	31	570	640
5	200	240	32	590	660
6	200	260	33	610	670
7	200	270	34	620	680
8	200	290	35	630	690
9	200	300	36	640	700
10	210	310	37	650	710
11	230	330	38	660	720
12	240	350	39	670	740
13	3105	360	40	670	750
14	330	380	41	680	760
15	350	390	42	690	770
16	360	400	43	700	790
17	370	420	44	700	800
18	380	440	45	720	
19	400	450	46	710	
20	420	460	47	730	
21	430	480	48	750	
22	450	500	49	760	
23	470	520	50	760	
24	490	530	51	770	
25	500	550	52	780	
26	510	560	53	790	
27	530	580	54	800	

TEST 3: Raw Score Conversion Table

Raw Score	Reading and Writing	Math	Raw Score	Reading and Writing	Math
1	200	200	28	540	600
2	200	200	29	550	610
3	200	200	30	560	620
4	200	220	31	570	630
5	200	240	32	590	640
6	220	260	33	610	660
7	230	270	34	620	670
8	240	290	35	630	680
9	250	300	36	640	700
10	270	310	37	650	710
11	280	330	38	660	720
12	300	350	39	670	740
13	310	360	40	680	750
14	330	380	41	690	760
15	350	390	42	700	770
16	360	400	43	710	780
17	370	420	44	720	800
18	380	440	45	730	
19	400	460	46	740	
20	420	480	47	750	
21	430	490	48	750	
22	450	510	49	760	
23	470	530	50	770	
24	490	550	51	780	
25	500	560	52	790	
26	510	570	53	790	
27	530	590	54	800	

TEST 4: Raw Score Conversion Table

Raw Score	Reading and Writing	Math	Raw Score	Reading and Writing	Math
1	200	200	28	540	580
2	200	200	29	560	600
3	200	200	30	570	610
4	200	220	31	580	630
5	200	240	32	600	650
6	220	260	33	610	660
7	230	270	34	620	670
8	240	290	35	630	690
9	250	300	36	640	680
10	270	310	37	650	700
11	280	330	38	660	710
12	300	350	39	660	730
13	310	360	40	670	740
14	330	380	41	680	760
15	350	390	42	690	780
16	360	400	43	690	790
17	370	420	44	700	800
18	380	440	45	720	
19	400	450	46	730	
20	420	470	47	740	
21	430	490	48	750	
22	450	500	49	760	
23	470	510	50	770	
24	490	520	51	780	
25	500	530	52	790	
26	510	550	53	790	
27	520	560	54	800	

TEST 5: Raw Score Conversion Table

Raw Score	Reading and Writing	Math	Raw Score	Reading and Writing	Math
1	200	200	28	540	590
2	200	200	29	550	600
3	200	200	30	560	620
4	200	220	31	570	630
5	200	240	32	590	650
6	220	260	33	610	660
7	230	270	34	620	680
8	240	290	35	630	690
9	250	300	36	640	700
10	270	310	37	650	710
11	280	330	38	660	720
12	300	350	39	660	740
13	310	360	40	680	750
14	330	380	41	690	770
15	350	390	42	690	780
16	360	400	43	710	790
17	370	420	44	710	800
18	380	440	45	720	
19	400	450	46	730	
20	420	470	47	740	
21	430	490	48	750	
22	450	510	49	750	
23	470	530	50	760	
24	490	550	51	770	
25	500	560	52	780	
26	510	570	53	780	
27	530	580	54	800	

TEST 6: Raw Score Conversion Table

Raw Score	Reading and Writing	Math	Raw Score	Reading and Writing	Math
1	200	200	28	540	600
2	200	200	29	550	620
3	200	200	30	560	630
4	200	220	31	570	640
5	200	240	32	590	650
6	220	260	33	610	660
7	230	270	34	620	670
8	240	290	35	630	680
9	250	300	36	650	690
10	270	310	37	650	710
11	280	330	38	660	720
12	300	350	39	670	740
13	310	360	40	670	750
14	330	380	41	690	760
15	350	390	42	700	770
16	360	400	43	710	780
17	370	420	44	720	800
18	380	440	45	730	
19	400	450	46	740	
20	420	470	47	750	
21	430	490	48	750	
22	450	510	49	760	
23	470	530	50	770	
24	490	540	51	780	
25	500	550	52	790	
26	510	570	53	790	
27	530	580	54	800	

TEST 7: Raw Score Conversion Table

Raw Score	Reading and Writing	Math	Raw Score	Reading and Writing	Math
1	200	200	28	540	610
2	200	200	29	550	620
3	200	200	30	560	630
4	200	220	31	570	650
5	200	240	32	590	660
6	220	260	33	600	670
7	230	270	34	610	680
8	240	290	35	620	690
9	250	300	36	630	700
10	270	310	37	650	710
11	280	330	38	660	730
12	300	350	39	670	750
13	310	360	40	680	760
14	330	380	41	680	770
15	350	390	42	690	780
16	360	400	43	700	790
17	370	420	44	720	800
18	380	440	45	730	
19	400	450	46	740	
20	420	470	47	750	
21	430	490	48	750	
22	450	510	49	760	
23	470	530	50	760	
24	490	550	51	770	
25	500	570	52	780	
26	510	580	53	790	
27	530	600	54	800	

40069029R00193